D1453396

The purpose of this book is to seek a fuller understanding of how the characterization of Paul in Acts would have been perceived by those who first read or heard the Lucan narrative. As the author makes clear, the careful reader of Acts should be amazed at the way St. Paul is portrayed therein. Dr. Lentz demonstrates, through a careful examination of particular texts, the great improbability that a Jew of strict Pharisaic background would have held, let alone been proud of, Roman citizenship and citizenship of the city of Tarsus. By investigating the social and legal expectations of the first century, the author shows that Paul is seen to be deferred to in matters of legal minutiae by those in positions of authority. He is given high social status and abundant moral virtue in order to attract to Christianity the high-ranking citizen who would recognize in Paul the classical cardinal virtues.

SOCIETY FOR NEW TESTAMENT STUDIES

MONOGRAPH SERIES

General Editor: Margaret E. Thrall

77

LUKE'S PORTRAIT OF PAUL

Luke's portrait of Paul

JOHN CLAYTON LENTZ, Jr.

*Associate Pastor, First Presbyterian
Church, Winchester, Virginia*

CAMBRIDGE
UNIVERSITY PRESS

Published by the Press Syndicate of the University of Cambridge
The Pitt Building, Trumpington Street, Cambridge CB2 1RP
40 West 20th Street, New York, NY 10011–4211, USA
10 Stamford Road, Oakleigh, Victoria 3166, Australia

© Cambridge University Press 1993

First published 1993

Printed in Great Britain at the University Press, Cambridge

A catalogue record for this book is available from the British Library

Library of Congress cataloguing in publication data

Lentz, John Clayton, Jr.
Luke's portrait of Paul / John Clayton Lentz, Jr.
        p.   cm. – (Monograph series / Society for New Testament Studies:
77)
Includes bibliographical references and index.
ISBN 0 521 43316 9
1. Paul, the Apostle, Saint.   2. Bible. N.T. Acts – Criticism, interpretation,
etc.   3. Sociology, Biblical.   I. Title.   II. Series: Monograph series
(Society for New Testament Studies): 77.
BS2506.L465   1993
226.6′092 – dc20   92–15802 CIP

ISBN 0 521 43316 9 hardback

CE

To my brother Peter (1954–1986) who told me to keep writing, and to my wife Deanne who made sure that I did.

CONTENTS

ACKNOWLEDGMENTS

Sincerest gratitude is expressed to Dr. David Mealand who supervised this study and to Professor J. C. O'Neill who added helpful criticism and support. Thanks too to the entire staff of New College, Edinburgh University. To the Reverend Donald D. M. Jones for retyping this manuscript, to The First Presbyterian Church of Winchester, Virginia USA which gave me time to complete the task and to my wife Deanne who read and re-read the various drafts – thank you!

ABBREVIATIONS

Unless otherwise noted all Latin and Greek references are taken from the Loeb Classical Library (London: William Heinemann, Ltd., 1908–)
   Unless otherwise noted all references from *The Testament of the Twelve Patriarchs* are taken from H. C. Kee's Translation.

ANRW	*Aufstieg und Niedergang der römischen Welt: Geschichte und Kultur Roms im Spiegel der neueren Forschung*, 33 vols. ed. H. Temporini and W. Hasse (Berlin: Walter de Gruyter, 1972–)
AJP	*American Journal of Philology*
ASR	*American Sociological Review*
BASOR	*Bulletin of the American School of Oriental Research*
Beginnings	*Beginnings of Christianity, part 1, The Acts of the Apostles*, 5 vol, ed. F. Jackson and K. Lake (London: The Macmillan Co., 1920–1933)
BGU	*Aegyptische Urkunden aus den königlichen Museum zu Berlin: Griechische Urkunden* vol. IV (Berlin: Weidmannsche Buchhandlaung, 1912)
BJRL	*Bulletin of the John Rylands Library*
BThB	*Biblical Theology Bulletin*
BZ	*Biblische Zeitschrift*
Catacombs and the Colosseum	*The Catacombs and the Colosseum: The Roman Empire as the Setting of Primitive Christianity*, ed. S. Benko and J. J. O'Rourke (Valley Forge, Pa: Judson Press, 1971)
CBQ	*Catholic Biblical Quarterly*
CIG	*Corpus Inscriptionum Graecarum*, 38 vols, ed. J. Franzius (Berlin: Vendit G. Reimeri Libraria, 1853)

CPJ	*Corpus Papyrorum Judaicarum*, 3 vols, ed. V. A. Tcherikover and A. Fuks (Cambridge: Harvard University Press, 1957)
ET	*The Expository Times*
EvTh	*Evangelische Theologie*
HTR	*Harvard Theological Review*
IESS	*International Encyclopedia of the Social Sciences*, ed. D. L. Sills, 17 vols. (New York: The Macmillan Co. and the Free Press, 1968)
JAAR	*Journal of the American Academy of Religion*
JAC	*Jahrbuch für Antike und Christentum*
JBL	*Journal of Biblical Literature*
JHS	*Journal of Hellenistic Studies*
JJS	*Journal of Jewish Studies*
JR	*Journal of Religion*
JRS	*Journal of Roman Studies*
JSNT	*Journal for the Study of the New Testament*
JST	*Journal for the Study of Judaism*
JTS	*Journal of Theological Studies*
NTS	*New Testament Studies*
New Docs	*New Documents Illustrating Early Christianity*, 4 vols., ed. G. H. R. Horsley (North Ryde, New South Wales: The Ancient History Documentary Research Centre, Macquarie University, 1981–)
New Perspectives	*Luke–Acts: New Perspectives From the Society of Biblical Literature*, ed. C. H. Talbert (New York: Crossroads, 1984)
NovT	*Novum Testamentum*
OCD	*The Oxford Classical Dictionary*, ed. N. G. L. Hammond and H. H. Scullard (Oxford: At the Clarendon Press, 1970)
OGIS	*Orientis Graeci Inscriptiones Selectae*, 2 vols., ed. W. Dittenberger (Lipsiae; Apud S. Hirzelium, 1903)
PBSR	*Papers of the British School at Rome*
Perspectives	*Perspectives on Luke–Acts*, ed. C. H. Talbert (Edinburgh: T. & T. Clark, 1978).
PLA	*Political Issues in Luke–Acts*, ed. R. J. Cassidy and P. J. Scharper (New York: Orbis Books, 1983)

PRE	*Paulys Real-Encyclopädie der Classischen Altertumswissenschaft*, 80 vols. (Stuttgart: J. B. Metzlerscher Verlag, 1894–1972).
PRE Supp	*Paulys Real-Encyclopädie Supplement*
RAC	*Reallexicon für Antike und Christentum. Sachwörterbuch zur Auseinandersetzung des Christentums mit der antiken Welt* (Stuttgart: Hiersemann, 1950–)
SBLDS	*Society of Biblical Literature Dissertation Series*
SBL Sem Pap	*Society of Biblical Literature Seminar Papers*
Schürer rev.	E. Schürer, *The History of the Jewish People in the Age of Jesus Christ*, rev. and ed. G. Vermes, F. Millar, and M. Black (Edinburgh: T. & T. Clark, 1973–87)
SEHHW	M. Rostovtzeff, *The Social and Economic History of the Hellenistic World*, 2 vols. (Oxford: Clarendon Press, 1959)
SIG	*Sylloge Inscriptionum Graecarum*, 4 vols., ed. W. Dittenberger, 3rd edn (Lipsiae: Apud S. Hirzelium, 1915)
SLA	*Studies on Luke–Acts*, ed. L. Keck and J. L. Martyn (New York: Abingdon Press, 1966).
Strack-Bill	H. L. Strack and P. Billerbeck, *Kommentar zum Neuen Testament aus Talmud und Midrasch*, 6 vols., (Munich: Beck'sche Verlagsbuchhandlung, 1926–)
Studies	M. Dibelius, *Studies in the Acts of the Apostles*, ed. H. Greeven (London: S.C.M. Press Ltd., 1956)
TDNT	*Theological Dictionary of the New Testament*, ed. G. Kittel, trans. G. W. Bromiley (Grand Rapids, Mich.: Eerdmans, 1964)
TL	*Theologische Literaturzeitung*
TRu	*Theologische Rundschau*
ZNW	*Zeitschrift für die neutestamentliche Wissenschaft*

1

THE PROBLEM

The careful reader of Acts should be confounded by the way St. Paul is portrayed. While every astute commentator acknowledges that Paul plays an exceedingly important role in Acts, attempts to understand the portrayal and how it serves Luke's larger aim are as inconclusive as they are unsatisfying. Some, like J. Jervell, R. Maddox, R. F. O'Toole, are convinced that Luke's foremost intention is to portray Paul as a loyal Jew.[1] While the Paul of Acts does indeed point with pride to his strict Jewish upbringing, he also is very proud of his Roman citizenship and his citizenship of the city of Tarsus. Not enough attention has been paid to this fact.

This lack of regard obscures a historical problem which is: what is the probability that a Jew of strict Pharisaic background would have held, let alone been proud of, these citizenships? This issue is important and requires careful consideration. While W. Ramsay, A. Deissmann, M. Dibelius, W. G. Kümmel, G. Bornkamm, and F. F. Bruce have offered well-known studies, their conclusions do not answer this pressing question.[2]

It has been argued that Luke's intention was to stress Paul's Jewishness in order to highlight early Christianity's continuity with Judaism and to assuage an inner church anxiety.[3] While there is continuity, there is also a Lucan concern to show how Christianity has grown beyond its Jewish roots. Furthermore, the mood of Acts is hardly anxious; rather, it is triumphant. As is well known, Jesus

[1] Jervell, *God's Christ and His People*; *Luke and the People of God*; "Paulus in der Apostelgeschichte," 378–392; "Paul in the Acts of the Apostles," pp. 297–305; *The Unknown Paul*; Maddox, *The Purpose of Luke-Acts*; O'Toole, "Luke's Position on Politics and Society." See also Burchard, "Paulus in der Apostelgeschichte"; 881–895; Löning, *Die Saulustradition in der Apostelgeschichte*.

[2] Ramsay, *St. Paul the Traveller*; Deissmann, *Paul*; Dibelius and Kümmel, *Paul*; Bornkamm, *Paul*; Bruce, *Paul: Apostle of the Free Spirit*.

[3] Karris, "Poor and Rich: The Lukan Sitz im Leben"; O'Toole, "Why Did Luke Write Acts (Luke-Acts)?", 66–77; Tiede, *Prophecy and History in Luke-Acts*.

presents the early church's "marching orders": "and you shall be my witnesses in Jerusalem and in all Judea and Samaria and to the end of the earth" (Acts 1:8).

Yet, what seems to be of greater concern to Luke is not just Paul the Jew, but Paul the Tarsian and Roman who showed himself to be comfortable in the company of the high and mighty of the first-century Greco-Roman world. In Acts, Paul is always in control. His authority is not only recognized among the Christians. He is also acknowledged as a man not to be taken lightly by the secular leaders as well. Luke is also intent on emphasizing that Paul, before his conversion, was a wild and zealous persecutor. Yet, after his conversion Paul is a model of sobriety, piety, and bravery.

It is obvious that, for most of the last eight chapters of Acts, Paul is on trial. Again, there have been several examinations of Luke's account of the Roman legal process from the time of Paul's arrest in Jerusalem to his house arrest in Rome.[4] All the analyses offer enlightening insight. However, all are equally tentative in reaching firm conclusions, due to lack of sufficient evidence. The following important questions are, if noted, passed over quite quickly: how likely was it that an individual in the Eastern provinces of the empire would have been treated with the respect that Paul was – even if that individual were a Roman citizen? Did a person's social status have anything to do with how that individual was treated?

There is no paucity of confusion among scholars concerning the nature of Paul's appeal. Furthermore, the honest commentator will admit that Luke's accounts of Paul's trials are not exact in all their details. Yet, no one has fully investigated how Luke's report might have reflected the social and legal expectations of the first century.

The consensus agrees that what can be concluded is that the description of the legal scenes in Acts shows Roman justice to be fair and protective, which was an advantage to Paul. Despite the common agreement, this assertion is difficult to prove. As will be shown, the representatives of Roman law and order are at best uneven in their ability to control the proceedings and all seem to defer to Paul in matters of legal minutiae.

In increasing numbers, students of the New Testament have become sensitive to socio-historical issues and have used socio-

---

[4] Most notably Sherwin-White, *Roman Society and Roman Law*; Jones, "I Appeal to Caesar," pp. 51–66; H. S. Tajra, *The Trial of St. Paul. A Juridical Exegesis of the Second Half of the Acts of the Apostles* (Tübingen: Mohr, 1989).

logical vocabulary to describe the early church.[5] However, no one has comprehensively and therefore adequately studied the Lucan portrayal of St. Paul in Acts with this sensitivity.

Many scholars have noted that Luke, in Acts, seems interested in showing that those of high social status were attracted to Christianity. Others, using Acts and Paul's letters, have attempted a social description of the apostle Paul.[6] But no one has formally studied the social status of Paul as presented in Acts alone with the intent of understanding how this portrayal might uncover a specific Lucan intention.

Furthermore, there has not been adequate attention paid to the fact that one's social standing was not only judged by specific social credentials, but also by the perception of moral character, or virtue. Admittedly scientific measurement of self-control, one of the cardinal virtues, is difficult if not impossible. But, in simply overlooking the unmeasurable, it is possible to miss significant information. This is particularly so in the legal scenes in Acts.

The thesis of this book is that Luke portrayed Paul as a man of high social status and moral virtue. In other words, the Lucan Paul possesses high social credentials and personifies what would have been recognized, by the first reader/hearer of Acts, as the classical cardinal virtues. Luke accomplished this task not only by using descriptive words and phrases but also by emphasizing Paul's high social status through the use of common rhetorical devices and through the construction of his narrative.

The broader purpose of this book is to consider how Luke reflects the social expectations of his first-century environment. The more focused aim in fulfilling the larger objective will be to investigate the portrayal of St. Paul in Acts. The specific, more immediate tasks which will provide evidence for the thesis include: an investigation of the historical probability of the biographical data on Paul provided by Luke; a study of the more subtle literary techniques that Luke used to highlight Paul's authority and control; an analysis of the relationship between social status and legal privilege, which in turn will help interpret the legal scenes in the last eight chapters of Acts.

---

[5] Judge, *Rank and Status*; *Social Pattern*; Kee, *Christian Origins in Sociological Perspective*; Meeks, *Urban Christians*; Theissen, *Social Setting*.
[6] Clark, "The Social Status of Paul," 110–111; Hock "Paul's Tentmaking," 555–564; S. K. Stowers, "Social Status, Public Speaking and Private Teaching: The Circumstances of Paul's Preaching Activities," *NovT* 26 (1984), 59–82.

In Acts one sees the movement from Palestine to Rome, from the parochial and the provincial to the capital of the civilized world. Of particular significance is the final section of Acts, 21:37 to 28:31. It is important because these final chapters possess a particular integrity that includes Paul's arrest and imprisonment prior to his arrival in Rome. In this section the reader is presented with a Lucan description of Paul that is fuller than earlier descriptions and places Paul on a pedestal above all others. His background and social standing, as will be shown, are impeccable by both Greco-Roman and Jewish standards. It is as if Luke intentionally presented Paul as one of the *splendidiores personae*.

The final section of Acts is significant, for it is longer than the section which describes Paul's mission. It will be assumed that just as Luke took consummate care in shaping his narrative throughout his two-volume work, so too, here at the conclusion, he is aware of the importance of this last picture the reader will receive. As R. Maddox has stated: "When we read Acts as a whole, rather than selectively, it is Paul the prisoner even more than Paul the missionary whom we are meant to remember."[7]

Even as a prisoner Paul is held up as the man representative of social credentials and moral virtue. With these characteristics in mind, Paul's arrival in Rome was important for Luke for, at last, his hero was where he belonged: in the captial, the center of power and prestige.

The question of how Christianity came to Rome is clearly secondary to Luke, for he writes at a time when these communities are already established. Of primary importance to Luke, particularly in the last eight chapters, is to show that Paul, and by extension, Christianity, belongs in the company of those of power and status.

As is true in our contemporary world, advertisements are directed not to those who possess what is advertised but to those who aspire to possess what is advertised. Luke's emphasis on Paul's high social status and moral virtue offered the reader a glimpse of the truly sophisticated, cosmopolitan Christian gentleman and extended to the status-conscious Greco-Roman world an invitation to join the ever-growing community of Christians which the Lucan Paul represented.

Admittedly the investigation of Luke's sensitivity to the issue of social status in Acts is not new. For example, H. J. Cadbury wrote:

[7]   Maddox, *The Purpose of Luke-Acts*, p. 70.

Furthermore our author is not above a sense of pride in the social standing of Paul's converts ... The Asiarchs were undoubtedly some of the "best people" in Ephesus – the richest and the most élite ... It is perhaps a mark of Luke's Greek view point, that this timarchic or economically aristocratic emphasis occurs so often in reference to the Apostle's converts.[8]

E. Haenchen takes for granted that the Paul of Acts is an idealized portrait and often notices the Lucan tendency to portray Paul as a man of high social standing and authority. For example, he commented:

What was significant for world history demanded as its framework high society, the world of the high and mighty ... and Luke was convinced that Christianity is of decisive significance for the whole world. But he could only express this conviction in the style of the literature of the period, and impart it to his own age, by making Paul again and again confront the statesmen and princes (even Caesar 27:24) and converse on friendly terms with the Asiarchs as with men of equal standing, and thus rising above the hole-in-the-corner existence in which great things cannot come about.[9]

While both of these scholars, among others, have mentioned the status of the converts, neither of them, in any systematic way, has offered a full discussion of the portrayal of the Paul of Acts paying specific attention to the status characteristics which Luke chose to describe. Their attention is ultimately directed elsewhere.

Before entering fully into the study of the relevant data, some brief, general comments about the presuppositions employed in this book are in order. Many scholars assume that an individual, whom tradition has called Luke, is the author/compiler of the two volumes that are known as Luke-Acts. Additionally, Luke should be taken at his word when he writes in his preface to Theophilus (Luke 1:1–4) that he has used sources, presumably both written and oral, some perhaps even from eye-witness accounts, to construct his narrative.

Furthermore, it is supposed by many modern Lucan scholars that Luke's narrative is only of secondary worth as an historical source

---

[8] Cadbury, *Book of Acts*, p. 43.
[9] Haenchen, *Acts*, p. 679. See also Plümacher, *Lukas*.

for the life, mission, and theology of Paul. This is not to say that Acts is worthless in this respect. Colin Hemer has recently shown that Luke offers precise geographical details and presents important material which can inform an historian about the world in which Luke lived.[10] However, proving that Luke knew details does not excuse Luke from possibly manipulating his sources and shaping his finished product.

The focus of this book is to seek a fuller understanding of how the characterization of Paul in Acts would have been perceived by those who first read or heard the Lucan narrative.

[10] C. J. Hemer, *The Book of Acts in the Setting of Hellenistic History* (Tübingen: J. C. B. Mohr, 1989).

2

DEFINING SOCIAL STATUS AND MORAL VIRTUE

The first readers of Luke-Acts were introduced to a panoply of individuals who would have appeared in the life of the cities, villages, and rural outposts of the Roman empire. The characters mentioned by Luke include individuals of every contemporary ethnic and political community. Furthermore, in his narrative Luke introduces shepherds, vinedressers, fisherfolk, tanners, silversmiths, purple-dye sellers, charismatic leaders and their followers, priests and scribes, prostitutes, tax-collectors, beggars, Roman soldiers of every rank, slaves and freemen, landowners, tenant farmers, stewards, representatives of Roman authority, local non-Roman officials, rich and poor, men, women, and children. These *dramatis personae* represent every position on the social scale, suggesting that it may be appropriate to use modern sociological terminology when studying Luke-Acts.

Social stratification

"Social status," "rank," and "class" are concepts that are often used indiscriminately; however, they should be more clearly distinguished. "Class" denotes a group of people who, from the standpoint of specific interests, have the same economic position. "Status" is a "quality of social honor or lack of it and is, in the main, conditioned as well as expressed through a specific style of life."[1] Hence, class is a term which more strictly defines economic earning power.

Social status is a term which possesses wider connotations denoting various levels of prestige, not limited in its definition by economic factors. A person's class is one factor in determining their social status, but it is not the only criterion. This point does have a

[1] Bendix and Lipset, *Class, Status and Power*, p. 31; Grant, "Social Setting," p. 17; Meeks, *Urban Christians*, p. 53.

bearing on the ancient world: a tax-collector and a centurion might have a similar economic standing, but possess differing social status within specific communities.

A person's "rank" in society is important for determining their social status. However, "rank" and "status" are not synonymous. One's rank marks any formally defined position in society. Status refers to positions of influence that may not correspond to the official pattern of the social order.[2] E. A. Judge notes that status tends to convert itself to rank which is "the fossilized status of the past . . . defending itself against the aspirations of those who have only status, often newly acquired."[3] The term "rank" is useful when discussing formal groups within the Greco-Roman world such as senators or equestrians. However, in Acts there is such a variety of individuals possessing differing status credentials that "rank" is not precise enough.

Furthermore, in the Greco-Roman world, the ideal man of social status possessed true dignity and moral virtue. Judgment concerning an individual's moral excellence should be included in a comprehensive understanding of a person's status. Of the three terms, "class," "status," and "rank," "status" is more dynamic, flexible, and inclusive than the other two and hence most appropriate for a discussion of the description of Paul in Acts.

There is yet another term, crucial to the study of the Roman world, which needs to be defined carefully: "social stratification." This is the sociological concept "that refers to the fact that both individuals and groups of individuals are conceived of as constituting higher and lower differentiated strata, or classes, in terms of some specific or generalized characteristic or set of characteristics."[4]

Inherent in this definition of social stratification is an evaluation of an individual's worth in society depending upon his or her placement on the social scale of that society. The Roman world perceived a moral distinction between those who were of the *ordo senatorius* (senators) and *ordo equester* (equestrians) on the one hand, and freedmen and slaves on the other.

R. Brown provides four criteria for a meaningful understanding of social stratification. First, a given population must be conscious of social division, and agree on number and membership; second, the styles of life are "strikingly uniform within the stratum" and clear contrasts between the strata are recognizable; third, social

---

[2] Judge, *Rank and Status*, p. 3.
[3] Judge, *Rank and Status*, p. 9.
[4] B. Barber, "Introduction to Social Stratification," in *IESS*, vol. XV, p. 289.

interaction is sharply patterned by stratum; fourth, "the boundaries suggested by the three kinds of data are coincident."[5]

These criteria give precision to what every student of the classical society intuitively recognizes: that the Greco-Roman world of the first century was socially stratified. Although overdramatic, M. Rostovtzeff's description of the stratification of the Mediterranean social order is useful:

> The senator and knights of the capital smiled at the boorishness of the municipal *gransignori*. The latter, in their turn despised the rich freedman and others. And separated from all stood the lower classes of the freeborn population, the mass of free peasants, free artisans, half-free farmers, and manual workers. Among the lower classes, again those resident in the city looked with a kind of contempt on the peasants, the *pagani* or *rustici*. In the background there was the enormous mass of slaves, servants, artisans, miners, agriculturalists, sailors and so forth.[6]

The sense of higher and lower status pressed heavily upon the people. In his influential evaluation of the legal privileges expected by and afforded to those of high social standing, P. Garnsey begins his study with the following recognition of the those of the social environment:

> The Romans saw men as subordinated to or raised up above one another by their involvement in conventional social relationship (as father was placed above son, a patron above a freedman, and a master above a slave); by their involvement in political relationships (the magistrate was placed above the private citizen); and by their respective positions in society.[7]

However, despite the rigid social barriers and the social hierarchy placed from above, it would be incorrect to conclude that there was no social mobility from below. Everybody, it seems, sought to improve their social position and it would be fair to say that those who most bitterly complained about the breakdown of the strict social hierarchy were those whose high social status was most threatened.

---

[5] R. Brown, *Social Psychology* (New York: Macmillan, 1965), p. 114.

[6] Rostovtzeff, *SEHHW*, vol. II, pp. 46f.

[7] Garnsey, *Social Status and Legal Privileges*, pp. 1–2.

Slaves worked hard for, and more often than not received, their freedom[8] (see Acts 6:9). Furthermore, if they had been owned by a Roman citizen, the slaves could expect to gain citizenship as well. Freedmen could amass vast fortunes and, in some cases, advance to positions of great authority.[9] However, while the freed slave was in a superior social position *vis-à-vis* those who had not yet been freed, it was hardly the case that he was a social equal of the one who had been freeborn. A slave's name often indicated his former status and it would take at least several generations for the ignominy of slavery to be forgotten.

Generally speaking, women as a group did not possess a high status and were subordinated to their husbands of fathers.[10] Yet, there are many examples of women who owned their businesses and were influential members of their communities. In Acts, Luke mentions Lydia who was a seller of purple goods (Acts 16:14), Priscilla, who, with her husband, was a tent-maker (Acts 18:3), and the women of Thessalonica and Beroea whose high status was acknowledged by Luke (Acts 17:4, 12).

Nevertheless, clear social boundaries remained and those individuals who succeeded in raising themselves above the station into which they were born were exceptions that proved the general rule. Therefore, while it is no doubt true that the world in which Luke lived and wrote can be described as one which was socially stratified, this concept is in need of further refinement.

Traditionally, the discussion of social stratification concerned the description of a single hierarchical structure within which each member of the society occupied a single position. For example, a senator held a recognized social position above an equestrian who, in turn, possessed a higher social status than that of the decurion, who was above the ordinary Roman citizen. At the lowest end of the

[8] For recent socio-historical studies of slavery see Bartchy, *Slavery*; P. R. C. Weaver, "Social Mobility in the Early Roman Empire: The Evidence of the Imperial Freedmen and Slaves," *Past and Present* 37 (1967), 3–20; P. R. C. Weaver, *Familia Caesaris: A Social Study of the Emperor's Freedmen and Slaves* (Cambridge: Cambridge University Press, 1972); Gager, "Religion and Social Class," pp. 9–12; M. B. Flory, "Family and Familia: A Study of Social Relations in Slavery," unpublished Ph.D. dissertation, Yale University, 1975; Koester, *History, Culture, and Religion*, pp. 54–67; Meeks, *Urban Christians*, pp. 20–22.

[9] Duff, *Freedmen*; Bartchy, *Slavery*; Gager, "Religion and Social Class," pp. 107–109; Macmullen, *Roman Social Relations*, p. 100; Meeks, *Urban Christians*, pp. 21–22.

[10] A. Oepke, "γυνή" in *TDNT*, vol. I, pp. 776–789; Pomery, *Goddesses*; Schüssler-Fiorenza, *In Memory of Her*; Meeks, *Urban Christians*, pp. 23–25.

social scale were women, children, and slaves. However, in the last thirty years it has been recognized that social stratification is best understood as a multi-dimensional phenomenon.[11] In other words proper discernment of an individual's social status requires measurements along each of the relevant, parallel, vertical, social hierarchies, or indices.

Luke presents a number of examples in Acts. Lydia as a single woman did not possess a high position in the social hierarchy in terms of sexual identity (Acts 16:14). Yet, as indicated by her professions, she probably possessed a fair amount of wealth and had relatively high economic status. If it could be discovered whether she was a slave, a freedwoman, or freeborn, an even more precise social description of Lydia's overall status could be achieved.

Felix, the governor, held a relatively high position on an occupation hierarchy. Since he was an equestrian he would possess a high degree of wealth. Yet, as tradition has it, he was a freedman and hence would not have been highly placed on a social hierarchy of pedigree.

The modern sociological discussion of this concept was pioneered by G. Lenski. In his study of social stratification and voting preference in Detroit, Lenski identified four relevant hierarchies of social status. According to Lenski they are: income, occupation, education, and ethnic background.[12] He found that individuals who had high status crystallization (who were "status consistent"), that is, who were highly placed on each of the social hierarchies, tended to vote for conservative politicians who would, for the most part, maintain the status quo. Conversely, Lenski found that those who were consistently not highly placed on the social hierarchies tended to support candidates who promised change. Lenski also advanced the contention that those individuals of low status crystallization, who were high on some status indices and low on others, were subjected to certain social pressures.

For example, a black (low ethnic status) doctor (high occupation, education, and income status) was not always accepted by his white contemporaries. Yet, his education, income, and occupation set him above the majority of blacks in Detroit. Since he was on the boundaries of potentially conflicting communities, he could become a "marginal" individual, one who was not accepted by either group. Lenski's conclusions have been widely accepted and other

---

11 Meeks, "The Social Context," 268.
12 Lenski, "Status Crystallization," 405–413.

sociologists have continued the study of status crystallization or status consistency in "terms of psychological stress and self-acceptance.[13]

It must be acknowledged that a potential methodological difficulty arises in simply appropriating vocabulary based on data gathered from twentieth-century Western, industrial societies and assuming that it describes the experience of first- and second-century, pre-industrial, Middle Eastern and Mediterranean communities. On the surface, there would seem to be a great dissimilarity between a black doctor in Detroit and, for example, a Jewish doctor in Antioch: doctors in antiquity had a much lower status than doctors of today. However, despite the dissimilarities, individuals of both historical eras would be confronted by similar social pressures. Therefore, with certain adjustments, the results of contemporary tests concerned with the dynamic concept of social status can be useful for an understanding of the first-century world which was probably more status conscious than ours.

At the outset of this book, the social hierarchies appropriate to Luke's historical context must be identified. As Wayne Meeks contends, wealth might count more heavily than having a rhetorical education, but being a scion of an old and famous family might count more than both.[14]

In a recent publication Meeks has written:

> Some of the indices of higher status were these: Roman citizenship, especially in the provinces in the early years of the empire when it was rare; citizenship in the local polis, compared with resident aliens; among the citizens, the decurions or city councillors of smaller cities; wealth, more and more, preferably inherited rather than worked for, and invested in land rather than trade; family and origin, though a freedman or even a slave of the emperor or of a senator was better off than many freeborn persons.[15]

Even a cursory glance at the literary and epigraphic evidence of the classical age shows that Meeks is correct.

Lack of citizenship was, in the words of E. A. Judge, "a humiliat-

---

[13] G. E. Lenski, "Social Participation and Status Crystallization," *ASR* 21 (1956), 458–464; E. Jackson, "Status Consistency and Symptoms of Stress," *ASR* 27 (1962), 469–480; C. A. Hornung, "Social Status, Status Inconsistency and Psychological Stress," *ASR* 42 (1977), 623–638.

[14] Meeks, "The Social Context," 268.

[15] Meeks, *The Moral World of the First Christians*, p. 34.

ing barrier to social acceptance in many cases."[16] Terms such as "stranger," "pilgrim," "sojourner," found in the biblical texts reflect the vocabulary of social exclusiveness.[17]

Those of the social élite separated the professions into the "liberal" and the "vulgar." Cicero wrote:

> Now in regard to trades and other means of livelihood, which ones are to be considered becoming to a gentleman and which ones are vulgar ... First, those means of livelihood are rejected as undesirable which incur people's ill-will, as those of tax-gatherers and usurers ... Least respectable of all those trades which cater for sensual pleasures: fishmongers, butchers, cooks, poulterers, and fishermen. But the professions in which either a higher degree of intelligence is required or from which no small benefit to society is derived – medicine and architecture, for example and teaching – these are proper for those whose social position they become.[18]

Although education and wealth were not, in and of themselves, enough to secure the individual a place among the élite, education and wealth were part and parcel of true social prestige.[19] In the eyes of those individuals of repute, the poor were morally weaker and, generally speaking, benevolence and gifts to the poor were a means of increasing one's prestige rather than an expression of moral compassion.[20]

Just how important one's pedigree was, in terms of social legitimation and acceptance, is reflected by the note or urgency in the words of Josephus as he indicates that he is not of ignoble birth: "My family is no ignoble one, tracing its descent far back to priestly ancestors."[21] About his father he writes: "Distinguished as he was by his noble birth, my father Matthias was even more esteemed for his upright character, being among the most notable men in

16 Judge, *Social Patterns*, p. 28.

17 Judge, *Social Patterns*, p. 28.

18 Cicero, *Concerning Offices*, 1.150; Macmullen, *Roman Social Relations*, p. 115.

19 Gager, "Religion and Social Class," p. 114; Plato, *Laws*, I, 641c–645c, believes that education brings excellence and improves the condition of the mind and the body. Right education invariably produces good men who "live nobly and vanquish their enemies in the field as well."

20 There were, no doubt, those in the first century who had great compassion for the poor. Strabo, *Geography*, xiv, 2, 5 (652) describes the quite generous inhabitants of Rhodes. See also Hands, *Charities and Social Aid*, pp. 62–75; Karris, 'Poor and Rich' p. 117.

21 Josephus, *The Life of Josephus*, trans. Thackery, Loeb Classical Library 1.

Jerusalem, our greatest city."[22] Josephus concludes his opening remarks: "With such a pedigree, which I cite as I find it recorded in the public registers, I can take leave of the would be detractors of my family."[23]

One can also see this concern in Luke-Acts. Paul is insulted when the tribune asks if he is an Egyptian (21:39). Moreover, Paul begins his speech to the Jews of Jerusalem with a statement about his Jewish background and credentials (22:3). Furthermore, despite his humble birth, the genealogy of Jesus (Luke 3:23ff.) shows his outstanding pedigree.

Finally, although not mentioned by Meeks, there was an important status distinction between rural and urban. The gospel stories of Jesus and his followers reflect primarily the life and experiences of rural men and women. To live off the land, totally dependent upon the conditions of weather and soil, was a meager existence. A bad year might mean the loss of all possessions with little hope for recovery. Away from the city, the rural dweller was less likely to be involved in the larger commercial and social life. Whether one was a tenant farmer on the estate of some great landowner or a hired fisherman working for one of the fishing collectives it was, more or less, a subsistence living. Rural folk would hardly have been considered privileged persons.[24]

In order to come to a more complete understanding of the social standing of Paul as portrayed by Luke in Acts, the following status characteristics which correspond to the status hierarchies described above will be used. They are: (1) pedigree, (2) education, (3) free, freed, or slave, (4) occupation, (5) wealth.

Yet the man who could truly claim to be a member of the *honestiores* also possessed the gentlemanly cardinal virtues of wisdom (φρόνησις), self-control (σωφροσύνη) righteousness (δικαιοσύνη) and bravery (ἀνδρεία). Therefore, a study of the portrayal of Paul in Acts must take into account how Luke shapes his narrative to highlight Paul's moral character. Close attention must be paid to the company Paul keeps and to the way Paul is juxtaposed with his antagonists. Likewise it is important to notice how characters in the narrative react to him, and how Paul responds to personal misfortune and trials.

The astute words of Meeks must be kept in mind. He writes: "it

[22] Josephus *Life*, 7.
[23] Josephus, *Life*, 6; Freyne, *Galilee*, p. 281.
[24] Freyne, *Galilee*, pp. 194–200.

would be a rare individual indeed who occupied exactly the same rank, in either his own view or that of others, in terms of all these factors. The generalized status of a person is a composite of his or her rank in all the relevant dimensions."[25]

An understanding of all the relevant factors of Luke's characterization of Paul will show just how rare an individual Paul is and, at the same time, indicate a possible purpose of this particular description.

Among other status attributes, Luke focuses on Paul's alleged Roman citizenship (16:36; 22:25, 26, 27, 29), reports Paul's claim to be a citizen of Tarsus (21:39), and emphasizes Paul's Pharisaic pedigree (22:3). These descriptive hereditary endowments add to Paul's overall "objective" or "attributive" status.

Objective status means those characteristics which concern generally recognized aspects of stratification which structure the environment.[26] In other words, the formal social hierarchies that have been identified above are means of measuring one's objective status. Paul's objective status, as described by Luke, is relatively high.

In addition, Luke describes Paul as a man of courage and sobriety which are characteristic cardinal virtues. These attributes contribute to the overall objective portrayal of Paul as well. However, as will be shown, Luke's general concern is to show that Paul became a man of moral virtue only *after* his conversion.

Besides emphasizing Paul's high objective status, Luke also sought to show that Paul's status and authority were acknowledged and deferred to by many of the characters whom Paul encounters. By way of illustration, that Paul continually attracts converts of high social standing confirms that he, and the faith which he represents, have been "accorded" or have "achieved" a high status. "Accorded" or "achieved" status is that prestige given to individuals or groups by others.[27] A further testimony to Paul's high accorded status is indicated by Luke when he reports that the tribune assigned a force of nearly 500 soldiers to escort Paul from Jerusalem to the governor in Caesarea (23:23). Likewise, the deference shown by the centurion Julius to Paul on the trip to Italy (27:3) assumes Paul's accorded status. Luke's description of the distinguished audience that gathered to hear Paul's defense before Festus

[25] Meeks, *Urban Christians*, p. 54.
[26] Lipsett, "Social Class," pp. 296–316.
[27] Lipsett, "Social Class," p. 299.

and Agrippa (25:23), as well as Festus' acceptance of Paul's request for a retrial in Rome (25:12), illustrates Luke's concern not only to portray Paul as a man of high social status but also to indicate that many others recognized and accepted his position.

Luke presents Paul as a man of high objective status who also has achieved a correspondingly high accorded status. Furthermore, in the three accounts of his conversion/call, Paul indicates how his "subjective" status vis-à-vis the church and God has changed. Once a persecutor of the Christians, now he perceives himself to be the missionary par excellence. "Subjective" status means "the personal sense of location within the social hierarchy."[28] Since Luke is constructing a narrative of sequential events, rather than focusing on the feelings of specific characters in Acts, it is difficult to judge the subjective status of any of the characters.

An appreciation of the three types of status is important because any individual is associated with various social groups. These individuals may have a different objective, accorded, and subjective social status within each of the communities to which they belong. Several factors must be kept clearly in focus. For example, a fisherman, a profession of low social status (low objective status) in the Greco-Roman world, would never be able to meet the social requirements needed to become a senator. Nevertheless, that same fisherman might become a relatively wealthy and respected leader within his village and hold a position of high social standing and high authority within his immediate community (high accorded status). Furthermore, within a new religious movement he might become a leading and authoritative member. Within the smaller community in which the fisherman is located his subjective status will probably coincide with his accorded status. As portrayed by Luke, Paul's objective status is relatively high in each of the three ethnic/political communities to which he belongs.

As long as individuals remained in their particular communities, where the boundaries of status were understood, little if any confusion arose. However, like the black doctor in Lenski's study, individuals in the first century who were of mixed status or crossed status boundaries faced inevitable difficulties. They would encounter the prejudice of those of recognized and long-standing status who were threatened by the "social climber" who sought to enter a higher social stratum. For example, Petronius describes the lavish,

28 Lipsett, "Social Class," p. 306.

lascivious, and gluttonous feast of the freedman Trimalchio with satirical disgust. That Petronius has exaggerated the opulence of Trimalchio is certain. However, this portrait of a freedman engaging in conspicuous consumption would no doubt amuse those of long-standing high objective social status who would know real-life, albeit lesser, examples of individuals who in their eyes had overstepped their place in society.

According to Petronius' portrait, Trimalchio had reached a high level of objective social status in terms of wealth. Yet, from Petronius' point of view, Trimalchio could hardly assume a high "accorded" status since his true crass and grotesque "objective" nature, which reflected his slave background, could never be hidden behind riches.[29]

There is an implicit expectation of an association between inherited status and noble character assumed by many Greek and Roman writers. As will be shown in more detail in a later chapter, Felix, the governor of Judaea, was another who could claim a high objective status which came as a result of his political position. However, in the eyes of Luke, Felix never exhibited the authority and self-control consonant with his appointment (24:25, 26).

On a less satirical note, it is clear that within the Christian community there were many believers whose objective secular status was not always coincidental with their accorded religious status. For example, the objective status of Priscilla and Aquila, the Jewish tent-makers, was not as high as, say, Apollos, who is described by Luke as an "eloquent man" from Alexandria (18:24).

Although little is known from Acts about his pedigree or profession, Luke's description of Apollos implies that he was a man trained in rhetoric and therefore possessed some level of sophistication. However, as teachers, Aquila and Priscilla have a high accorded status in the opinion of Christians. In contrast, Apollos, in spite of his objective status in terms of secular society, does not have as high an accorded status as that of his teachers (18:26).

Wayne Meeks has argued, as have many others, that early Christianity included individuals representing a variety of positions in the social hierarchy who were mixed together in the early church.[30] Individuals of relatively high objective social status (for example, a freeborn male, Roman citizen who owned a fishing co-operative in

[29] Petronius, *Satyricon*, xxvi–lxxix; Reekman, "Juvenal's View on Social Change," 117–161.

[30] Grant, "The Social Setting," pp. 16–29; G. Theissen, *Social Setting*, p. 33.

his coastal city) might conceivably be taught and placed under the authority of one of low objective but high accorded social status (for example, a freed slave who fished for the co-operative). This fact is surely illustrated in Acts where the first authoritative leaders are perceived as unsophisticated followers of a wandering charismatic. The early church included Peter and Cornelius the centurion, Simon the tanner, a minister of the queen of the Ethiopians (8:27), Sergius Paulus (13:7), and a member of the court of Herod (13:1).

The mixing of individuals of varying degrees of social status around the communion table and the crossing of the social boundaries could be problematic, as G. Theissen has perceptively shown in his study of the Corinthian community.[31] Yet, as Meeks has indicated, this mixing was probably an appealing aspect of the new faith, either for those who did not possess high status in the non-Christian community, or for those "status inconsistents" who found it difficult to locate themselves within a homogeneous secular community.

Maintaining disparate levels of social status could lead to what is called "status dissonance" or "marginality."[32] Meeks assumes that individuals who suffered from the ambiguities of status inconsistency and therefore confronted status dissonance "brought with them not only anxiety but also loneliness, in a society in which social position was important and usually rigid."[33]

Meeks also believes that the presence of a group of Gentiles who adhered to the synagogue ("Godfearers") "testifies to some kind of dissonance between them and their society."[34] In his study of the apparent division within the Christian congregation at Corinth, Theissen shows that Christianity offered the Gentile who was sympathetic to but not a proselyte of Judaism, "the possibility of acknowledging monotheism and high moral principles and at the same time attaining full religious equality without circumcision, without ritual demands, without restraints which would negatively affect their social status."[35] It is interesting to note that these Godfearing Gentiles are often mentioned in Luke-Acts (Luke 7:5; Acts 10:2; 16:14; 17:4).

Whoever the first readers/hearers of Luke-Acts were, Luke has Paul claim that he was a citizen of Rome and Tarsus. In so doing,

---

31   Theissen, *Social Setting*, pp. 70–73.
32   Lenski, "Status Crystallization," p. 107; Meeks, *Urban Christians*, pp. 53–54.
33   Meeks, *Urban Christians*, p. 191.
34   Meeks, *Urban Christians*, p. 221.
35   Theissen, *Social Setting*, p. 104.

the Lucan Paul represents an individual of secular status and success. Luke also stresses Paul's strict Pharisaic Jewish pedigree. In the next chapter these three claims will be studied in more detail. For the present discussion it will suffice to say that Luke, through the highlighting of Paul the Pharisee, offered to his audience an example of one who could combine righteousness before the law with high secular status. Likewise, Luke describes a faith community in which all are welcome and those of high status do not need to relinquish their secular prestige.

Black doctors in the twentieth century, freedmen with skills but stigmatized by their origins, independent women of moderate wealth, Jews who lived in Hellenized cities in the first century, and Gentiles who were drawn to the synagogue, all had to come to terms with the various communities of which they were a part. It may be that Luke wrote with such individuals in mind. Luke holds up Paul as an example to those who were seeking to increase or maintain their social status.

Yet Luke's purpose in presenting Paul's high objective and accorded secular and religious status with such prominence contains a deeper significance. Luke was asserting not only that the church could attract those of relatively high social status but also that it could offer the believer, upon conversion, a new accorded status which would, in turn, be recognized by the unbeliever as a mark of significant social distinction.

In Acts, Paul is the definite example of one who experiences a change of status through conversion. On three occasions Paul tells of the event on the road to Damascus where he was changed from persecutor to missionary. It is significant that Paul confesses that while he was a persecutor he was enraged and embittered. Yet, after his conversion Paul becomes a man of sobriety and self-control (26:25). These two qualities would have been recognized as cardinal virtues. It is also germane to note that the community in Jerusalem recognized Paul's new status (9:26) only when he had proven himself worthy (9:28). The Jerusalem church did not accord Paul the status that corresponded to his new objective status as a Christian in the sight of God.

Although in the concluding chapters of Acts Luke portrays Paul as a man who possesses high objective social status, it is important to mention that Luke does not offer the reader a full description of Paul's status characteristics until well after his conversion in Acts 9. It would not be too far fetched to presume that this was done intentionally. Luke wanted to suggest that true status and virtue were given to the believer by God through the Holy Spirit at conversion. This contention will receive a more detailed discussion in a later chapter.

The point advanced here is initially confirmed by a recognition that the Holy Spirit is the agent that conveys a new accorded status to the believer and confirms a new objective status inside the Christian community. That this is the case is evident from the outset of Luke's gospel. Mary recognizes that her original humble status is forever transformed by God in her response to the Holy Spirit: "For he has looked with favor on the lowliness of his servant. Surely, from now on all generations will call me blessed" (Luke 1:48). Mary further acknowledges, and by it Luke gives notice to his readers, that Jesus will be the cause of the rise of the humble and the fall of those in political authority ("He has brought down the powerful from their thrones, and lifted up the lowly" – 1:52) In passing, it would not be irrelevant to suggest that this passage, which is explicitly threatening to secular authority, counts against the traditional argument which held that Luke had a particularly positive view of Roman sovereignty. Even if Luke inherited this more radical motif from one of his sources, he has included it and so endorsed it.

Later in Luke's gospel Jesus promises his disciples that, when they are brought before powers and authorities to witness, his Spirit will give them wisdom (21:15). Mark and Matthew do not include wisdom as a gift of the Spirit in their accounts of Jesus' words (Mark 13:11; Matt. 10:19). Wisdom, as will be shown in chapter 4, is closely related to σωφροσύνη, which was the premier cardinal virtue. Hence, once again Luke reveals his interest in showing that the Spirit gives the believer a new objective religious status which has implications for their accorded and objective secular status as well. The Spirit brings power, wisdom, and courage.

The discussion of objective and accorded status has important implications for Luke's portrayal of Jesus. A full investigation of this issue would confuse the specific intent of this book which is to investigate the Paul of Acts. Nevertheless, it appears that part of Luke's aim was to show that Jesus, who was of humble objective status by human standards, was of the highest objective status in the sight of God. Furthermore, Luke indicates that God designated Jesus Lord and Christ at the resurrection (Acts 2:33).

In Acts the first thing that the disciples await is the Spirit which will give them power (1:8). It is also to be noted that Peter and John, even though they were considered to be simple uneducated fisherfolk of low objective and accorded status, are transformed through the Spirit into men who speak with an authority that amazes the Sanhedrin (4:13).

In the Greco-Roman world, those who held positions of authority, and therefore could speak with boldness, were usually those of high social status. The term, "boldness" might suggest presumption, but the reference in the context to a "sign" suggests a divine authorization. Here, in Luke and Acts, the Spirit empowers the lowly and increases their standing and prestige.

In Peter's first speech at Pentecost he promises his listeners that if they repent and are baptized, they will receive the gift of the Holy Spirit (2:38). To Luke, one of the main gifts of the Holy Spirit is a new accorded and subjective status which is given by God to the believer through faith which, in turn, gives a new objective status to the believer as a member of the Kingdom of God.

By way of summary, those who would have read Acts include both those of relatively high and those of relatively low status. Luke did not dismiss those of high social status. Indeed throughout Acts he offered examples of persons who were of high objective social status throughout Acts and responded favorably to the gospel. Yet, Luke does not ignore those of low objective social status either. Luke wanted to show that religious conversion brought with it increased prestige, social standing, and virtue.

In Acts not all individuals of high objective secular social status convert. Furthermore, it would be incorrect to say that for Luke social standing was a prerequisite for belief. However, status attributes such as wealth, good pedigree, education, and vocation were not to be rejected. Despite Jesus' words to the rich young ruler (Luke 18:22), and Luke's positive description of the early Christian community of goods in Jerusalem (Acts 4:32ff.), in the concluding chapters of Acts Luke indicated that those of authority and wealth would not have to lose or lessen their secular objective status to become a Christian. The prerequisite was recognition of the ultimate status and authority of Jesus as the Christ. To these potential believers, Paul represents the paragon of status and virtue. Likewise, those who sought to increase their status would be offered the definitive way of doing so. Through faith those of low status would be accepted as social equals and mix freely with those of higher status. Luke's is an inclusive gospel.

Conclusion

In conclusion, three assumptions have been made in this chapter. The first is that the Greco-Roman world of the first century was both consciously and unconsciously shaped by the pressures of social status. Therefore it was important to offer a brief investigation of the vocabulary used to discuss this issue.

The second assumption, which follows from the first, is that Luke was a writer of his age and hence reflects the issues which were important to the larger social world. Therefore it was important to identify those status indices which were significant for Luke's social environment. The first readers/hearers of Acts would have intuitively recognized those characteristics that would have marked an individual as being of high status and moral virtue. Luke's audience would have understood the inferences and implications of his character description, as well as the subtle and dramatic effects of the movement of the narrative.

The third assumption, which is the only contentious one, is that Luke shaped the characterization of Paul in Acts with a particular concern to show him to be one of high social status. It is now necessary to study the text of Acts in the attempt to understand the social description of Paul.

3

PAUL AS GREEK, ROMAN, PHARISEE

In Acts 21–23 Luke describes Paul in two ways which seem to be at odds with one another. On the one hand, Paul is described as a Jew, on the other as a citizen of the Greek city of Tarsus (21:39). Paul claims that, from an early age, he was brought up in Jerusalem at the feet of Gamaliel (22:3). Furthermore, Paul is quick to assert that he is both a Roman citizen (22:25,27,28), and a strict Pharisee from a Pharisaic family (23:6). This description presents difficulties.

The purpose of this chapter will be to show that in Acts 21:27 to 23:11 Luke has described Paul in such a way as to make him a most striking figure in the first-century Greco-Roman world. As has been stressed in the previous chapter, and will be indicated in the chapters to come, the Greco-Roman world placed great significance upon one's breeding, one's social status, one's prestige, and one's authority.

In both what is explicitly stated and what is implicitly presented, Luke is concerned to show that Paul was just such a man of prestige, status, and authority. Therefore a proper understanding of the biographical data presented by Luke in 21:17 to 23:11, is crucial to a correct comprehension of all subsequent events recorded in Acts.

As indicated in the introductory chapter, the fact that Paul is highlighted in Acts in order to serve a particular Lucan purpose is not debated by anyone. Furthermore, that Luke has presented a portrait of Paul which, in its final form, is not historically accurate in all its individual parts is hardly an innovative observation. One merely has to scan the numerous articles and books on the comparison of the Paul of Acts with the Paul of the letters to realize that.

However, what is somewhat surprising is that although so many have questioned Luke's chronological and theological portrait of Paul, relatively few have recognized fully the difficulty of harmonizing the biographical details of Paul given in Acts.[1] Of those who have recognized the problems, few have adequately appropriated them into a convincing discussion about Luke's portrayal of Paul. For example, H. J. Schoeps in his study of Paul acknowledges that there would have been few if any Roman-citizen Pharisees: *"civis Romanus* and 'Pharisee of the Pharisees' was no doubt a rare one in Palestine and confronts us with an extraordinary phenomenon of the Diaspora."[2]

However, having made note of the "extraordinary phenomenon" he does not press on, nor do many others, to investigate the implications of his statement. Furthermore, he does not even mention Paul's citizenship of Tarsus which, due to various civic and social obligations, would probably have been even more problematic than just the Roman citizenship.

It is highly improbable that a strict Pharisee, who had come from a rigorous Pharisaic family from Tarsus, would also have possessed citizenships. Each of the religious and civic claims made by Paul in Acts would have, in and of themselves, carried a high degree of prestige and respectability relative to particular communities. For example, Pharisees were recognized for their strict observance of the Torah in matters of cultic cleanliness and table fellowship, and had the reputation of separating themselves from the larger community. The Pharisees, as shown by the sources, were both respected by some and dismissed by others for their conscientious interpretation of the Torah. They possessed a high degree of religious status. Josephus wrote that "they make no concessions to luxury."[3] Although Pharisees were not, as a rule, wealthy, some were highly educated and their adherence to the law made them an esteemed group. In the writings of Josephus, the Pharisees played a particularly prominent role in first-century Judaism and had the support of the majority of Jews in Jerusalem.[4]

In the gospels the Pharisees are notorious but, nonetheless, recog-

[1] Vielhauer, "On the Paulinisms of Acts," pp. 33–50; V. Wilkens, "Interpreting Luke-Acts in a Period of Existential Theology," in *SLA*, pp. 60–83; P. Borgen, "From Paul to Luke," 168–182.; C. K. Barrett, *New Testament Essays* (London: SPCK 1972), pp. 70–115; Knox, *Chapters in a Life of Paul*; R. Jewett, *A Chronology of Paul's life*; Corley, *Colloquy on New Testament Studies*, especially part 4: "Seminar on Pauline Chronology"; Lüdemann, *Paul: Apostle to the Gentiles*.

[2] H. J. Schoeps, *Paul: The Theology of the Apostle Paul in the Light of Jewish Religious History*, English translation by H. Knight (London: Lutterworth Press, 1961), p. 25; Theissen, *Social Setting*; Meeks, *Urban Christians*, pp. 14, 38.

[3] Josephus, *Antiquities*, xviii, 12.

[4] Josephus, *Jewish Wars*, i, 110–114; ii, 162–4; *Antiquities*, xiii, 408–410.

nized for their reputation and authority. In Acts, the Pharisees, represented by the person of Gamaliel – who was held in honor by all the people (Acts 5:34) – are favorably represented. As indicated in the previous chapter, social status is not strictly defined in terms of wealth. Therefore, it is not improper to suggest that, at least to those who would have read Josephus, the gospels, and Acts, Pharisees had high visibility and a correspondingly high religious and social status.

Not everyone in the Greco-Roman world could claim citizenship of their city (πόλις). For Paul, as he indicates in Acts, to be a citizen of Tarsus was a mark of distinction. For Paul to be a full citizen yet claim a strict Jewish, if not Pharisaic, upbringing is problematic.

While communities of Jews did possess a recognized civic status in the cities of the Diaspora as members of a πολίτευμα, they did not automatically possess full citizenship. Full citizenship in the Greek cities implied loyalty to the local gods and participation in Greek education. Jews possessed certain civic rights which allowed them to follow their own customs and not to participate in the celebrations of the city. But these particular charters of special civic status do not necessarily prove full citizenship.

Formal citizenship was not determined simply by residence, or by birth in a given location. Citizenship in the cities such as Alexandria, Antioch, Cyrene, and Tarsus was always limited, and therefore carried with it a high degree of social superiority and implied wealth and importance.

Although Roman citizenship became increasingly common through the first three centuries, for Paul to have citizenship in the first century is a mark of distinction. Before the more lenient policy of Claudius, citizenship of Rome in the eastern provinces was bestowed only by individual grants and was very rare.[5] As affirmed in Acts, Paul's citizenship was inherited, which means that Paul's family earned or was given the citizenship during the reign of Augustus, if not before. For a family from Tarsus to have Roman citizenship implies a status and prestige that would have been shared with a very small number of individuals in the eastern provinces of the Roman empire. W. Ramsay has admitted that for Paul's family to possess both citizenships would probably have placed them among the governing élite of the empire![6]

The combination of Roman citizenship with Greek citizenship

---

[5] Sherwin-White, *The Roman Citizenship*, p. 273.
[6] Ramsay, *The Cities of St. Paul*, p. 227.

was not uncommon. Yet both of these citizenships would have implied a degree of Hellenization which would have made strict Pharisaic practice diffficult, if not impossible. The problem, simply stated, is whether it is probable that Paul could have lived in a Pharisaic family from birth, and have been a citizen of Tarsus and a Roman citizen in the manner presented by Luke. When studying the description of Paul in Acts, one receives the distinct impression that the whole of the portrayal of Paul is greater than the sum of each of the parts. It appears as if Paul is presented in Acts in such a way as to stress his social credentials for a particular purpose.

Before beginning a detailed discussion of these problematic issues, some preliminary remarks are in order. Despite what has been suggested above, acceptance of the historicity of the Lucan portrayal of Paul remains persuasive to many for two reasons. First, the Paul of Acts supports the ecclesiastical tradition of Paul as the perfect "chosen vessel," able to bridge both Hellenistic and Jewish worlds. Paul himself exclaims: "To the Jews I became as a Jew ... To those outside the law I became as one outside the law ... so that I might win those outside the law" (1 Cor. 9:20–1). Scholars who have not looked closely enough at the biographical details presented by Luke argue that there is no reason to question the data in Acts. The second persuasive reason, perhaps even more forceful than the first, is that the unique characterization of Paul suggests historicity. Luke would not have had an adequate motive for creating such a portrayal.

While there is much in the traditions behind the sources used by Luke which is trustworthy, not enough attention has been paid to certain added features of the Lucan portrayal of Paul which are historically problematic. Furthermore, to say that Luke highlighted certain aspects of his portrayal of Paul in order to present him as a man of high social standing and moral virtue does not necessarily take away from Paul's unique genius, his eclectic upbringing, or his position as missionary to the Gentiles *par excellence*.

That Paul came from Tarsus, moved to Jerusalem, and was at home in both the Greek and Jewish world may indeed be true. But a careful reading of Acts indicates that Luke was concerned to show more than that. Comments concerning Luke's motive will be saved for a more general conclusion after the evidence is investigated.

One of the main tasks of this chapter is to look closely at the manner in which the character of Paul is presented by Luke in Acts 21:17 to 23:11, paying particular attention to his social description.

It is probable that Luke used and shaped the biographical material he acquired in order to draw attention to Paul's impressive social credentials. The task is to identify both the explicit statements and implicit allusions which Luke used in order to convey Paul's pedigree, education, wealth, and overall social status.

Before investigating the biographical data in Acts, it is necessary, for the purpose of comparison, to note the autobiographical details provided by Paul in his letters. The reader is confronted by the dearth of information about Paul's birth and upbringing which could serve to corroborate all of the specific claims which Luke had Paul make in Acts. There is no explicit evidence that Paul was ever born in Tarsus or, for that matter, that he was a Roman citizen. In Galatians 1:21 Paul reports that he went into the regions of Cilicia after seeing Peter and James in Jerusalem but this is hardly tantamount to a confession of his birthplace.

Some have tried to find a reference to his Roman citizenship in Philippians 1:13–26 where Paul writes that he has a choice to make about life or death. J. F. Collange, in his commentary on Philippians, believes that Paul's dilemma involves a decision whether or not to disclose his Roman citizenship. To Collange, if Paul does decide to offer this information, he will be freed to continue his mission.[7] Collange's reconstruction goes far beyond the evidence of those verses.

It has been argued that Paul does not mention his citizenship in his letters either because the context of the letter does not call for this self-disclosure or because he is too modest to do so. While these are possibilities, they are no more than conjecture. Furthermore, that Paul does not speak of his Roman citizenship due to modesty seems to contradict the fact that the Paul of the letters, in defense of his gospel, never hesitates to proclaim his credentials.

What does appear with great clarity in the letters is that Paul saw himself as an Israelite, and a descendant of Abraham from the tribe of Benjamin (Rom. 11:1). Paul declares that he was circumcised on the eighth day and that he was a "Hebrew of Hebrews; as to the law a Pharisee" (Phil. 3:5). He even recalls with pride that he was advanced in Judaism beyond his contemporaries and that he was extremely zealous (Gal. 1:14). It was this zeal that led him to persecute the early church. Paul is proud of his Jewish pedigree and does not hesitate to proclaim it. Hence, in the letters the only explicit

[7] J. F. Collange, *The Epistle of St. Paul to the Philippians*, trans. A. W. Heathcote (London: Epworth Press, 1979).

biographical data concerning Paul show that he was a strict Jew –
and a zealous one at that.

Having thus noted the biographical data presented in the letters,
it is necessary to return to the portrayal of Paul in Acts and
investigate the claims in the order in which they appear in Acts 21 to
23. First the evidence concerning the possession of Greek citizenship by Jews (21:39) will be discussed. Second, the data concerned
with his alleged Roman citizenship (22:25) will be studied. Third,
the data concerning strict Pharisaism in the Diaspora and the
meaning of the phrase "a son of Pharisees" (23:6) will be investigated. When this preliminary study is complete, certain other passages which add to the totality of the Lucan portrayal of Paul will be
examined. Then the original query will be asked again about the
probability that Paul could have combined such characteristics in
the way Luke relates. It is important to note that each of the first
three claims of Paul will be studied in the context of the scenes in
Acts in which it is made. In so doing it will be shown that Luke was
cognizant of the social significance of the claims being expressed.

Paul, the Greek citizen (21:39)

In an attempt to quell the riot that ensues upon the accusation that
Paul has taken a Gentile into the Temple, the Roman guards carry
Paul to safety, and when away from the crowd, they bind Paul with
two chains (21:33). Out of immediate danger Paul requests to speak
to those who would have taken his life.[8] Haenchen has remarked
that Paul's request to the tribune ("May I say something to you" –
21:37) is spoken with "elaborate politeness."[9]

The centurion is taken aback upon hearing such Greek and
responds: "You know Greek?" (21:37). Such an introduction to
Paul's speech is a wonderfully devised piece and it places Paul on
center stage. The tribune believed that he had caught the "Egyptian" but the official's perception, roused by the disheveled Paul, was
far off the mark.

Commentators disagree on the historicity of the scene. For
example, H. Conzelmann is convinced that this scene, as it is
recorded in Acts, is not historical, and many would agree.[10] F. F.
Bruce, on the other hand, sees no reason to dismiss this scene as

---

[8] Haenchen, *Acts*, p. 620.
[9] Haenchen, *Acts*, p. 619.
[10] Conzelmann, *Acts*, p. 123; Haenchen, *Acts*, p. 622.

Luke's redactional invention.[11] The identification of "the Egyptian" is somewhat problematic.[12] However, most attention is placed upon the last clause of Paul's response: "I am a Jew, from Tarsus in Cilicia, a citizen of an important city" (21:39). This clause is, in the words of Cadbury, "entirely idiomatic" in form and application, which is expressive of Greek pride and indicates that the city in question is predominantly Greek.[13]

Some astute commentators have realized that Paul's claim to be a citizen of "no mean city" suggests a fairly high level of social status.[14] F. F. Bruce realizes that for Paul to be a citizen of Tarsus and a Roman citizen, which Paul has already alluded to in Acts 16, "placed him among the élite of the citizens of Tarsus."[15]

Yet, few have investigated, in any depth, the data which would support or deny the statement that Paul possessed the citizenship of Tarsus. Furthermore, while most commentators acknowledge the explicit status juxtaposition of Greek and Egyptian, the observation is given secondary importance. The primary importance of the scene, according to Haenchen, is that "it constitutes the first acquittal of Christendom ... Christianity has nothing to do with political Messianism."[16] This comment reflects Haenchen's, and most others', insistence that Luke is writing to impress upon his audience Christianity's peaceful and law-abiding nature. However, the important status juxtaposition must be emphasized and the claim being made here brought to the forefront.

The reaction of Paul to his mistaken identity is representative of Luke's sensitivity to the issue of Paul's social status throughout these last chapters in Acts. Being mistaken for an Egyptian was an immense social slur. Jews who lived in Alexandria resented being identified as Greek citizens although they were not as a group given the franchise. The Greek citizens maintained their social distance from the larger Egyptian population through their tax exemptions and other privileges.[17] These perquisites were sought after, but not gained, by the higher-status Jews of Alexandria.

---

11 Bruce, *Acts*, p. 399–400; Marshall, *Acts*, p. 352.

12 H. Cadbury, *Book of Acts*, p. 32; Josephus, *Jewish Wars*, ii, 261–263 and *Beginnings* vol. II, pp. 357ff. The Egyptian of Josephus is not necessarily the Egyptian the Centurion believed he had caught. Eusebius, *Church History*, trans. A. C. McGiffert, ii, 21; Bruce, *Acts*, p. 398.

13 Cadbury, *Book of Acts*, p. 33.

14 Rackham, *Acts*, p. 420; *Beginnings*, IV, pp. 276–278.

15 Bruce, *Acts*, p. 398.

16 Haenchen, *Acts*, p. 622; Marshall, *Acts*, p. 382.

17 On Jewish privileges in Alexandria see *CPJ*, no. 151 on Jewish exemptions in Alexandria; Philo, *Legatio ad Gaium*, trans. E. M. Smallwood, pp. 8f; Smallwood,

Josephus mentions that Egyptians were the only ones refused any citizen rights at all from Rome.[18] In a papyrus, being called an Egyptian was likened to being called a barbarian.[19] Philo was even more scathing in his criticism of Egyptian natives. He showed contempt for Egyptian religion and described the Egyptian as passionate, unstable, rebellious, and unreasonable.[20]

Strabo was likewise harsh. He called the Egyptians "savage, not inclined to be civil, and numerous."[21] The social and political changes instigated by the Romans had, at least to Strabo, begun to put things right; but there was still no good wine![22] It is no wonder that Luke would want to distinguish Paul from the Egyptian rebel.

In the account in Acts, Paul immediately takes offense at this social slander and is quick to proclaim his status and his credentials. His fluency in Greek is explained by his birth in Tarsus of Cilicia. This was no idle boast since Tarsus was, with Alexandria and Athens, arguably one of the three chief centers of learning in the ancient world. Tarsus was also the capital of Cilicia and a free city of the empire.[23]

In Acts, Paul asserts that he was not just a native of the city but a citizen. Paul's Tarsian citizenship made no great impression on the tribune but this is only an indication of the tribune's boorishness. Dio Chrysostom in his first Tarsic discourse writes:

> The fact is, my friends, that you consider yourselves fortunate and blessed because your home is in a great city and you occupy a fertile land, because you find the needs of life supplied for you in greatest abundance and profusion, because you have this river flowing through the heart of your city, and because, moreover, Tarsus is the capital of all the people of Cilicia.[24]

The Jews Under Roman Rule, pp. 230–2; L. H. Feldman, "Orthodoxy of the Jews," 215–237; N. Lewis, *Life in Egypt under Roman Rule* (Oxford: Clarendon Press, 1985).

[18] Josephus, *Against Apion*, ii, 41.

[19] Oxyrhynchus Papyri 1681 93rd col., 11, 4f.

[20] Philo, *Allegorical Interpretation*, ii, 84; iii, 13, 37f, 81, 87 (particularly iii, 38); *On Dreams*, ii, 255. He also calls them uneducated. *On the Preliminary Studies*, 20; *On Dreams*, i, 240.

[21] Strabo, *Geography*, xvii, 1,12.

[22] *Geography*, xvii, 1,13.

[23] Jones, *The Greek City*, p. 207; Ramsay, *Cities of St. Paul*, pp. 85–116; Ramsay "Tarsus"; T. B. Mitford, "Roman Rough Cilicia," in H. Temporini and W. Haase, *ANRW*, vol. II, 7.2 (1980) pp. 1,230–1,261.

[24] Dio Chrysostom, *The Tarsic Discourses*, xxxiii 17; Xenophon, *Anabasis*, i, 2, 22–33; Josephus, *Antiquities*, i, 6, 7; Jones, *Cities of the Eastern Roman Provinces*, pp. 192–215; Dio Chrysostom, *Tarsic Discourses*, xxxiii, 49.

Although Dio's remarks on Tarsus are on the whole critical, the faults attributed by him are those that, in the words of Sir William Ramsay, "accompany overflowing prosperity."[25] Strabo, on the other hand, praises Tarsus as a city of high intellectual repute:

> The people at Tarsus have devoted themselves so eagerly, not only to philosophy, but also to the whole round of education in general, that they have surpassed Athens, Alexandria, or any other place that can be named where there have been schools and lectures of philosophers ... Further, the city of Tarsus has all kinds of schools of rhetoric, and in general it not only has a flourishing population but also is most powerful, thus keeping up the reputation of the mother city.[26]

The history of the citizenship of Tarsus is complicated and the historical development of the civic rights of the Jews in that city, as in other cities in the Greco-Roman world, is even more so. Before the reforms of Athenodorus (15 B.C.E.?), Tarsus had a democratic constitution that included all native free males as citizens. That this democracy recognized the equal status of the Jewish settlers is doubtful.

Athenodorus reformed the constitution and required a payment of 500 drachmae for the privilege of full citizenship.[27] This act effectively disenfranchised the majority of the population by removing some of the craftsmen and most of the linen workers from the list of citizens. As Dio's remarks suggest, the citizens of Tarsus, in the post-Athenodorus reform, were concerned and embarrassed by the numerous linen workers who were for the most part underpaid and made up the bulk of the day laborers of the city: "And some are accustomed to call them 'linen workers', and at times the citizens are irritated by them and assert that they are a useless rabble and responsible for the tumult and disorders in Tarsus."[28]

Dio, in expressing his democratic inclination, is highly critical of the fact that, in Tarsus, wealth was the only criterion of citizenship.[29] However, Dio's remarks also indicate how the citizenship of Tarsus would have been understood during Paul's lifetime and, of even more importance for this study, how the citizenship of Tarsus

[25] Ramsay, *Cities of St. Paul*, p. 232.
[26] Strabo, *Geography*, xiv, 5, 12–15.
[27] Jones, *The Greek City*, p. 174.
[28] Dio Chrysostom, *Tarsic Discourses*, xxxiv, 23.
[29] *Ibid.*

would have been understood by those who read Luke-Acts. Tarsus was a major city and one had to possess at least moderate wealth to be considered for citizenship.

Tarsus' apparent affluence is alluded to again by Philostratus, who writes: "for nowhere are men more addicted than here to luxury."[30] The gulf which separated those who could enjoy the wealth of the city from the large number of linen workers and craftsmen who lived in relative poverty must have been large indeed. To claim the citizenship of Tarsus in the middle decades of the first century was a social distinction of no small degree.

Jews in Tarsus

According to H. Böhlig, there had been Jews in Tarsus from the time of Antiochus IV, Epiphanes (171 B.C.E.).[31] Böhlig assumes that Antiochus IV, following the precedent of Seleucus I and Antiochus II, who gave Jews civic rights in other cities, presented Jews in Tarsus with the same liberal rights and protection.[32] Hence, to Böhlig, Jews were full-standing citizens of Tarsus from the founding of the city.

Although there is no evidence to prove Böhlig wrong, there are two immediate problems which count against Böhlig's description. First, and importantly, since Böhlig's study it has been shown that in the other cities of the Greco-Roman world certain civic rights possessed by the Jews did not constitute full citizenship.[33] Rather, Jews held a middle status. They were better off, in most cases, than the non-Greek inhabitants [κατοίκοι] but they did not, as a group, have the same status as Greek citizens. Second, it is important to note that Antiochus IV's program of Hellenization in Jerusalem caused bitter opposition.

Antiochus Epiphanes holds a particularly notorious status in Jewish literature: he is described as the worst tyrant in history (Dan. 11:36). One can only wonder if law-abiding Jews in Tarsus would have accepted the citizenship which would have required certain obligations in terms of service to the local gods and participation in

---

[30] Philostratus, trans. F. C. Conybeare, *Life of Apollonius of Tyana*, i. 7.

[31] Böhlig, *Tarsos*, p. 128; Philo, *Allegorical Interpretation*, 281; Welles, "Hellenistic Tarsus," 41–75; Schürer rev., vol. III, pp. 33–4.

[32] Böhlig, *Tarsos*, p. 129, depends upon Josephus, *Antiquities*, xii, 121, 124, yet questions the overall trustworthiness of Josephus' account!

[33] Tarn, *Hellenistic Civilization*, pp. 211ff.; Tcherikover, *Hellenistic Civilization and the Jews*, trans. S. Applebaum, pp. 297–332.

education and civic festivals. In other words, it cannot be assumed that Jews could have possessed the citizenship on equal footing with the Greek inhabitants without to some extent compromising their Jewishness.

Citizenship in the Greek cities was not simply acquired by everyone upon birth in a given locale. Rather, citizenship throughout the Greek cities of the empire was earned, bought, or inherited. Becoming a citizen of a polis, "depended upon hereditary possession of citizenship, or on a special grant, honorary or otherwise by the city authority ... but citizenship still remained an exclusive privilege which could not be obtained automatically or as a matter of course."[34] Full citizenship in a Greek city was reserved, even in the city of Tarsus which was known for its love of luxury, for those of landed wealth and was a mark of status that many longed for but few achieved.

At this point two critical questions are raised. First, what was the probability that Jews were citizens of Greek cities? Second, what was the probability that Paul was a citizen of Tarsus? E. M. Smallwood calls Jews who coveted Greek citizenship "modernists" and those Jews who paraded their Hellenization "no better than apostates."[35] The traditional portrait of the Jews based on the classical literature as world-haters and anti-social separatists has come under constant attack.[36] Many scholars today reject the traditional simplistic definition that Jews separated themselves from all forms of Hellenization.[37] Furthermore, the evidence seems to suggest that there were Jews who were both conscious of their religious identity and also at home in the Hellenistic environment.

J. Goldstein, in his study on Jews in the Diaspora, argues that far from distancing themselves from Hellenization many Jews welcomed the Greek influence and actively sought assimilation without consciously intending to reject their Judaism. Goldstein goes so far as to argue that since the Torah had nothing specifically to say about much of what is considered hellenistic culture, Hellenization did not threaten Jewish identity.[38] While all this may be true, it is interesting to observe that Goldstein himself wants to maintain that participation in the gymnasium and unlimited association with

[34] Applebaum, "Legal Status," pp. 26–7.
[35] Smallwood, *The Jews Under Roman Rule*, p. 235.
[36] Stern, *Greek and Latin Authors*; Gager, *The Origins of Anti-Semitism*.
[37] Smith "Fences and Neighbors," vol. II, pp. 1–26; Kraabel, "The Roman Diaspora," 445–464
[38] Goldstein, "Jewish Acceptance," pp. 64–87.

Greeks in terms of religious celebrations would have been acknowledged as taboo by strict Jews.[39]

The important work of A. T. Kraabel and the even more recent study of the evidence by P. Trebilco have shown that, at least in Sardis, Goldstein's thesis does not go far enough.[40] In Sardis in Lydia, the remains of a late third-century synagogue have been uncovered.[41] The synagogue, which had been before its remodeling a judicial tribunal for the city, was an integral and prominent part of a bath–gymnasium complex. This proximity of the synagogue to the bath–gymnasium is, in the words of Trebilco, "completely unparalleled in the ancient world."[42]

Kraabel has described the large colonnaded forecourt and the public hall that could hold 1,000 people[43]. Moreover, eighty inscriptions, many of which recorded donations to the synagogue, were discovered. Often, but not always, these inscriptions include the title "Sardianos." There is even one office holder mentioned: Aurelios Basileides who was a "former procurator," an official of the provincial governor responsible for collecting revenues. As Trebilco points out, the procurator was, strictly speaking, a personal agent of the emperor and was often an imperial freedman. Kraabel, one of the excavators of the synagogue, wrote that here is "a Jewish community quite integrated into the social, economic and political life of a major Anatolian city ... Nothing in the archaeological or epigraphical evidence would suggest exclusiveness of any kind; they participate fully in the community life."[44]

Trebilco offers two late third-century inscriptions from Acmoneia in Phrygia which tell of two Jewish men, Aurelios Phrugianus and Tiberius Flavius Alexandros, who held numerous civic positions in that city.[45] Furthermore, Trebilco uses Paul as evidence for this general Jewish assimilation.

---

[39] Goldstein, "Jewish Acceptance," pp. 66–67.

[40] Goldstein, "Jewish Acceptance," p. 67; *2 Maccabees* 4:9–15; Josephus, *Antiquities* xv, 267ff; Tarn, *Hellenistic Civilization*, p. 221; Harris, *Greek Athletics*, Appendix "Jews with Greek or Roman Names," pp. 102–106.

[41] Kraabel, "Paganism and Judaism," pp. 13–33; Schürer rev., vol. III, pp. 21ff; Trebilco, *Jewish Communities*; G. M. A. Hanfmann, *Sardis*.

[42] Trebilco, *Jewish Communities*.

[43] A. T. Kraabel and A. R. Seager, "The Synagogue and the Jewish Community," in Hanfmann, *Sardis*, pp. 168–190; Kraabel, "Social Systems."

[44] Kraabel, "Six Questionable Assumptions," p. 448; L. Roberts, *Nouvelles Inscriptions de Sardes* (Paris: A. Maisonneuve, 1972).

[45] Trebilco, *Jewish Communities*, pp. 6–7; Smallwood, *The Jews Under Roman Rule*, p. 503.

This evidence does indeed call into question the traditional consensus that the Jews of the Diaspora were forced either to assimilate and thereby apostatize, or seek to remove themselves entirely from the life of their cities in order to maintain cultic purity. However, just as one can no longer contend that all Diaspora Jews sought to erect protective walls around their faith, neither should one go to the opposite extreme and say that all Jews, in all places, became fully involved in all aspects of the social and political life of their city. The diversity of Judaism both before and after the destruction of the Temple is far too complicated to allow for an uncritical acceptance of either position.

A middle course is preferable. While one may admit that there were some Jews who could comfortably balance their faith with their secular life, the literary evidence should not be totally ignored. Furthermore, what is strict Judaism to one group is not necessarily strict Judaism to another. One only has to remember that the compilation of the Mishnah was going on at the same time as these liberal Jews were living in Sardis.

While important, the late dating and the very uniqueness of the Sardis evidence should be kept in mind. Perhaps the Jewish community that worshiped at that magnificent synagogue represents the exception that proves the rule. Furthermore, all the evidence presented comes from the late third century. It had been at least fifty years since Caracalla's edict included just about all free males within the empire as Roman citizens. Aurelios Basileides and Aurelios Phrygianus probably took their names from the emperor when they or their ancestors became citizens. It is not necessarily the case that the condition of the Jewish communities in a city as far west as Sardis, 200 years after the destruction of the Temple and over 100 years since Hadrian had renamed Jerusalem Aelia Capitolina, represents the condition of Diaspora Judaism in cities which were to the far east of Sardis at the end of the first century C.E. In other words, there are major historical and geographical issues to be decided.

Moreover, one should not necessarily assume that all the names on the inscriptions are Jewish. There were pious non-Jews who had given to that synagogue as well. The fact that the city gave the building to the Jews suggests non-Jewish support for this endeavor. Even if all the names on the inscriptional list of donors were Jewish only some of them note that they came from Sardis. This designation does not necessarily imply full citizenship status. As will be shown, some of the Jews of Alexandria called themselves "Alexandrians" without possessing citizenship. Yet even if all the Jews who call themselves Sardinians were citizens of that town, this only serves to substantiate the contention that Jews who possessed the citizenship of their city were in the wealthy minority of their fellows. This evidence also seems to demonstrate that Jews, as a group, were not automatically included in the citizenship. If they were, why make mention of it on the inscription?

While some Jews would have been able to maintain a dual identity, not all Jews would have been as open to hellenistic pressures. One can safely assume that just as there are varying degrees of orthodoxy in present-day Judaism and in the Judaism of Jerusalem in the days of Jesus and Paul, so too it can be assumed that the Judaism of the Diaspora was varied in its expression. A contention, which must be tested, is that the more likely it is that Paul was of a Pharisaic family, the less likely it is that he inherited full citizenship of Tarsus.

A city's municipal life was intimately connected to its cultic celebrations because Greek religion, as is commonly acknowledged, embraced politics.[46] Each Greek city had its tutelary god or goddess and recognition of the deity was fundamental to civic identity. The importance of Pallas Athene to Athens is well known and documented. Aristophanes in the fifth century B.C.E. acknowledges Pallas' primacy and Aelius Aristides in the second century C.E. used similar language in his speech to the Panathenaic festival.[47]

An inscription, found in Eretria (308 B.C.E.), commemorating the departure of the Macedonians from the city, is illuminating in that it acknowledges the fundamental connection between civic and religious celebrations.[48] The inscription furthermore identifies and thereby differentiates citizen (πολίτης) from an inhabitant (ἔνοικος) in the city. The declaration invites all persons residing in Eretria to join the celebration. However, only the citizens will receive their garland at public expense. Probably the cost of an individual garland was not high. Nevertheless, an important distinction is made: all inhabitants were not citizens, even though Eretria is considered a democracy. In the light of this fact, one cannot assume

---

[46] Böhlig, *Tarsos*, p. 144.
[47] Aristophanes, *Knights* 581f; Ferguson, *Greek and Roman Religion* pp. 61–89; W. Burkert, *Greek Religion* (Oxford: Basil Blackwell, 1985); Aelius Aristides, i, 40–48; Ferguson, *Greek and Roman Religion*, p. 63.
[48] *SIG* no. 323.

that because Tarsus was founded as a democracy all inhabitants were automatically given citizenship.

One hardly need mention the significance of the cults of the Greek kings and later of the Roman emperors in the life of cities throughout the Greco-Roman world.[49] The religious festivals and associations were fundamental to every Greek city and even the most skeptical citizen would acknowledge the cultic significance of such religious celebrations.[50]

Considering Greek education, religion, and athletic celebrations, it seems highly unlikely that a Jew who prided himself on following the strict Pharisaic interpretation of the Torah would also seek citizenship or boast of its acquisition. Paul's claim, in Acts, that he was a citizen of Tarsus must be seen in context of the larger discussion concerned with the civic rights and privileges of Jews throughout the Diaspora. Although the status of Jews in the Diaspora has been discussed in detail by numerous historians this century, the conclusions have not, as a rule, been appropriated by those who study the portrayal of Paul in Acts.

The issue of Jewish political and civic rights in Greek cities of the Diaspora is a complicated one; yet the evidence does show that entire Jewish communities, in Greek cities, *did not* possess full citizens' rights as members of the πόλις.[51] Smyrna, for example, granted citizenship to all persons living in Magnesia, "provided they are free and Hellenes."[52] In most ancient cities of Phoenicia, Syria, and Asia Minor, as in Greece itself, immigrant Jews occupied the position of non-citizen aliens.[53] That Jewish religious observances were protected and that Jews in many cities did possess a civic status which gave them certain privileges may be true. However, civic recognition and religious freedom do not necessarily imply full citizenship.

Traditionally those who believed that Jews did possess the citizenship of many of the major Greek cities have relied upon the evidence of Josephus. In a number of places Josephus reports that Greek

---

49 Ferguson, *Religions*, p. 77; J. H. W. G. Liebeschuetz, *Continuity and Change in Roman Religion* (Oxford: Clarendon Press, 1979), pp. 197–200.

50 Ferguson, *Religions*, p. 77.

51 Jones, *The Greek City*.

52 Philo, *Legatio ad Gaium*, trans. Smallwood. The introduction is the most full discussion of this issue; Smallwood, *The Jews Under Roman Rule*; Applebaum, "Legal Status," vol. I, pp. 420–463; Applebaum, "The Organization of the Jewish Community," vol. I, pp. 464–503; Applebaum, "Social and Economic Status," vol. II, pp. 701–727; Rabello, "Legal Condition," pp. 662–762; Schürer rev., vol. III, pp. 126–129.

53 *OGIS* no. 229, 1, 45; Schürer rev., vol. III, pp. 126–132.

citizens of several cities attempted to limit certain of the Jewish privileges. In these accounts, language is used which would seem to suggest that the Jewish inhabitants in the cities of Alexandria, Antioch, Ionia, and Sardis had equal and full citizenship status. Furthermore, apparently Jews were exempted from religious and cultic observances of the city and their rights to worship according to their own customs were protected.

For example, Josephus reports that the Greek citizens of both Alexandria and Antioch sought to have the long-standing protected citizen status of the Jew revoked.[54] Likewise, Josephus offers an account of the petition from the Ionians to Marcus Agrippa, requesting that they alone, and not the Jews, should enjoy the benefits of citizenship (πολιτεία).[55] The petition insists that if the Jews desired to be their fellows, they should worship the Ionian gods. Here, Josephus seems to be implying that the Ionians wanted to revoke Jewish citizenship, which they had been granted, because they did not worship the gods.

The account of the same event in a later book of *Antiquities* is enlightening for the proper understanding of what actually took place.[56] In this second, more detailed report, it is the Jews who appeal to Marcus Agrippa, not the Ionians. The Jews claim that they had been denied the protection which had been granted to them. They had been deprived of the monies sent as an offering to Jerusalem, and they had been forced to participate in military service and civic duties, which was not in accordance with their own laws.[57]

What is at stake, as indicated in the speech of Nicolas of Damascus, who was the advocate for the Jews, is the protection of religious observances and maintenance of traditional customs – *not citizen rights*. The Jews were resident aliens, not full citizens, who, relying upon Roman protection, sought to improve their status![58] It seems as if Josephus' concern to emphasize the high status of Jews through the Diaspora and the Roman protection of Jewish civic rights led him to confuse the terminology of citizenship.

In another place, Josephus notes the decree of Sardis which begins: "Whereas those Jews who are our fellow-citizens (πολῖται) and inhabitants (κάτοικοι) of this city ... "[59] W. W. Tarn remarked

54 Josephus, *Antiquities*, xii, 121.
55 *Antiquities*, xii, 125–127; xvi, 27–60.
56 *Antiquities*, xvi, 27–60.
57 *Antiquities*, xvi, 28.
58 Smallwood, *The Jews Under Roman Rule*, pp. 140–141.
59 Josephus, *Antiquities*, xiv, 259.

that "inhabitants" and "citizens" were mutually exclusive technical terms for differing municipal status. Therefore, "citizens" was a "self-evident" interpolation.[60] Incidentally, Tarn was adamant in his insistence that Paul was not a citizen of Tarsus![61] That Jews in Sardis had civic rights as "inhabitants" is probable; that they possessed the full citizenship as Greek citizens is less certain.

Likewise, the evidence of Josephus concerning the Jews of Antioch is problematic. V. Tcherikover points out that there is no irrefutable evidence outside of Josephus that fully substantiates Josephus' claim that Jews possessed the citizenship of Antioch or of any other Greek city in the first century. Moreover, the privileges that Josephus alludes to could equally refer to the privileges and protection of the immigrant community.[62]

The status of the Jewish community in Alexandria has been the source of much discussion. Both Josephus and Philo use language that would seem to indicate that Jews possessed full citizenship of the city although, almost without exception, scholars of this century have concluded that they did not, in fact, possess equal status with the Greek inhabitants.[63] The issues have been discussed in detail by so many that a full analysis would be redundant. However, the results of the scholars who have studied the evidence are so important to the question of Paul's status in Tarsus that a brief summary of the conclusions must be noted.

First, Josephus would like to claim that Jews had been given the citizenship of Alexandria by Ptolemy. Furthermore, Josephus alleges that Caesar had reiterated these rights by engraving them upon bronze tablets.[64] However, as the edict of Claudius makes clear, Jews were not full citizens. Claudius differentiates the Alexandrians from the Jews and speaks of the Jews as living "in a city not their own."[65] When Josephus, in his admitted paraphrase of the edict, uses the term "equal civic rights,"[66] he may in fact be referring to a recognition of the Jewish community as an autonomous ethnic

[60] Tarn, *Hellenistic Civilization*, p. 176 n.1.

[61] Tarn, *Hellenistic Civilization*, p. 177.

[62] Tcherikover, *Hellenistic Civilization and the Jews*, pp. 328–329.

[63] Philo, *Flaccus*, 53; Josephus, *Antiquities*, xii, 1; xix, 5; *Against Apion* ii, 38–39; Smallwood, *Legatio ad Gaium*, pp. 4–10.

[64] Josephus, *Antiquities*, xii, 8; xiv, 188.

[65] I. H. Bell, *Jews and Christians in Egypt: The Jewish Troubles in Alexandria and the Athanasian Controversy* (London: Bernard Quaritch, 1924); A. S. Hunt and C. C. Edgar, *Select Papyri II* (London: William Heinemann, 1934), no. 212, pp. 79–89; Line 95 of the edict.

[66] Josephus, *Antiquities*, xix, 281.

community (πολίτευμα) that would have basic rights and protection without possessing the citizenship of the city.

Second, that Jews lived in Alexandria from the beginning may be the case but that fact did not necessarily entitle them to citizenship. Jews may have been regarded as Alexandrians in that they resided in that city but they were not necessarily Alexandrian citizens in the formal sense of citizenship. A papyrus dating from the reign of Augustus offers an important example. The Jew who petitioned the Roman Governor Gaius Turannius called himself an Alexandrian. However, a second hand corrected that claim to read "a Jew from Alexandria." A clarification has been made to clear up any ambiguity of status.[67] Likewise, it is interesting to note that Josephus reports that Apion is astonished at the idea of Jews being called "Alexandrians."[68] Apion's surprised response indicates that Jews did not have a legal basis for such a designation.

Third, what the evidence seems to suggest is that Jewish communities in Alexandria, and other Greek cities throughout the Mediterranean world, were recognized as a specific ethnic group which had their particular religious customs protected by law. Jews, like other ethnic groups in the cities of the Diaspora, formed semi-autonomous civic organizations called πολιτεύματα.[69] Each πολίτευμα was a corporation of aliens with the right of residence in the city. Furthermore, it was a quasi-autonomous civic organization with administrative and judicial powers over the community. In short, the πολίτευμα became the focus of civic, religious, and ethnic identity.

The evidence indicates that there was a πολίτευμα of Caunians at Sidon, of Phrygians in Alexandria, and foreigners of unknown nationality at Cos.[70] The Papyri collection of the Berlin Museum records that the Jews of Alexandria had their own Jewish record office.[71] The Jews at Berenice in Cyrenaica formed a πολίτευμα as did the Syrians and Jews of Seleucia-on-Tigris.[72] Furthermore, in Acts 18:12, there is evidence that the Jews maintained legal jurisdiction in certain matters in Corinth as the Proconsul Gallio insists that the Jews take care of the case against Paul (Acts 18:15).

[67] *BGU*, vol. IV no. 1140; Tcherikover, *Hellenistic Civilization and the Jews*, p. 312.
[68] Josephus, *Against Apion*, ii, 38.
[69] Tcherikover, *Hellenistic Civilization and the Jews*, pp. 313–317; Schürer rev., vol. III, pp. 76–79.
[70] *OGIS* 592, 658.
[71] *BGU*, IV, 1151, 7–8; Josephus, *Antiquities*, xiv, 235.
[72] *CIG*, no. 5361; Josephus, *Antiquities*, xviii, 372, 378; Schürer rev., vol. III, p. 90.

Fourth, the Jews in the Diaspora cities, because of their protected status, were relatively privileged compared to the majority of inhabitants but they were not recognized as citizens. The third book of Maccabees (2:30) reflects the "almost but not quite" citizen status of Jews. It reports that if the Jews wanted to return to their former restricted status then they would be branded by fire with the sign of the ivy leaf, the emblem of Dionysus. But if they wanted to worship the gods they would be treated as full citizens.

What appears to be the case is that the Greek citizens of Alexandria and, as mentioned above, Antioch and Ionia as well, were concerned that the Jews were attempting to put on airs of citizenship while maintaining their special protected status. That Greek citizens of Alexandria, but not Jews and Egyptians, were exempt from the *lagiographia* of Augustus is further evidence that Jews did not, as an ethnic group, possess the citizenship of the city.[73]

Strabo, providing evidence from a city other than Alexandria, identified four groups of residents in Cyrene: the citizens of the city, the farmers, the resident aliens, and *then the Jews.*[74]

S. Applebaum, who has recently studied the evidence concerning the Jews in Cyrene, writes that the timocratic constitution strongly favored the upper-income groups, "revealing a pronouncedly conservative prejudice against craftsmen, traders and other non-landholding elements . . . clearly, the Jewish settlers would not easily have obtained Cyrenean citizenship, or the right to acquire land in the city's territory."[75] These comments about Cyrene are interesting in that they coincide with Dio Chrysostom's remarks about prejudice against linen workers in Tarsus.[76] One must assume that the Jews of Tarsus would not have held a higher status than the Jews of almost every other city in the empire.

It is apparent that the terms citizen (πολίτης) and citizenship (πολιτεία) are ambiguous and were used either to identify full members of a Greek πόλις or to identify members of one of the πολιτεύματα.[77] It is interesting to note that in Philippians 3:20 Paul uses the word πολίτευμα, not πολιτεία, to describe the community that Christians will have in heaven. F. Lyall is confident that the use

---

[73] Smallwood, *The Jews Under Roman Rule*, pp. 230–232; Feldman, "Orthodoxy of Jews," 215–237.

[74] Josephus, *Antiquities* xiv. 115.

[75] Applebaum, "Social and Economic Status," p. 709; Rostovtzeff, *SEHHW*, vol. I, pp. 277–281.

[76] *Tarsic Discourses*, xxxiv, 21.

[77] Josephus, *Antiquities*, xiv, 259–261; Smallwood, *Legatio ad Gaium*, p. 10.

of this term indicates Paul's Roman citizenship.[78] This is hardly likely and more probably the word used by Paul reflects a knowledge of the ethnic grouping of a πολίτευμα.

Although there is scant evidence concerning the life of the Jews in Tarsus, the evidence of the status of the Jew in Ionia, Alexandria, and Cyrene, suggests that the Jews of Tarsus did not possess citizenship as a group. Hence, the claim attributed to Paul in Acts places him among a significant minority of Jews who possessed citizenship.

So far we have argued that most Jews would not have the full citizenship of their city and would most probably have achieved whatever protection they had as members of the Jewish πολίτευμα. However, this is not to deny that some Jews aspired to and achieved citizenship of the Greek cities of the Diaspora in which they lived. For example, Philo's nephew Tiberius Julius Alexander was a Greek citizen, although Josephus is critical of him for forgetting the laws of the fathers.[79] It is unknown whether Philo himself was a citizen of Alexandria.

Dositheus, son of Drimylus, mentioned in 3 Maccabees 1:3, was a Jew by birth who later renounced the law, abandoned his ancestral beliefs, and became a citizen. Antiochus, who obtained Greek citizenship and held a magistracy, denounced his father, a member of the *gerousia* of the Jewish community in Antioch, and other Jews to the Greek assembly for allegedly plotting to set fire to the city.[80]

Although it cannot be correct that all Jews who gained the citizenship were as infamous as Tiberius, Dositheus, and Antiochus, the contention here is that only a minority of highly Hellenized and presumably wealthy Jews possessed the citizenship and appreciated the status and prestige commensurate with the honor.[81] For example, an inscription from Smyrna, from the reign of Hadrian, lists a number of citizens who had made benefactions to the city. Mentioned in the inscription are "the former Jews." Obviously there had been Jews who had apostatized to become citizens.[82]

In summary, the evidence indicates four important points.

[78] Lyall, "Roman Law," 9.
[79] Josephus, *Antiquities*, xx, 100; *OGIS*, 669; Tacitus, trans. J. Jackson, *The Annals*, xv, 28, 4; Josephus, *Jewish Wars*, ii, 309, 492; iv, 616. He was a Roman equestrian as well as a Greek citizen of Alexandria; E. G. Turner, "Tiberius Iulius Alexander", *JRS* 44 (1954), 54–64.
[80] Josephus, *Against Apion*, ii, 38–39; *Jewish Wars*, vii, 46–53.
[81] Schürer rev., vol. I, p. 136 n.43; Tcherikover, *Hellenistic Civilization and the Jews*, p. 49 n.4.
[82] *CIG* 3148; Smallwood, *The Jews Under Roman Rule*, p. 234 n.59; Kraabel, "Six Questionable Assumptions", 458.

Citizenship in the Greek cities, including the citizenship of Tarsus, was not held by everyone. Possession of citizenship was a distinction of no small degree and was jealousy guarded. Jews, as a whole, did not possess full citizenship of the Greek cities in the Diaspora. In general Jews gained their civic recognition and religious protection as part of the Jewish πολίτευμα in the city. While Jewish customs and religious rites were recognized and protected, this status should not be equated with full citizenship.

Those Jews who did obtain citizenship can hardly be called strict Pharisaic Jews. They might have perceived themselves as loyal to Judaism and in some cases they might still have participated in Jewish ceremony. However, it would be exceedingly difficult for a strict, law-abiding Jew to take on citizenship with its corresponding obligations. Tarsus was indeed "no mean city." It was the premier city of Cilicia and one of the foremost cities of the Mediterranean. To claim citizenship of a renowned city such as Tarsus was an indication of personal standing and prestige.

In the light of these conclusions, several important questions are raised about the Lucan portrayal of Paul. How does Paul's claim to Tarsian citizenship coincide with his strict upbringing in the Pharisaic family? Furthermore, how does Paul's pride in his citizenship coincide with his statement that he was raised in Jerusalem (22:3)? How does Paul's assertion that he possessed the citizenship of Rome shape the overall portrayal of Paul in Acts?

At this juncture, the suggestion that Luke portrayed Paul as a man of social prestige has some merit.

Paul, the Roman citizen (22:25,7,8)

To the reader of the first century an even more dramatic example of Paul's status is contained in his response to the centurion with regard to his impending examination under the lash (Greek – μάστιξ; Latin – *flagrum* or *flagellum*). While Paul is being secured, he makes a startling declaration: he is a Roman citizen. The lash was used on slaves and non-Roman troublemakers in order to force a confession. According to the *lex Julia*, it was illegal to beat a Roman citizen, although it will be shown that this exemption was not always enforced.

Most commentators focus their attention upon the legal issues involved with the text and discuss this scene in relation to Acts 16:37 which relates the story of Paul's and Silas' experience in Philippi.

The various issues concerned with a Roman citizen's legal rights are complicated yet crucial to the overall argument of this book. Therefore, those scenes in Acts where Paul assumed legal privileges and appealed to the court of the emperor will be discussed in full in later chapters. At this point it is sufficient to say that Paul's Roman citizenship saves him from a thrashing and places those in authority in an uncomfortable position.

The subsequent dialogue between Paul and the tribune, who is a man of high military rank and a Roman citizen as well, reveals the Lucan interest in describing Paul as a man of high social standing. An explicit status comparison is being made which would be obvious to the audience of Acts. Paul's claim that he was a Roman citizen by birth is neatly contrasted with the tribune's embarrassed revelation: "It cost me a large sum of money to get my citizenship" (22:28).

Most astute commentators discuss the import of the tribune's confession. During the reign of the Emperor Claudius (C.E. 45–54), there seems to have been a traffic in Roman citizenships, thereby lowering the prestige of this honor.[83] The name of the tribune is Claudius Lysias (23:26) and it is most likely that he acquired his citizenship during Claudius' tenure. It was customary to honor the one from whom the citizenship came by taking his name, in much the same way as a freedman would adopt the pronomen of the one who freed him.

Dio Cassius comments that during Claudius' first years as emperor, a potential citizen might offer large sums to an official in order to buy his influence, but that later anyone bringing "even a broken piece of glassware" might become a citizen.[84] Certainly Dio is exaggerating the apparent devaluation of Roman citizenship, yet his point is clear. It is important to note here an interesting textual variation. The Latin recension of Codex Bezae expands the verse at this point and the ensuing interpretation is that the tribune was sarcastically remarking that citizenship was so cheap that even one like Paul might obtain it.[85] Regardless of the text used, that Lysias was willing to pay a great sum for the citizenship indicates just how much of a status symbol it was. Likewise, that Paul was born a Roman citizen is an impressive and prestigious assertion. As

---

[83] Judge, "St. Paul and Classical Society," 25; Sherwin-White, "The Roman Citizenship," I, 2, pp. 23–58.

[84] *Dio's Roman History*, trans. E. Cary, lx, 17, 5f.

[85] J. H. Ropes, in *Beginnings*, vol. III, p. 215; Bruce, *Acts*, p. 407.

H. Cadbury so aptly concludes: "The phrase merely indicates the usual but illogical preference of human nature for rank obtained by inheritance rather than purchase."[86]

What Cadbury and most other commentators fail to perceive is that Luke, throughout the last eight chapters of Acts, stresses this "usual but illogical" concern for status in the narrative. Obviously, to the centurion and to the tribune, Paul's status as an inheritor of a Roman citizenship caused immense embarrassment. In this scene Luke juxtaposes the Roman tribune, the chief executive of Roman authority in Jerusalem directly responsible to the procurator at Caesarea, with Paul, who is hardly an Egyptian terrorist.

What is also of interest in this scene is that Lysias is a tribune, which was a rank of significant status. In both the legion and auxiliary, possession of Roman citizenship was a prerequisite for attaining the rank of tribune.[87] Aside from the prestige of the rank, a legionary tribune received more than sixteen times the amount in wages of a common soldier. Moreover, after the middle of the first century, the position of tribune of a cohort was a prerequisite of the entire *cursus honorum*, although before this time the rank of tribune was often filled by veteran centurions.[88] Holding the rank of tribune made entering the equestrian order a possibility. What is odd is that a tribune would admit to having bought the citizenship!

The issue of Jews possessing the citizenship of Rome is less problematic than possession of the citizenship of a Greek city. For citizens outside Rome there were few obligations. Aside from the social status associated with the citizenship, there were few practical advantages. Philo writes that there were numerous Jews in Rome who had been brought to the city as slaves and who, when manumitted, became citizens.[89] Josephus claims that Jewish Roman citizens were exempt from military service and reports that there were Jerusalem Jews who were also members of the *ordo*

[86] *Beginnings*, vol. IV, p. 284.

[87] T. R. S. Broughton, "The Roman Army," *Beginnings*, vol. V, 427–441; Cadbury, *Book of Acts*, p. 79; G. R. Watson, *The Roman Soldier* (London: Thames and Hudson, 1969), p. 99; L. Keppie, *The Making of the Roman Army From Republic to Empire* (London: B. T. Batsford, 1984), p. 112; G. Webster, *The Roman Imperial Army of the First and Second Centuries*, 3rd edn (London: Adam and Charles Black, 1985), p. 219.

[88] Cadbury, *Book of Acts*, p. 79.

[89] Philo, *Legation to Gaius*, xxiii, 155–157; Josephus, *Antiquities*, xvii, 300; H. J. Leon, *The Jews of Ancient Rome* (Philadelphia: Jewish Publication Society, 1960), pp. 6ff; Smallwood, *The Jews Under Roman Rule*, pp. 131–135; Ramsay, *Cities of St. Paul*, pp. 169ff.

equester.[90] Acts makes mention of a synagogue of freedmen in Jerusalem (6:9) who were, probably, Roman citizens.

An inscription (C.E. 24) listing the names of subscribers to the repair of the synagogue in Berenice, makes mention of Marcus Laelius Onasion who was given the title of ἄρχος of the Jewish πολίτευμα.[91] The editors of the revision of Schürer are convinced that Marcus is Jewish, but the possibility must be left open that he is a pious Gentile who made a benefaction to the synagogue. Hence, in this case, ἄρχος is an honorary title not an actual office. Herod Antipater and his son Herod were Roman citizens and Josephus asserts that he was granted the citizenship personally by Titus.[92]

Unfortunately, Luke does not relate how Paul's father (grandfather?) acquired his citizenship, if indeed he ever knew himself. The advice of most Acts scholars is that speculation is fruitless. While the matter of Paul's possessing the citizenship of Rome is enigmatic, speculation concerning how he obtained his citizenship is far from fruitless. Understanding how a Jew, who allegedly was a citizen of Tarsus, also received the citizenship of Rome can help uncover the impression that Luke was trying to convey to his readers. For throughout it has been stressed that Luke was more concerned to give an impression rather than to offer, in every instance, exact biographical and historical data.

There were three legally recognized ways in which a Jew of the Diaspora might have received the Roman citizenship. Paul's forefathers might have served in the army of Rome. One of Paul's direct ancestors might have been a freed slave of a Roman citizen, receiving the citizenship when manumitted. Paul's nearest kin might have been given the citizenship as a personal gift in reward for special services rendered.

It is unlikely that Paul's forefather received the citizenship from serving in the army. Although Josephus and the writer of 1 Maccabees report that Jews served in the army of the Ptolemies and Seleucids, Josephus is adamant in pointing out that Jewish Roman citizens were released from their military obligation in the Roman legions and auxiliary forces. In 49 B.C.E. Lucius Lentulus exempted Jewish Roman citizens in Ephesus and later throughout Asia. The decree, as written in *Antiquities*, is as follows: "Those Jews who are

90   Josephus, *Antiquities*, xiv, 228, 232, 234, 237, 240; xix, 52; *Jewish Wars*, ii, 308.
91   Schürer rev., vol. III, p. 133.
92   Josephus, *Jewish Wars*, i, 194; ii, 308; *Antiquities* xiv, 137; *Life*, 76.

Roman citizens and observe Jewish rites and practice them in Ephesus, I release from military service before the tribunal on the twelfth day before the Kalends of October in consideration of their religious scruples, in the consulship of Lucius Lentulus and Gaius Marcellus."[93]

Dollabella (43 B.C.E.) renewed the privilege.[94] Evidently this exemption extended throughout Asia Minor. In the words of the revisers of Schürer: "Jewish Sabbath and Roman discipline were irreconcilably opposed."[95] Yet given the pro-Roman emphasis throughout *Antiquities* one wonders whether Josephus is speaking of an exemption made by the Romans out of respect for Jewish custom, or whether Josephus' account indicates that the Romans realized that trying to raise and discipline an army made up of Jews was pointless. S. Applebaum has made a similar observation: "Roman army life revolved extensively round the ruler cult, the consecrated standard and the auguria; this and the constant tension between the Jews and the Roman power made Jews as reluctant to enlist as it made authorities reluctant to accept them."[96] In any case, E. M. Smallwood believes that the number of Jews included in such a decree would have been "infinitesimally small."[97]

A more likely explanation of how Paul acquired the citizenship is that his ancestors received the citizenship of Rome through manumission.[98] There were three formal methods of manumitting a slave which would lead to an automatic grant of citizenship. These three methods were by rod (*vindicta*), by census (*censu*), and by will (*testamento*). Being freed by the rod was a ceremony performed before the praetor, or other competent authority. Being manumitted by census could be achieved only when the censor was in office registering the number of citizens. Being freed by will was the most popular as the master kept the slave throughout his own life and left the expense and formalities of freedom to the heirs. Apparently there were so many slaves being freed by these three methods that

---

[93] Josephus, *Antiquities*, xiv. 228.
[94] *Antiquities*, xiv. 226.
[95] Schürer rev., vol. II, p. 475.
[96] Applebaum, "Legal Status," p. 459; C. Nicolet, *Le Métier de citoyen dans la Rome républicaine* (Paris: Editions Gallimard, 1976), pp. 122–131; Stegemann, "War der Apostel Paulus ein römischer Bürger?," p. 225.
[97] Smallwood, *The Jews Under Roman Rule*, p. 128.
[98] Duff, *Freedmen*; Bartchy, *Slavery*; P. R. C. Weaver, "Social Mobility in the Early Roman Empire: The Evidence of the Imperial Freedmen and Slaves," *Past and Present* 37 (1967), 3–20.

Augustus passed legislation intended to lessen the flow of slave/citizens into the empire.[99]

If there is truth in the tradition behind Acts that Paul was a Roman citizen, then it is most likely that Paul inherited the citizenship because his parents or grandparents had at one time been slaves and subsequently manumitted.

However, two important points are raised which have a bearing upon the portrayal of Paul in Acts. First, a Roman citizen of slave origin carried the name of his master who had released him and the stigma of slavery remained for much longer than one generation. It is argued in this work that the biographical details Luke provides are part of an overall constructive argument that runs throughout the last eight chapters, emphasizing Paul's high social standing and moral virtue. As is well known and often observed, Luke takes pains to show that Paul converts women and men of high social standing (17:4,12) and mentions that Asiarchs are among Paul's friends (19:31). As the scene is set up in Acts, Paul's credentials are being compared with those of Claudius Lysias. Being descended from a slave family does not coincide with the total picture of Paul as a citizen of high standing.

Second, if Paul acquired the citizenship of Rome because of his father's manumission from slavery to a Roman citizen, it does not necessarily follow that Paul would have also automatically gained the citizenship of Tarsus. Furthermore, being a slave of a Roman citizen seems to suggest that Paul's ancestors came from another location. This hypothesis would be supported by the tradition found in Jerome that Paul came with his family from Giscalis in Galilee.[100] This tradition would affirm Paul's Tarsian connection and better explain, as will be shown, Paul's Pharisaic ancestry.

Jerome's source does not coincide with Paul's claim in Acts and it makes it almost impossible that Paul would have become a citizen of Tarsus. However, there may be more to the tradition found in Jerome than is usually recognized. That Paul's father was personally granted the citizenship is extremely unlikely given that only those who were of the most prominent families received the honor.

Rome attempted to cultivate the loyalty of the ruling classes in the

[99] Goodfellow, "Roman Citizenship," pp. 112ff.; Lüdemann, *Das frühe Christentum*, pp. 240–250.

[100] Jerome, *De viris illustribus*, trans. E. C. Richardson, in *The Nicene and Post-Nicene Fathers*, 2nd edn (Grand Rapids: Eerdmans, 1892), vol. III, p. 362.

provinces by granting to them rights and privileges. Caesar, it is reported, was generous in giving out citizenships, but most of these grants were given to wealthy individuals in Gaul and Spain, not in the East.[101] Furthermore, even given Caesar's generosity, it was difficult for anyone without wealth and influence to obtain such an honor. The propertied classes were the ones who benefited.

E. R. Goodenough conjectures that if Paul's father had been given the citizenship personally, he must have received it under either Augustus or Tiberius which, to Goodenough, was "so unlikely as to be incredible." Paul's father would have had to be one of the "few great benefactors of the new regime."[102] Goodenough concluded, "If Paul had been born a citizen, then it would mean that he whom Acts itself calls a tentmaker by trade was from one of the greatest families in the East.[103]

Those who would have been granted the Roman citizenship would have made up an inner aristocracy in the Greek cities. For only those families which had "raised themselves so conspicuously in the city by wealth or by high office or, as usually was the case, by both, [were] to be admitted into the governing class of the Empire."[104] Hence, although it is most unlikely that a strict Jew from Tarsus would have been among the governing élite to be given the Roman citizenship, this is, apparently, what Luke wishes to imply when he has Paul claim first, that he is a citizen of Tarsus and second, that he inherited the Roman citizenship.

It has traditionally been assumed that Paul's name is sufficient proof of Roman citizenship. However, a name alone tells little, especially without the other names of the formal Roman *tria nomina*.[105] Names can be of assistance in discussing social status only as a secondary piece of evidence; little is gained by them alone. C. E. B. Cranfield considers it unlikely that Paul took his name in Acts 13:9 from Sergius Paulus, although Jerome believed that this was the

101 E. Kornemann, "Civitas," *PRE* Supplement, cols. 304–317; Goodfellow, "Roman Citizenship," pp. 90–108; Sherwin-White, *The Roman Citizenship*, p. 338.

102 E. R. Goodenough, "The Perspective of Acts," p. 55; E. Renan, *Saint Paul* (Paris: Michel Levy Frères, 1869), pp. 527–527 n.1.

103 Goodenough, "The Perspective of Acts," p. 55; Hock, "Paul's Tentmaking," pp. 555–564; A. Burford, *Craftsmen in Greek and Roman Society* (London: Thames and Hudson, 1972); R. F. Hock, *The Social Context of Paul's Ministry: Tentmaking and Apostleship*; P. Lampe, "Paulus-Zeltmacher," 256–260.

104 Ramsay, *Cities of St. Paul*, p. 127; Cicero, trans. R. Gardner, *Pro Balbo*, xi, 28; Sherwin-White, *The Roman Citizenship*, p. 245; Schürer rev., vol. III, p. 134 n.31.

105 Meeks, *Urban Christians*, pp. 55–63.

case.[106] Rather, Cranfield assumes that Paul was a Roman citizen and, therefore, had the formal *tria nomina* that consisted of the *praenomen*, or personal name, the *nomen*, or clan name, and a *cognomen*, or family name. Likewise, the name Saul would have been Paul's *signum* or *supernomen* – an unofficial, informal name. Although Paul is considered a "good" Roman name, Cranfield is correct to point out that,

> had Paul not been a Roman citizen, it would have been natural to suppose that 'Paul' was simply a Gentile name possessed by him from childhood alongside his Jewish name Saul; for the use of a Gentile name in addition to a Jewish, particularly one more or less like-sounding, was by N. T. times a well-established custom among Hellenistic Jews.[107]

G. H. R. Horsley has recently compiled a table of those individuals in the New Testament who had a Jewish name and a Roman name. Besides Saul–Paul, there is John–Mark, Jesus–Justus, Symeon–Niger, and Josephus–Justus.[108]

Sherwin-White admits: "Paul's double name is not proof that his family was enfranchised in his own lifetime. It is just a matter of local usage."[109] Furthermore, Sherwin-White points out that the phrase "But Saul, also known as Paul" (Acts 13:9) is more natural in a first-generation citizen than in a member of a long-established family.[110]

It was fairly common for a non-Roman citizen to possess a Roman name. The Emperor Claudius decreed the illegal use of the Roman *tria nomina* a capital offense.[111] This shows, on one hand, that Rome wanted to protect the exclusive rights of its citizens. But, on the other hand, this evidence also shows that people in the empire wanted to usurp privileges without pedigree and that some who possessed what sounded like a good Roman name were not citizens.

Luke knows and uses the name Saul until 13:9 but does not give any indication that he knew Paul's other Roman names if indeed he

[106] Cranfield, *Romans*, pp. 48–50; Cadbury, *Book of Acts*, p. 69; Sherwin-White, *Roman Society and Roman Law*, p. 152; Jerome, *De viris illustribus*, v.
[107] Cranfield, *Romans*, p. 49; H. Harris, "Jews with Greek or Roman Names," pp. 102–106.
[108] Horsley, *New Docs*, pp. 93–4.
[109] Sherwin-White, *Roman Society and Roman Law*, p. 152.
[110] *Roman Society and Roman Law*, p. 152.
[111] Suetonius, *Claudius* 25.

had those appellations. Furthermore, in his epistles, Paul uses only his non-Jewish name. It can be inferred that Saul was an appropriate name to give a Jew of Benjaminite descent. From the evidence it would seem that Paul was given two names, like many Jews of the Diaspora, and hence, was simply and always called Saul–Paul. Therefore, one could argue that where Paul's mission extended to Gentile and Hellenistic areas the use of his name Paul would be to his advantage.

The scenes described in chapters 21 and 22 vividly show Luke's interest in establishing Paul's status.[112] Taken aback by the insult that he is an Egyptian troublemaker, Paul adamantly claims his credentials and Luke thereby served notice to the reader that this Roman Tarsian and, as is shortly to be indicated, Pharisaic Jew is not to be taken lightly. It is of great importance that Luke establishes Paul's status early on in this final section as Paul lives out the programmatic prophecy of Jesus: "They will arrest you and persecute you; they will hand you over to the Synagogue and prisons, and you will be brought before kings and governors because of my name. This will give you an opportunity to testify" (Luke 21:12–13). Paul, from now until the end of Acts, will confront those of high social status and political prestige and Luke is making clear beforehand that Paul will never be at a social disadvantage.

Paul, the Pharisee (23:6)

Paul claims in Acts that he was raised in Jerusalem and trained as a Pharisee (22:3, 23:6, 26:5). Moreover, he states his former allegiance to the Pharisaic school in his Philippian correspondence. However, there is significant disagreement concerning the exact nature of Paul's Pharisaic upbringing. Since the main effort of this study is to understand how Luke's portrayal of Paul serves the author's larger aim, the riddle of Paul's formal Pharisaic background will be left to others.[113]

---

[112] Haenchen, *Acts*, p. 638; Lüdemann, *Apostelgeschichte*, p. 251; Pesch, *Apostelgeschichte*, vol. II, p. 243.

[113] Lüdemann, *Apostelgeschichte*, 251; A. Schweitzer, *Paul and His Interpreters*, trans. W. Montgomery (London: Adam and Charles Black, 1912); Davies, *Paul and Rabbinic Judaism*, p. 1; Montefiore, *Judaism and St. Paul*, p. 95; Enslin, "Paul and Gamaliel," 360–375; H. Maccoby, *The Myth Maker: Paul and the Invention of Christianity* (London: Weidenfeld and Nicolson, 1986), p. 17; A. Schweitzer, *The Mysticism of Paul the Apostle*, trans. W. Montgomery, 2nd edn (London: Adam and Charles Black, 1953); Neusner, "Two Pictures of the Pharisees," 525–538; van Unnik, *Tarsus or Jerusalem?*

Of immediate concern is the interpretation of a hardly discussed but extremely important phrase in Acts 23:6. Paul claims that he is a Pharisee and then adds that he is also "a son of Pharisees." Haenchen has paraphrased the sentence: "I am a Pharisee from a devoted family of Pharisees."[114] This understanding of the phrase, which reflects the intention of Luke, raises problems.

To restate what has been mentioned in numerous places throughout this chapter: while there were individual Jews who would have attained the citizenship of their Greek city, and there were Jews who could claim to have the Roman citizenship, for a strict Pharisee these status claims would seem to have been incompatible with Pharisaism.

J. Jeremias, in an attempt to dismiss the difficulty, writes: "but these last two words [υἱὸς φαρισαίων] could equally mean that he [Paul] was a pupil of a Pharisaic teacher or a member of a Pharisaic association." Jeremias presents evidence of parallel uses of the "sons of ... " formula. For example, Jeremias has shown that the phrase "sons of high priests" means simply "one of the high priests" and therefore "son of Pharisees" means simply that Paul was a Pharisee.[115] At first glance, it is a convincing argument, and one can think of numerous "son of ... " combinations in the Old and New Testaments that would add substance to Jeremias' thesis. Jeremias concludes, "In other words, the term 'son of ... ' denotes not descent but membership of a class."[116]

If Jeremias is correct, then here, in Acts, Paul is not claiming that his father and grandfather were Pharisees, which would raise a number of difficulties; rather, Paul is stating that at one point in his life he chose to become a Pharisee. Yet it must be pointed out that the specific term "son of Pharisees" is found nowhere else in either the rabbinic or biblical material and therefore, while enlightening, Jeremias' contention is not conclusive.

Although the editors of Schürer do not discuss the phrase "son of Pharisees," they do, like Jeremias, focus upon the meaning of the phrase "sons of the high priests."[117] Schürer's editors argue that the term "sons of high priests" is a title not only of membership of a group but of distinctive pedigree. For, as they point out, the prestige

---

[114] Haenchen, *Apostelgeschichte*, p. 571; Wendt, *Apostelgeschichte*, p. 466.

[115] Jeremias, *Jerusalem*, p. 252 n.26.

[116] Jeremias, *Jerusalem*, p. 177; Schweizer, υἱός, *TDNT*, vol. VIII, p. 365; J. B. Lightfoot, *St. Paul's Epistle to the Philippians* (London: Macmillan and Co., 1890), p. 148.

[117] Schürer rev., vol. II, pp. 234, 249–250.

of the high priesthood was the prerogative of a few, wealthy, high-status Jewish families (as Jeremias concedes). The point is made: "the mere fact of belonging to one of the privileged families must have conferred a particular distinction."[118] The editors of Schürer are correct. Josephus was well aware of both the status and the pedigree implied when, naming the three sons of Ishmael the high priest, he uses the phrase, "sons of the high priest."[119]

Also, there was the custom of sons following in the footsteps of their father's livelihood. Hence the phrase "son of a carpenter" meant either that the person was a carpenter, or that he came from a line of carpenters, or, presumably, both. A papyrus preserves the claim "I am an Alexandrine, the son of an Alexandrine."[120] Therefore, although Jeremias may be correct that "son of Pharisees" can simply mean "a Pharisee", he is incorrect to limit the meaning to this. Moreover, since Paul claims that his Tarsian and Roman citizenships are his by birth, it is likely that Luke completed the triad of pedigree assertions by stressing the birthright of Paul's Pharisaic claim.

It must be admitted that before the destruction of the Temple, the Sadducees, not the Pharisees, possessed the highest social status in terms of wealth and rank. However, after C.E. 70, the high priests and Sadducees ceased to be recognizable groups while the Pharisees, who had maintained their organization to some degree after the destruction of the Temple, could claim to represent Jerusalem Judaism. In the writings of Josephus, the Pharisees became the sect which had the support of the masses and Josephus himself claims that he selected the Pharisaic school as the best of the Jewish sects.[121]

If the consensus opinion that Acts was written in the last part of the first century is accepted, it would be unlikely that Luke's audience in the Greco-Roman world would recognize the potential discrepancy of a strict Pharisee also being a citizen of Tarsus and Rome. To the Lucan readership, Paul's claim of Pharisaic upbringing bespeaks a solid pedigree in what might have been recognized as a type of philosophical school. Hence, here in Acts, Luke has Paul claim that he was born in Tarsus of a Pharisaic family of the Diaspora, and that his father and perhaps his grandfather were Pharisees.

118 Schürer rev., vol. II, p. 234.
119 Josephus, *Jewish Wars*, vi, 114.
120 *BGU*, 1140.
121 Josephus, *Antiquities*, xiii, 297–298, 401–406; xiii, 288; xvii, 41–46; *Life*, 191; Jeremias, *Jerusalem*, p. 246.

This claim raises two further highly problematic questions: (1) Were Pharisees found in the Diaspora? (2) How probable is it that Pharisees would also be citizens of a Greek city? The first of these issues is tremendously complicated. Jacob Neusner has written: "I don't know what to make of Pharisees born overseas which, by definition, is unclean. If Pharisees are worried about the cultic cleanness at home, they cannot pursue their discipline outside of the Holy Land ... as to other parts of the Diaspora, Paul is the sole testimony I can think of."[122]

Josephus makes mention of a strict (ἀκριβής) Jew, Eleazer, who convinces the king of Adiabene that to become a Jew he must be circumcised.[123] Josephus never calls Eleazer a Pharisee, but he does use ἀκριβής to describe the Pharisees elsewhere.[124] Hence, it might be argued that Eleazer was a Pharisee. However, it can hardly be the case that only Pharisaic Jews were strict or enforced circumcision.

Hillel, the famous sage who was a Pharisee, came from Babylon.[125] But the tradition does not maintain that he began his Pharisaic career in Babylon. Both Philo and Josephus write that Essenes were found in every town and, by extension, it might be argued that Pharisees and other strict Jewish groups would be found in the Diaspora.[126] In addition, the woe proclaimed by Jesus to the Pharisees suggests traveling Pharisaic missions (Matt. 23:15), although this has not been accepted by all scholars.[127]

Hence, there is some evidence that suggests the presence of Pharisees outside of Palestine before the destruction of the Temple. However, until evidence comes forth specifically naming Pharisaic groups in the Diaspora in the early decades of the first century, the suggestion that Paul was from a Pharisaic family from Tarsus can hardly be accepted without serious reservations.

Even Paul's own testimony in Philippians 3:5 is not conclusive

---

[122] In a personal letter dated 18 November 1986; E. P. Sanders, *Jesus and Judaism* (London: S.C.M. Press, 1985); J. Neusner, *Formative Judaism III* (Providence, R.I.: Brown University Press, 1983).

[123] Josephus, *Antiquities*, xx, 38–41.

[124] Josephus, *Jewish Wars*, i, 110; ii, 162–166; *Life* 191.

[125] J. Neusner, *The Rabbinic Traditions About the Pharisees before 70 C.E.*, part 1: "The Masters" (Leiden: E. J. Brill, 1971).

[126] Philo, *Every Good Man is Free*, 75–91; Josephus, *Jewish Wars*, ii, 119–161.

[127] F. W. Beare, *The Gospel According to Matthew* (Oxford: Basil Blackwell, 1981), pp. 453–454; E. Lerle, *Proselytenwerbung und Urchristentum* (Berlin: Evangelishe Verlag-Anst, 1960); D. R. A. Hare, *The Theme of Jewish Persecution of Christians in the Gospel According to St. Matthew* (Cambridge: Cambridge University Press, 1967); Schürer rev., vol. III, pp. 159–160.

evidence. After asserting his strict Jewish credentials, Paul adds that he is "according to the law a Pharisee." While this is a straightforward admission, it is the only time that Paul, in his letters, mentions his Pharisaism. This is somewhat odd considering his list of credentials in Romans 11:1, 2 Corinthians 11:22, and Galatians 1:14. One might expect him to mention his Pharisaic upbringing in these places.

It could be that, in his letter to the Philippians, Paul was not saying that he was a Pharisee, but only that the party whose views were closest to his views were the Pharisees. One can imagine that this admission, shared with the community at Philippi, might become the basis for the tradition of Paul's strict Pharisaism. But, even if the traditional interpretation of Philippians 3:5 is accepted, the important point is that Paul makes no explicit claim outside of Acts to have been born into a Pharisaic family.

The point is this: while it is highly probable that there were strict Jews in the Diaspora, it is less probable that there were Pharisees outside of Palestine in the years preceding the Jewish war. The second issue which sharpens the difficulty of Paul's possessing the full citizenship of Tarsus is whether a Pharisee would possess or want to have the citizenship of a Greek city.

The sources indicate that the Pharisees of the first century were concerned with strictness of interpretation of the law, were guardians of ancestral customs, and particularly intent upon the purity of their table fellowship.[128] Josephus, who describes the Pharisees as a philosophic sect, writes that they "excel the rest of the nation in observance of religion as exact exponents of the law."[129] The same impression of the Pharisees, albeit from a cynical polemical viewpoint, is received from the gospel accounts. The rabbinic literature seems to place most emphasis on the rules of ritual purity.

Epiphanius of Salamis, who, in the fourth century, gathered traditions of various heretical groups, described the Pharisees as ascetics who were constantly at prayer, who fasted twice a week and separated themselves from the larger society.[130] Although Epiphanius is not renowned for his reliability, his description of the

---

[128] T. W. Manson, "Sadducee and Pharisee: The Origin and Significance of the Names," *BJRL* 22 (1938); H. Hübner, *Law in Paul's Thought*, trans. J. C. G. Greig (Edinburgh: T.&T. Clark, 1984), p. 23.

[129] Josephus, *Antiquities*, i, 110.

[130] Ed. and trans. F. Williams, *The Panarion of Epiphanius of Salamis*, book 1 (sections 1–46) (Leiden: E. J. Brill, 1987), no. 16, p. 38.

Pharisees is not far removed from the other traditions found in the gospels and Josephus.

In this century, Jeremias has called the Pharisees a "holy community of Jerusalem"[131] and Vermes, even more recently, has described the Pharisees as "in short, a fairly small pious enclave within Jewish society."[132] These Pharisaic concerns for ancestral law, ritual purity, table fellowship, and strict interpretation of Torah would seem diametrically opposed to holding Greek citizenship which assumes loyalty to the local gods, tacit acceptance of the gymnasium, and assimilation of Hellenistic culture. Can it be imagined that Paul, who prides himself on being from the strictest of Pharisaic backgrounds, could be any less strict than Peter who says to Cornelius and his household: "You yourselves know that it is unlawful for a Jew to associate with or to visit a Gentile" (Acts 10:28).

In conclusion, that Paul at one time in his life was a Pharisee is a highly credible possibility. That there were Pharisaic Jews in Tarsus is less likely, although the evidence is far from conclusive. However, that Paul was born into a Pharisaic family in Tarsus and also possessed the citizenship of that Greek city and could claim that he had inherited the Roman citizenship is highly improbable. Yet this is precisely what Luke has Paul claim.

Paul's other objective status characteristics in Acts

In the light of Paul's Greek, Roman, and Jewish claims, which would have placed him among the élite of the empire, it would not have been necessary for Luke to stress Paul's wealth and education – his citizenships and strict Pharisaic upbringing would imply both these things. However, within Acts 21:17 to 23:10, Luke alludes to Paul's piety, wealth, and education which would, no doubt, have added to the overall portrait of his hero. For example, the mention made by Luke that Paul participated in and paid for the purifying rite for four Nazirites (21:23) indicates not only Paul's piety but also his wealth. The payment of the vow of four men who did not have the means to pay implies possession of considerable wealth.

Josephus reports that when Agrippa arrived in Jerusalem, to take over the kingdom given to him by Claudius, he paid for "a considerable number of Nazirites to be shorn" in order to impress upon his

131 Jeremias, *Jerusalem*, p. 246.
132 G. Vermes, *The Dead Sea Scrolls: Qumran in Perspective* (London: S.C.M. Press, 1982), p. 120.

subjects that he was a pious, rich, and generous Jew.[133] That Paul, upon his entrance into Jerusalem, would undertake financial responsibility for this activity indicates his piety and personal wealth.

It was expensive to pay for a Nazirite's vow. A he-lamb, a ewe-lamb, a ram, the fine-meal, and many pints of wine and oil would have to be provided for the sacrifices at the end of the time of the vow.[134] Providing these requirements for just one Nazirite would have been expensive; having the resources to pay for four Nazirites implies great wealth. Those from Jewish backgrounds who read Luke would have recognized the cost of such a benefaction. Likewise, as witnessed by numerous stelae, the Greco-Roman reader would, no doubt, have also been acquainted with the cost of many pious obligations![135] The assumption that the Paul portrayed by Luke in Acts was wealthy is strengthened as the narrative proceeds and it is reported that Paul maintained himself in Caesarea, that Felix expected a bribe (24:26), that Paul would have had to pay for his travel and appeal to Rome (25:11) and, finally, that he rented a house in the capital for two years (28:30). How Paul paid for his expenses, if indeed Luke has accurately portrayed the various scenes, and whether or not the historical Paul was a man of wealth remains unclear. Furthermore, it is unknown if Luke was unaware of, or deliberately chose not to report, the details of Paul's financial status. However, as the various scenes are presented in Acts, Luke's portrayal suggests that Paul was, at the very least, financially secure, if not wealthy. In addition, that Paul's friends included Asiarchs (19:31) and the leading women and men of the city (17:4,12) adds to the impression that Luke was determined to show that Paul was a man of wealth and standing.

Even Paul's claims in Acts 22:3 that he had been born in Tarsus but had been raised in Jerusalem and taught by Gamaliel suggest a proper pious upbringing and education. It is important to note that although Luke stressed Paul's Jewish credentials, he used a Greek

[133] Josephus, *Antiquities*, xix, 292–294; *Beginnings*, vol. IV, p. 272; F. W. Danker, *Benefactor: Epigraphic Study of a Greco-Roman and New Testament Semantic Field* (St. Louis, Mo.: Clayton Publishing House, 1982).

[134] G. B. Gray, *Sacrifice in the Old Testament: Its Theory and Practice* (Oxford: Clarendon Press, 1925), pp. 38–39.

[135] Horsley, *New Docs 1978*, pp. 73–74; *New Docs 1976*, p. 24; R. L. Fox, *Pagan and Christian* (New York: Viking Press, 1986). Fox provides numerous examples of costly piety.

literary motif to do so.[136] Van Unnik writes: "They fit completely into the pictures of Greek upbringing and education."[137] Of the many examples Van Unnik offers, two, taken from Plutarch and Philo, are particularly interesting. Of the Gracchi Plutarch writes: "Of all the Romans they were the most disposed to virtue, and they received a most excellent upbringing and education."[138] He compares Agia and Cleomenes with the Gracchi and notes: "Agis and Cleomenes also were by nature richly gifted, but in their case the essentials of a right upbringing had been wanting: Their disposition appears to have been more vigorous than the Gracchi inasmuch they did not receive a sound education and were trained to manners and customs that had corrupted the elders before them."[139] In the scene in Acts where Paul stands before the Jews of Jerusalem, he wants to stress that he was disposed to virtue because he had received the best upbringing and the strictest training.

Philo, in his book devoted to the life of Moses, comments that Moses' parents were among the "most excellent persons of their time."[140] His upbringing and education, under the supervision of the Egyptians, allowed Moses to be free from "dissolute lusts" and made him σώφρων, which was one of the classical cardinal virtues. Again, in Acts, Luke wants to stress Paul's status by indicating that he was perfectly well bred and had received an excellent education. The one important difference between Philo's account of Moses and Luke's account of Paul concerns the fact that Paul is not σώφρων until after his conversion (26:25). This important point will be discussed in the next chapter. Finally, although Paul probably was, in fact, bilingual, that he switches from immaculate Greek (21:37) to Hebrew (21:40) would not discredit his education or upbringing, or Luke's overall portrayal of Paul in Acts.

Conclusion

Within a relatively short space Paul has not only declared his civic status, but also intimated his solid upbringing and strict education as well as alluded to his piety and wealth. While it is ultimately impossible to discern, with any degree of certainty, the precise

---

[136] Van Unnik, *Tarsus or Jerusalem*, pp. 17–45; Conzelmann, *Apostelgeschichte*, p. 125; Haenchen, *Acts* pp. 624–625.
[137] Van Unnik, *Tarsus or Jerusalem*, p. 33.
[138] Plutarch quoted by Van Unnik, *Tarsus or Jerusalem*, p. 22.
[139] Van Unnik, *Tarsus or Jerusalem*, p. 22.
[140] Philo, *The Life of Moses*, i, 17.

historical data which lay behind the Lucan portrayal of Paul in Acts, it seems certain that Luke was deliberate in what he did present. In the foregoing pages three particular claims made by the Lucan Paul were considered. Attention was focused upon this specific block of material because all the action and dialogue of this section takes place in Jerusalem. It marks a transition from Paul's missionary journeys (Acts 13 to 21:16) to his trials before the Roman authorities and his final journey to Rome (23:12 to 28:31). Furthermore, this portion of Acts serves as an introduction to Paul. It is no coincidence that within relatively few verses, covering three scenes, the character of Paul has been made the focus of great attention.

Of even greater importance than the events in the narrative is the composite description of Paul that the reader receives. In these chapters Paul is described as a citizen of his home city of Tarsus, a Roman citizen, and a zealous Pharisee. Moreover, there are several allusions to his wealth, education, and piety.

At the outset of this chapter the following question was posed: is it probable that Paul could have been born into a Pharisaic family and also have been a citizen of Tarsus and a Roman citizen in the manner in which Luke presented it in Acts? The explicit auto-biographical data gleaned from Paul's letters emphasized Paul's strict Jewish background but offered nothing to confirm, with a high degree of probability, the pedigree claims that the author of Acts has Paul make. Therefore, the probability of Paul's claims in Acts concerning his citizenships of Tarsus and Rome needed to be judged.

Given the evidence noted earlier in this chapter, it seems that an individual possessing the citizenship of Tarsus, or the citizenship of any Greek city, would have had at least tacitly, to accept the religious, political, and educational institutions of the πόλις. Hence, for one to claim to be a strict Jew from a Pharisaic family and possess the citizenship of a Greek city is problematic. Possessing the citizenship of any Greek city, particularly the citizenship of Athens, Alexandria, and Tarsus, was an indication of high social status and implied wealth and prestige.

Possessing the citizenship of Rome, while not as problematic for a Jew, was hardly common in the East during the first decades of the first century. If Paul was a Roman citizen, it is most likely that he was descended from a slave family who had been manumitted. While this alternative cannot be dismissed as an historical impossibility, in Acts the reader is not presented with any indication that Paul was descended from a slave family. In the light of the obvious status comparison that occurs between the tribune's citizenship, which was "bought," and Paul's citizenship, which was inherited, it is clear that Luke had a particular intention in mind for presenting Paul the way he did. Despite the claims of Josephus, the number of Jews who would have had both citizenship of their city and Roman citizenship would have been small indeed, and the impression that the reader receives from the double claim of Tarsian and Roman citizenship is that Paul is a man of high social standing.

It is admitted that there were some Jews who would have had the citizenship of their Greek city and other Jews who would have possessed the citizenship of Rome and still others who, presumably, would have held both. However, the evidence indicates that Jews who would have aspired to or held these citizenships were not, as a rule, included among those who would have been perceived as among the strictest, more zealous, law-abiding Jews. Yet, this is precisely the difficulty of the portrayal of Paul in Acts – he claims that he has been all three from birth! In other words, while each of the specific claims, in and of itself, is not problematic, the combination of the three in one person is doubtful.

Of course, in positing the problematic three-fold description of the Paul of Acts, the obvious question mentioned at the outset needs to be answered. If it were so improbable for Paul to combine the citizenships of Tarsus and Rome as well as a Pharisaic upbringing, why would Luke have shaped the portrayal of Paul in such a manner? Who would have believed it?

The most likely answer is that Luke's audience and perhaps Luke himself would not necessarily have recognized the discrepancies. The exact distinctions between strict Jewish groups would have been rather remote by the end of the first century. Furthermore, from Acts alone there is little indication that Pharisees would have found citizenship of a Greek city abhorrent. Gamaliel seems an enlightened and fair leader, "respected by all the people" (5:33). In Acts, the only explicit indication of a specific Pharisaic belief is that they believed in the resurrection of the dead (23:6). The readers of Acts would have had no reason to suppose that Luke painted an improbable picture. Rather, they would have recognized the description of an individual of the highest social and religious credentials. This answer, if it is correct, may provide a clue to Luke's initial audience. But that issue is better left for another place.

With the explicit claims thus examined other, more implicit, ways in which Luke emphasized not only Paul's social status but also his moral virtue must be investigated. In so doing it will be shown that Luke's concern to highlight Paul's social standing is matched by a concern to draw attention to his moral credentials. For an individual of ideal status possessed both.

4

PAUL, THE MAN OF VIRTUE

The Greco-Roman world was, to a great extent, conscious of and indeed built upon a hierarchical system of social status where each person had a place. Furthermore, men of wealth, education, and good pedigree were those who held power. Given this fact, it is no wonder that Luke seemed intent on emphasizing his hero's social credentials. According to his portrayal in Acts, Paul was a man of wealth, good birth, and education who was proud of his standing in his city of Tarsus, relied upon the advantages of an inherited Roman citizenship, and was also a strict Pharisee. It is evident that each of these attributes possessed correspondingly high prestige or status. However, Luke's description of Paul as a Greek citizen of Tarsus, a strict Pharisee, and a Roman citizen raises many problems. It appears that in these last chapters of Acts, Luke was not simply recording historical facts but was intentionally portraying Paul as a man of high social status.

However, Luke was not satisfied to testify to Paul's social credentials alone. He also set Paul forth as an individual who exhibited, particularly after his conversion, the various cardinal virtues of φρόνησις, σωφροσύνη, ἀνδρεία, and δικαιοσύνη. It was recognized by the various philosophical traditions which interested those of power and wealth of the day, that the advantages of good pedigree, wealth, and education were no guarantees of virtuous action. Likewise, acquired social position and accumulated wealth did not necessarily produce self-control or righteousness, bravery, or wisdom. Trimalchio is perhaps the best-known example of an individual who had achieved wealth but who had not refined his baser instincts of gluttony and debauchery.[1]

Wealth, position, and glory were external advantages to be enjoyed by the one who possessed them. However, an aristocratic

---

[1] Petronius, *Satyricon.*

disdain and mistrust are evident for those who sought to cultivate riches and status at the expense of virtuous conduct in personal and civic relationships. An ideal citizen of the Greco-Roman world combined both secular social status and philosophical virtue and excellence. It seems certain that Luke, or his source, was consciously portraying Paul in such a manner that he exemplified an ideal man of status and virtue (ἀρετή).

This chapter will be divided into four parts. First, a brief discussion indicating the importance of virtue in the classical world will be presented. Second, the conversation of Paul and Festus in Acts 26 will be re-interpreted in order to show the significance of this scene for a proper understanding of Luke's characterization of Paul as a man of virtue. Third, it will be argued that one of Luke's main purposes in including the third account of Paul's conversion , and the discussion with Festus which follows, was to emphasize a fundamental relationship between conversion and virtue. Fourth, and finally, it will be demonstrated that Luke, or his source, not only used explicit descriptive words and phrases to indicate Paul's social standing and virtuous character, but implied Paul's status and moral worth by comparing his hero with the antagonists in the narrative. Implicit comparison of characters was a common literary technique. In so doing Luke highlighted the excellence of Paul and stressed the meanness of the others. In Luke's case, he sought to highlight Paul's virtue and suggest the shortcomings of Paul's antagonists.

The first readers/hearers of Luke-Acts would have naturally recognized the portrayal of Paul for what it was, and would have responded positively to this man who possessed both social status and moral virtue. Luke held Paul to be the model Christian. Therefore, the last eight chapters of Acts are encomiastic in nature in that, in praising Paul, Luke offers an example for his readers to respect and imitate.

In formal rhetorical terms, encomium was that part of epideictic oratory which was concerned with praise in order to influence a response from the hearer to imitate the example of the one being praised.[2] Plato, in his *Protagoras*, shows the essential function of praise. He writes that young boys were given: "Eulogies of good men in times past, that the boy in envy may imitate and yearn to

---

[2] Cicero, *On Behalf of Marcellus*, is one of the classic panegyrics; Aristotle, *Rhetoric*, i, 9, 33 defines encomium; F. Cairns, *Generic Composition in Greek and Roman Poetry*, (Edinburgh: University Press, 1972), especially chapter 3.

become even as they."[3] The desire to imitate virtue was not limited to children, nor to those before the turn of the eras. Epictetus used the illustration of a purple thread in a white cloth as a metaphor to show how the one of excellence stands out from all others as an example to be followed. He wrote: "And what good does the red do in a mantle? What else than that it stands out conspicuous in it as red, and is displayed as a goodly example to the rest."[4] Seneca, who quotes Epicurus, wrote: "Cherish some man of high character, and keep him ever before your eyes, living as if he were watching you and ordering all your actions as if he beheld them."[5] And again, from the same letter, added:

> One who can so revere another, will soon be himself worthy of reverence. Choose therefore a Cato; or, if Cato seems too severe a model choose some Laelius, a gentler spirit. Choose a master whose life, conversation and soul-expressing face have satisfied you. Picture him always to yourself as your protector or your pattern. For we must indeed have someone according to whom we may regulate our characters, you can never straighten that which is crooked unless you use a ruler.[6]

Just as Seneca held Cato up for praise and imitation, Luke, in Acts, extolled Paul for a similar purpose. Plutarch, a contemporary of Luke and Epictetus, was a man of wealth and education. Writing for an audience made up primarily of his social equals, he believed that at the philosopher's words the heart of the hearer must feel anguish and be convicted. Plutarch continued:

> but more than that, the man who is truly making progress comparing himself with the deeds and conduct of a good and perfect man, and being pricked by the consciousness of his own shortcomings, yet at the same time rejoicing because of his hope and yearning, and being filled with an urging that is never still is ready in the words of Simonides, "to run like a weanling colt beside its dam," so great is his craving all but to merge his own identity in that of the good man.[7]

[3] Plato, *Protagoras*, 326A; Dio Chrysostom, *Tarsic Discourses*, v,4,5.
[4] Epictetus, *Discourses*, i, 2, 22.
[5] Seneca, *Epistles*, ix, 9–10; Xenophon, *Memorabilia*, 1, 2, 3.
[6] Seneca, *Epistles*, ix, 9–10.
[7] Plutarch, *How A Man May Become Aware of His Progress in Virtue*, 84D.

In the literature of Hellenistic Judaism a similar relationship between praise and imitation is exhibited. For example, Eleazar, his sons, and especially his wife, are praised by the author of 4 Maccabees for their faith and courage in the face of death. Eleazer's dying son exclaims to his brothers, "imitate me, brothers" (9:23). The purpose of the exhortation was to strengthen others who faced similar experiences and the purpose of the entire work was to praise the courage of Eleazar's family as representatives of the true virtue of their faith. Although far different in tone, the conclusion of the letter of Aristeas to Philocrates, which exalted the wisdom of the Jewish translators and glorified the Jewish religion, concluded with these words, which suggest a mimetic intent:

> There you have Philocrates, as I promised, my narrative. These matters I think delight you more that the books of the mythologists, for your inclination lies in the direction of concern for things that benefit the mind, and to them you devote the greater time. I will also attempt to write down the remainder of what is worthwhile, in order that in going through it you may achieve the very noble reward of your purpose.[8]

Although there is considerable disagreement concerning the provenance and date of the *Testament of the Twelve Patriarchs*, the character of Joseph is extolled as the paradigm of righteousness to be imitated throughout.[9] For example, in the *Testament of Dan*, Joseph is praised as a man who is "true and good."[10] In the *Testament of Simeon* the speaker describes Joseph as a "good man having the spirit of God within him."[11] Simeon continued: "Guard yourselves therefore, my children, from all jealousy and envy. Live in the integrity of your heart so that God might give you grace and glory and blessing upon your heads, just as you observed in Joseph."[12]

The *Testament of Benjamin*, too, offers the portrait of Joseph as the definitive example of virtue. Benjamin exhorts his children: "Now, my children, love the Lord God of heaven and earth; keep

---

[8] *Letter of Aristeas*, 322f.
[9] M. de Jonge, *The Testament of the Twelve Patriarchs: A Critical Edition of the Greek Text* (Leiden: E. J. Brill, 1978); Hollander and de Jonge, *Commentary*; *Sirach* 44.
[10] *Testament of Dan*, 1:4.
[11] *Testament of Simeon*, 4.4.
[12] *Ibid.*, 4.5.

his commandments; pattern your life after the good and pious man Joseph."[13]

The readers are to imitate Joseph's piety in keeping the law of the Lord and walking in holiness before the face of the Lord.[14] Just as Joseph bore no malice to anyone while in Egypt, the one seeking to imitate Joseph should likewise express no bitterness or resentment against his neighbor.[15] Joseph is even praised for guarding himself from women.[16] In the *Testament of Asher*, the patriarch warns his children not to be like the man who is two-faced.[17] What is apparent is that the virtuous man is the holy man who does not seek riches, who lives in peace and is self-sufficient.[18]

It is clear that Luke seeks to portray Paul as a righteous, pious, law-abiding Jew. Yet the portrait of Paul, which is developed in the last eight chapters of Acts, is much more cosmopolitan than the ideal man of virtue in the *Testaments*. Both the author of the *Testaments* and the author of Luke-Acts are familiar with the concepts and vocabulary of the Hellenistic world. But, whereas the *Testaments* clothe their hero in the garb of Hellenistic Judaism, in Acts Paul is fitted out for the urban Greco-Roman world.

Furthermore, there is a marked discontinuity between the example of discipleship presented in the gospels and the example of discipleship presented by Luke in his portrait of Paul in the last eight chapters of Acts. In the gospels the model disciples dispossessed themselves of riches and became followers of a charismatic leader. In Acts, the paradigm of discipleship is Paul who, as portrayed by Luke, takes advantage of his alleged high social standing, uses his wealth, and interacts easily with the high and mighty.

Once the narrative moves beyond Jerusalem and the portrayal of Paul becomes central, it does not appear that Luke expects his readers to sacrifice much of anything in the way of wealth, status or power. In Acts, Paul is the representative of a new, high-society Christian.

Likewise, there is an apparent discrepancy between the Paul of the letters, who takes pride in the fact that there are not many who are wise or powerful or well born (1 Cor. 1:26), and the portrayal of

---

[13] *Testament of Benjamin*, 3.1
[14] *Ibid.*, 10.11.
[15] *Testament of Zebulon*, 8.5.
[16] *Testament of Reuben*, 4.8–10.
[17] *Testament of Asher*, 3.1–2.
[18] Hollander and de Jonge, *Commentary*, 41–46.

Paul and many of his followers in Acts, who are described as possessing just these attributes.

The difference between the social program of Paul expressed in
his letters and Luke's sensitivity to social status in Acts may be
expressed as the difference of perspective from below and from
above. In his letters, Paul indicates that faith in Christ breaks down
social barriers so that there is neither slave nor free, neither male nor
female. Furthermore, he reverses worldly expectations so that the
wise are the foolish and the foolish are the wise.

In Acts, Luke seems to offer a different message which sets out to
raise Christians above their former status level to join Paul who is
the model of the cosmopolitan Christian. Luke seeks to build up the
status of the Christians so that the faith will be attractive to the
cosmopolitan, status-conscious world. Paul, in his epistles, on the
contrary, levels status distinction altogether. Hence, when Paul, for
example, writes, "I appeal to you then, be imitators of me" (1 Cor.
4:16) he is not offering the same model as presented by Luke in Acts.[19]

Before drawing conclusions concerning the various ways in which
Luke shaped his narrative in order to praise Paul, it is necessary to
construct a portrait of an ideal man of social status and moral virtue
from a sample of classical authors from the time of Aristotle to the
second century C.E. Given the confines of this book, this will not be
an exhaustive survey. Yet, there is such a similarity of description
throughout the classical world that exact differentiations between
philosophers and rhetoricians are not needed.

It is well known that Plutarch disagreed with some from the Stoa
precisely on the unity of the virtues. However, Plutarch, Zeno, and
Chrysippus would all have agreed that it is better to be prudent
rather than rash, self-controlled rather than incontinent, just rather
than rapacious, and brave rather than cowardly. Furthermore, to be
too formal in the distinctions between the schools of philosophy
would be inappropriate given that the lay public who read Acts
would not be specialists in any one school but would rather accept,
consciously or unconsciously, an eclectic smattering of various
approaches.

Finally, the intention is much more modest than a formal philosophical discussion. The point is to show that Paul as portrayed in
Acts, exhibits the characteristics of the ideal man of social status
and moral virtue that would have been recognized by the first
readers of Luke's work.

[19] O'Toole, "Luke's Notion," 155–161.

The cardinal virtues

In *Merit and Responsibility*, A. Adkins contends that

> The noun *arete* and the adjective *agathos* ... are ... the most powerful words of commendation used of a man both in Homer and in later Greek. Being the most powerful words of commendation used of a man, they imply the possession by anyone to whom they are applied of all the qualities most highly valued at any time by Greek society.[20]

Likewise, W. Jaeger wrote that in the aristocratic world of Greece there was a "definite ideal of human perfection to which the élite of the race was constantly trained."[21] This ideal of human perfection was no less true for republican and imperial Rome.[22]

The history and development of the concept ἀρετή in regard to morals and ethics in Greek philosophy, and the translation of this concept into Latin for Roman society by Cicero, and into Hellenistic Judaism by Philo, and hence into Christianity in the works of Clement of Alexandria and Origen, is worthy of a detailed study in and of itself. Indeed many scholars have made just such an investigation.[23] This wealth of secondary literature on the subject, and the equally lengthy list of classical authors who have discussed the virtues, proves that the identification and explication of what makes a man virtuous was one of the single most important themes of classical literature and philosophy.

Furthermore, the various works devoted to a discussion of virtue and the virtues suggest that this was not simply an esoteric or academic debate. The words of the classical authors on the subject both reflected and shaped the fundamental notion that Greek society recognized and praised certain values in men and women. These moral values, or virtues included φρόνησις (*prudentia*, wisdom or prudence); ἀνδρεία (*fortitudo, magnitudo animi*, courage or endurance); δικαιοσύνη (*iustitia*, justice, righteousness) and σωφροσύνη (*temperantia, moderatio, verecundia*, self-knowledge or self-control).

In the various philosophers, poets and rhetoricians there are slight variations in terms of order, importance, and specific vocabu-

---

[20] Adkins, *Merit and Responsibility*, pp. 31, 60; J. R. Fears, "The Cult of Virtues and Roman Imperial Ideology," *ANRW*, vol. II, 17.2 827–948.

[21] Jaeger, *Paideia*, p. 1.

[22] Leeman, "Die ideale bürger," 43–65.

[23] O. Bauernfeind, "APETH," *TDNT*, vol. I, 457–461; Spicq, "APETH," 161–176.

lary, but what is significant is the essential integrity and continuity of the terms and concepts pertaining to moral excellence from the time of Homer into the second century of the Common Era and beyond. These moral virtues were the attributes of outstanding individuals. Just as Luke purposefully portrays Paul as a man of high social status, so too does he want Paul to possess and exhibit the ideal virtues that would be easily recognized by the reader/ hearer of Luke-Acts.

Ἀρετή, the noun, can mean "goodness," "excellence," or "virtue." For example, Josephus describes the lands of Samaria and Judea as virtuous, meaning that they have abundant natural resources.[24] Furthermore, ἀρεταί could mean "the glorious deeds," "the wonders," or "the miracles" of the gods,[25] or the heroic qualities of the warrior.[26] Hence, the collection and writing down of the miracles of gods and especially gifted heroic men became known as aretalogies. The glorification of personal honor and prestige was fundamental to the Greek world, at least from the time of Homer, when a man of ἀρετή personified warlike valor.

As shown by Strabo and Josephus, the older definitions of ἀρετή remained meaningful into the first century of the Common Era.[27] Yet, by their time, ἀρετή had developed to include the less bellicose virtues necessary for maintaining social order.

The development can be seen as early as the sixth century B.C.E. in the writings of Aeschylus, who described an individual as a "wise, just, good, pious man."[28] His emphasis is less on the qualities of the warrior and more on the virtues of self-control, justice, and piety. Xenophon (470?–355? B.C.E.), in his *Memorabilia*, depicted his mentor Socrates (470?–399 B.C.E.) discoursing upon the virtues:[29] "Between wisdom and prudence he drew no distinction; but if a man knows and practices what is beautiful and good, knows and avoids the base, that man is judged to be both wise and prudent."[30]

In the same monologue he concluded, "Justice and every other form of virtue is wisdom."[31]

Furthermore, Socrates contrasted wisdom with madness, which

---

24 Josephus, *Jewish Wars* iii, 50; *Antiquities* iii, 302; xvii, 171.
25 *SIG* 1172; Strabo, *Geography*, xvii.1.17.
26 Homer, *Iliad*, 20.411; Josephus, *Jewish Wars*, i.193.
27 *War*, i.193.
28 Aeschylus, *Seven Against Thebes*, 610.
29 Xenophon, *Memorabilia*, iii, 9, 1–5; iv, 6, 1–12.
30 *Ibid.*, iii, 9, 4.
31 *Ibid.*, iii, 9, 5.

was understood to mean a lack of self-knowledge. The identification of madness as the antonym of virtue is significant and will be referred to again in the discussion of Acts 26, when Paul admits that he was mad before his conversion and wise after it.

Besides Socrates and Xenophon, the primary systematic discussions of virtue were developed in the writings of the fourth-century philosophers Plato and Aristotle. Aristotle's *Nicomachean Ethics* is devoted to a discussion of the moral virtues and their value to society. He is also interested in the man to whom these virtues have been given; Aristotle calls them "great-souled men". To this "great-souled" man comes honor, "For Honor is the prize of virtue; it is the tribute paid to men of ability"[32]. Yet this begs the question; what was it to be a "man of ability"? For Aristotle, the man of ability, or the "good man," excelled in each of the virtues. This concept of a man excelling in the virtues continued to play an important part in ethical discussion through the centuries. Luke, although not directly influenced by Aristotle or using the technical term, was concerned to show Paul as a " great-souled man" to his audience.

Plato took for granted that the virtues of wisdom, self-control, justice, piety, and bravery directed the man towards the good. Such a man of virtue was of great value to the polis. Plato wrote: "And wisdom, in turn, has first place among the goods that are divine, and rational temperance of soul comes second; from these two, when united with courage, there issues justice, as the third; and the fourth is courage."[33]

Each virtue possessed a distinct quality. However, all the virtues were naturally connected; hence, the man who was truly wise was also self-controlled, just, and brave. The essential connectedness of the virtues was fundamental to most ethical systems and particularly to the ethical thought of Zeno and the Stoics.[34]

To Plato, this knowledge or practical wisdom, which was the crown of virtues, naturally produced a man of "self-control," "moderation," "temperance," and "obedience." The most grievous sin, and antithesis of self-control and temperance, was hubris, which was to lose all self-knowledge and aspire above the human station. "Self-control" also developed as the opposite of violence, sexual licentiousness, and drunkenness. Xenophon believed that this moral self-control was the foundation of the palace of

---

[32] Aristotle, *Nicomachean Ethics*, iv, 3, 15.

[33] *Laws*, i, 631c.

[34] J. von Arnim, *Stoicorum Veterum Fragmenta* (Lipsiae; Aedibus B. G. Teubneri, 1921).

virtue.[35] In *Cyropaedia*, Xenophon wrote that without self-control other virtues were useless.[36] Democritus opined that "self-control increases delight and makes pleasure greater."[37]

Plato believed that the man who had self-knowledge and self-control was absolutely good.[38] Therefore, although true wisdom was always the goal of philosophy and was always the highest and most noble virtue, self-control, σωφροσύνη, became the most important practical virtue and was fundamental to society and all relationships. Its importance should not be underestimated.

σωφροσύνη is the virtue Paul possesses after his conversion, as described by Luke in Acts 26. The importance of σωφροσύνη as a mediating and controlling virtue developed further with Aristotle. His entire discussion concerning the virtues presumes that virtue is, by definition, the mean between the extremes, which are vices. This Aristotelian notion has come down through the centuries in one form or another as "in all things moderation."[39] This concept of a virtuous mean is also found in Philo who called virtue "The middle way."[40] In the letter of Aristeas, a similar sense is detected: "And yet, in everyone moderation is a good thing."[41]

The third cardinal virtue was ἀνδρεία (courage) but, as the word itself shows, it is more literally translated "manliness." In Homer "manliness" was the primary virtue. The warrior who achieved prowess as a fighter was the man of virtue. In later writings courage became a more general quality of facing danger. Xenophon used this term to describe the condemned Socrates who faced his death with equanimity.[42]

Aristotle defined courage as the mean between cowardly fear and over-confidence and wrote that "courage" was "the quality of reason of which men are disposed to do noble actions in times of danger, as the law commands; cowardice is the opposite."[43] In another place Aristotle added that "to act in a courageous manner for that which is noble is the full accomplishment of virtue."[44] It is

---

[35] *Memorabilia*, i, 5, 4; i, 5, 5.
[36] *Cyropaedia*, iii, 1, 16.
[37] H. Diels, *Die Fragmente der Vorsokratiker*, 3 vols. (Berlin: Weidmannsche Verlagsbuchhandlung, 1952), frag. 211.
[38] *Gorgias*, 507 a–c.
[39] *Letters* i, 18, 9; Philo, *On the Unchangeableness of God*, 164; Plutarch, *On Moral Virtue*, 444c.
[40] Philo, *On the Unchangeableness of God*, 164.
[41] *Letter of Aristeas*, 223.
[42] *Memorabilia*, iv, 6, 11.
[43] *Rhetoric*, i, 9, 8.
[44] *Nicomachean Ethics*, iii, 6, 3.

important to note that Aristotle's comments, on the one hand, reflect the traditional sense of courage (i.e. acts of bravery); yet on the other hand Aristotle stressed that these acts of courage should be controlled by the law and performed only at appropriate times of need – not simply as a retributive response to bruised honor.

In the Hellenistic Jewish writings and for the Greek and Latin church fathers, this manly courage developed into the strength to resist temptation, to endure the agony of persecution, and to face martyrdom with calm assurance. Endurance (ὑπομονή) became the most important attribute of a courageous person.

The fourth of the cardinal virtues was δικαιοσύνη. To the Jew, this word was the translation of *tsedeq* which meant personal right-eousness, being in the right relationship with God, and fulfilling his commandments. In Latin this concept was translated by *iustitia* which emphasized fairness and equity. Righteousness, as used in the Greek literature that has been studied, seems to have defined the individual who followed the accepted way, who respected order, constancy, and the ways of nature. J. Ferguson defines one who is righteous as a man who respects the "justified claims" of the other, be it another individual, his city, or the gods. Included in this defi-nition was the sense of obligation.[45] Of course, the concept of right-eousness included piety; for piety was the "right relationship to the higher powers."[46]

From these basic definitions of the virtues one can easily detect how they overlap one another. Their very connectedness adds to the essential richness of the concepts. Ferguson concludes: "The ideal personality is one in which reason rules, temper is courageous, self-control is established throughout. The just man is the man in whom these conditions fully prevail."[47]

The Stoic school founded by Zeno (fourth to third century B.C.E.), whose followers included Chrysippus, Cleanthes, and Hecato, accepted, according to Diogenes Laertius, the primary virtues mentioned above. For the Stoic, to be virtuous was to live in harmony with reason (φρόνησις), for to live in harmony with reason made one independent of fortune. To be absolutely brave (ἀνδρεία) was to ignore pain and death. To be absolutely content (σωφροσύνη) was not to seek after pleasure as the ideal good. To be absolutely just (δικαιοσύνη) was to be free from the influence of prejudice and

45 Ferguson, *Moral Values*, p. 18.
46 *Ibid.*, p. 42.
47 *Ibid.*, p. 44.

favor. The Stoics made it explicit that the virtues were distinct yet interconnected. An individual who has one virtue has all the virtues. As Diogenes Laertius wrote: "They hold that the virtues involve one another, and that the possessor of one is the possessor of all."[48]

It would be misleading to imply that Luke was a Stoic. However, he does seem to share this understanding of the essential unity of the virtues. This will become important when the scene in Acts in which Paul stands before Festus is investigated.

Cicero is important to the discussion for several reasons. First, he was a Roman public servant of high status and wealth who lived in the first century B.C.E. and, no doubt, reflected the sensitivity of the Roman élite. Second, Cicero, of all Roman writers, specifically attempted to translate Greek philosophical language into Latin. Third, he wrote about the virtues both in a theoretical way and, even more importantly, in a very practical way, emphasizing the importance of self-control and the other virtues to his son Marcus.[49]

Cicero, in another of his works presented a noteworthy definition of the cardinal virtues:

> Nature has engendered in man the desire to discern the truth ... from this starting point we are led to the love of all truth, that is all that is trustworthy, straightforward and unchanging, and to the corresponding hatred of all that is idle, false, and deceitful, such as guile, perjury, malice, and injustice ... Reason further contains a noble, glorious element, fitted for ruling rather than obeying, in such a way as to look on our mortal lot as trivial and easily endurable – a lofty and exalted element, which fears nothing, gives in to no one and is for ever unconquerable ... Mark these three aspects of morality. A fourth follows. It enjoys loveliness and is formed from the other three. To it belongs order and self-control. We can see something that resembles it in physical objects, when they are beautiful in appearance, and from there we pass to moral beauty in word and deed. It derives from those three admirable qualities I have already mentioned. It shrinks from rash action, and is not so shamefaced as to harm anyone by wanton word or action. It fears to act or speak in a manner untrustworthy of a man.[50]

48 Diogenes Laertius, vii, 92.
49 Cicero, *Concerning Offices*.
50 *De finibus*, ii, 14, 46–7, translated J. Ferguson, *Moral Values*, p.45.

Cicero, although he would not have called himself a Stoic philosopher, shared with the Stoics the understanding that the pursuit of wisdom was the highest calling. Furthermore, like the Stoics, he considered the virtues to be naturally connected.

Plutarch was born in the middle decades of the first century (46–47 C.E.), during the last years of the reign of Claudius, and died during the first few years of Hadrian (120 C.E.). His life spanned the Lucan era and reflects the understanding of members of the Greek aristocratic and cultural élite.[51] Furthermore, he was well known in Rome and mirrored certain ethical concerns of the educated people of that city. He wrote a number of homilies and essays on the subject of moral virtue. An admirer of Plato and Aristotle and a self-professed critic of the Stoics and Epicureans, his writing was instructive and popular. His constant concern was to emphasize that the virtues have practical application and that a man should strive to make progress in virtuous action. As mentioned above, it is in Plutarch's essay "How One May become Aware Of His Progress in Virtue" that he stressed the importance of imitating one who exemplified virtue. In his essay on ethical virtue, and in other places, Plutarch attacks the Stoics for depriving the virtues of "both plurality and difference."[52] However, Plutarch too suggests the essential unity of the cardinal virtues in his essay "Concerning Chance." He writes that σωφροσύνη is a kind of intelligence (φρόνησις) which renders men virtuous in the midst of pleasure. In perils and labors such prudence is called courage. In private and public relationships prudence is called piety and righteousness.[53]

The Wisdom of Solomon and 4 Maccabees provide examples that show that Greek ethical and philosophical terms were not unknown to the Hellenistic Jews. The author of 4 Maccabees shows himself to be fully at home with Greek philosophical language as he states clearly at the outset that his work is a eulogy to the greatest of virtues, namely φρόνησις (vv. 1–6). Furthermore, from this prudence comes "righteousness and self-control" (v. 6) which in turn controls the passions. The characters in whom these virtues are exemplified are Eleazar, and his wife and sons. Eleazar and his kin died "for virtue's sake" providing that "reason is Lord of the passions" (v. 10). Eleazer is a "great-souled man" (6:5). The list of

51 Betz, *Plutarch's Ethical Writings*; C. P. Jones, *Plutrarch and Rome* (Oxford: Clarendon Press, 1971).
52 Plutarch, *On Moral Virtue*, 440e.
53 Plutarch, *On Fortune*, 97e.

cardinal virtues is made explicit in 1:18 and 5:23 and it is important
to note that 4 Maccabees exhibits how the virtue "courage" has
taken on a particular importance for martyrdom.

Another important development, one also detected in Philo and
in the later apologists, is that the virtues, before they were explicated
by the Philosophers, were apparent in the Law of Moses. In 5:23 the
author of 4 Maccabbees wrote that, even though non-believers
mock the Law, the Law teaches "temperance" (or self-control) in
order that one might control "the pleasures and desires." Furthermore, one is trained in "courage" in order to endure hardship. The
Law also instructs one to be "just" and "pious." The Fourth Book
of Maccabees particularly praises Eleazar's wife who overcame her
passionate feelings with pious reason which gave her "manly
courage" to transcend her love for her children (15:23).'

Another interesting stylistic point, one that will be important to
the study of Paul in Acts, is the implicit comparison of the king and
his soldiers with Eleazar and his family. Eleazar possesses true
virtue; the king and his attendants, by comparison, are shown to
have few of the virtues expected of a ruler. As will be shown, similar
comparisons are being made between Paul, Felix, and Festus.

The most intriguing fact about 4 Maccabees is that in praising
Eleazar for remaining faithful to the Torah and not sharing the
Greek style of life, his panegyric is cast in full Hellenic garb. This
offers at least one indication of the extent to which Jews assimilated
to Hellenism. The author aggressively usurps the Greek philosophical language and claims it as his own, yet detests the fact that Jason,
who was appointed High Priest by Antiochus Epiphanes, built a
gymnasium on the Temple mount (4:20). Likewise, it would have
been anathema for a Jew, like Paul who prided himself on the
strictest of upbringings, to involve himself in the civic celebrations
of the Greek city.

To the author of 4 Maccabees, true virtue is ideally expressed in
pious acts of martyrdom. This does not seem to be the case in Acts
where the martyrdom of Paul is, at best, alluded to but not
reported.[54] One can see a certain similarity of thought, but not to
the same extent, in Luke's description of the martyrdom of Stephen.
Luke reports that Stephen was "full of grace and power" and was a
man of "wisdom and inspiration" (6:10). While none of the specific
cardinal virtues is mentioned, the characterization of Stephen as a

---

[54] Maddox, *Purpose of Luke-Acts*, p. 97; Haenchen, *Acts*, p. 732.

man of ἀρετη seems obvious. His vision of the Son of Man confirms his piety. Furthermore, the virtue which Stephen possesses is dramatically contrasted to the frenzy and total lack of control of the crowd who rushed upon him and stoned him. The virtue of Stephen is also contrasted with Saul who approved of the stoning (7:58; 8:1).

This description of Stephen has certain similarities to the description of the pious martyrs described by Eusebius several centuries later. However, Luke's interest in Paul does not include a description of his martyrdom. It is interesting to note that Clement, in *Stromateis*, wrote that the practice of σωφροσύνη was a preparation for death.[55] Perhaps Luke was alluding to Paul's death in Acts 26 when Paul claims that he is not mad but is a man of σωφροσύνη. Whatever the reason it seems clear that Luke was not interested in portraying Paul as a pious martyr. However, Luke is concerned to place in sharp contrast Saul before his conversion, who does not possess σωφροσυνη, with Paul after his conversion, who is a character of ideal virtue.

The Wisdom of Solomon, like 4 Maccabees, possesses a natural affinity with the language of Greek virtues, for the book opens with the words; "Love justice ... set your mind upon the Lord" (NEB), and immediately juxtaposes "fools" with those who have wisdom (1:3b–4a). Wisdom and justice are recognized as controls of lawlessness and passion. To search for wisdom is "perfect prudence" for wisdom teaches "self-control," "wisdom," "righteousness," and "bravery" (8:7). True virtue (ἀρετή) is both the source and the goal of wisdom.

Philo's concern with and discussion of virtue and the virtues is so prevalent in his writings that a full study of his use of the terminology could more than occupy the rest of this study. Hence, the following comments concerning virtue in Philo will hardly reflect the extent to which he used the term.[56] Suffice it to state the obvious: Philo's writings exhibit a fluency in the Greek philosophical discussion and an intimate knowledge of Jewish literature and tradition. To Philo, the Ten Commandments corresponded to Greek ethical teaching and the true "examples of virtue" came from the Hebrew scripture.[57]

Philo, commenting upon Genesis 2:10–14, suggests that each of

---

[55] Clement, *Stromateis*, iv, 8, 58, 2–4.
[56] H. A. Wolfson, *Philo*, 3 vols. 2nd edn (Cambridge: Cambridge University Press, 1948) vol. II, pp. 200–201.
[57] *Allegorical Laws*, iv, 25, 134; 34, 179.

the cardinal virtues is derived from one of the rivers flowing from the garden of Eden. The river Pheison gives rise to φρόνησις; ἀνδρεια springs forth from Gehon; σωφροσύνη is identified with the Tigris, and the Euphrates represents δικαιοσύνη.[58]

Philo uses the standard terms from the Platonic tradition which separated the virtues into the "intellectual virtues" (the divine virtues), the "virtues of the soul," the "virtues of the body," and the "external advantages." The intellectual or divine virtues have God as their object and the vocabulary includes "piety," "godliness," "holiness," and "faith." The virtues of the body include health, strength, dexterity, and the like. The "external advantages" include such things as wealth, glory, status and birth.[59] To Philo, piety is the highest virtue and the virtue of faith was "the perfect good." The true man of virtue (e.g. Moses, Abraham, Joseph) was rare indeed; "For virtue does not often spring in mortal creatures."[60]

One point that takes on considerable importance is the proposition in Hellenistic Judaism that true knowledge leads to God, from whom all the other virtues come. Jewish roots for this lie, for example, in Proverbs:

> The fear of the Lord is the beginning of wisdom.
> And all who practice this have good understanding.
> And piety towards God is the beginning of discernment:
> but the wicked despise wisdom and instruction. (1:7)

Likewise, in the letter of Aristeas, the author wrote, "Take the fear of God as your guiding principle and you will not fail in anything."[61] One can even detect the connection between knowledge of God and true wisdom and courage in the account in Acts 4:13 where the Sanhedrin is amazed by the boldness with which the disciples speak about salvation, knowing that the apostles are, by human standards "uneducated and ordinary men" (RSV). It is no accident that later in Acts Luke indicates that Paul becomes a man of σωφροσύνη, which has its genesis in the proper knowledge and fear of God.

As has already been mentioned, Josephus used "virtue" in its several common meanings and, like Philo, claimed that the Greek

---

[58] *Allegorical Laws*, i, 63; *Questions and Answers on Genesis*, i, 12; Philo, *Every Good Man is Free*, 67.

[59] *On Sobriety*, xii, 61; *Allegorical Laws*, iv, 27, 147; 25, 135; *On Rewards and Punishments*, 9, 53.

[60] *On the Virtues*, 13; *Every Good Man is Free*, 63.

[61] *Letter of Aristeas*, translated R. J. H. Shutt, 189.

philosophers learned of the cardinal virtues from Moses.[62] Yet, Josephus does not present any full discussion of them. This fact is, no doubt, in keeping with the nature of his writings which are not philosophical but historical in nature. However, it is apparent that the cardinal virtues were well known to him. Agrippa and Vespasian were virtuous leaders who were, by nature, men of σωφροσύνη.[63] Josephus, in his retelling of the attempted seduction of Josephus by Petephres' (also known as Potiphar) wife, uses σωφροσύνη in its full range of meanings.[64] In another place, Haman shows himself to be a man of σωφροσύνη and δικαιοσύνη.[65] Herod is praised for his wisdom,[66] and the Essenes are recognized for their temperance and the control of their passions.[67]

Obviously, from the brief review of the literature thus offered, the virtues were fundamental to any philosophical and ethical discussion. Furthermore, many historians, rhetoricians, and essayists freely used the terminology. It is also true that in the traditional apologetic literature of the post-apostolic church, writers were keen to translate the cardinal virtues in Christian terms in much the same way that Philo and the author of 4 Maccabees did in Jewish terms. Given this, it is rather surprising that these nouns and adjectives of excellence are not found in abundance in the New Testament literature.[68]

It is true that the noun ἀρετή is employed sparingly in the New Testament. "Virtue" is found four times in the literature, and only once in the authors mentioned above is it used in a way that reflects the sense of cardinal virtues. Paul uses the term once, in Philippians 4:8, in his parting remarks to the church there. He exhorts his listeners to consider as important those things which are true, honorable, just, pure, pleasing, commendable, excellent, and worthy of praise. Of significance is Paul's admonition to the Philippians to imitate what they have heard and seen from him. Luke also hopes, by his characterization of Paul, to evoke a mimetic response from his readers.

"Virtue" is found three times in the Petrine epistles. In 1 Peter 2:9 the author refers to the "virtues" of God, meaning by it, God's wonderful acts. As one would expect there is a different sense altogether in the second epistle. In 2 Peter 1:3 there is a suggestion

---

[62] *Against Apion*, ii, 168–170.
[63] *Jewish Wars* ii, 208; iv, 596.
[64] *Antiquities*, ii, 58–9.
[65] *Ibid.*, xi, 217.
[66] *Ibid.*, xvii, 247.
[67] *Jewish Wars*, ii, 120.
[68] Spicq, "APETH", p. 174.

that the believer shares in the virtues of God, who is the source of everything that is needed to live a devout and pious life. As a result of sharing God's excellent virtue, the believer is set free from the "consuming lust of the world." The discussion continues in 2 Peter 1:5–7 reflecting the ethical and philosophical language of the Greek philosophers. The author writes: "For this very reason, you must take every effort to support your faith with virtue, and virtue with knowledge, and knowledge with self-control, and self-control with endurance, and endurance with godliness, and godliness with mutual affection, and mutual affection with love."

It is important to note that here "virtue" heads the list which includes "knowledge," which is fully within the semantic range of "wisdom," "self-control," "endurance" which is part of bravery, and "godliness" which is part of a proper respect and acknowledgement of God. O. Bauernfeind is correct when he concludes, "here a notable formal analogy points us to the secular world."[69]

It is this understanding of virtue that is reflected in Acts and it is these virtues that Paul personifies. Like this passage in 2 Peter and the examples given in the Hellenistic Jewish literature, Luke recognizes and demonstrates through the action in the narrative, that these virtues come from God.

Looking up the classical cardinal virtues in the New Testament literature does not provide much in the way of evidence. Of course δικαιοσύνη and its derivatives are common, yet most of these reflect an Old Testament antecedent, not Greco-Roman ethical language, although the two are not mutually exclusive. The participle form of the verb σωφρονέω is found in Mark 5:15 (par. Luke 8:35) to describe the demoniac who is healed and sits "in his right mind." In Romans 12:3 Paul uses the word to indicate that the believer is not to think of himself too highly but with "sober judgment" to judge himself according to the amount of faith God has given. In 2 Corinthians 5:13 Paul writes: "For if we are beside ourselves, it is for God; if we are in our right minds it is for you." The contrast between insanity ("beside ourselves") and sanity ("in our right minds") reflects a similar understanding of Luke's use of the words μανία and σωφροσύνη in Acts 26. Again, in 1 Peter 4:7, the author tells his audience to be "self-controlled" as they await the end of all things. σωφροσύνη is used once by Luke in Acts 26:25 but, as has been indicated in a number of places, its inclusion at that point in the narrative is of the utmost importance.

[69] Bauernfeind, "APETH", p. 460.

It is interesting to note that of the eighteen times σωφρονέω and its derivatives appear in the New Testament, ten are in the pastoral epistles. φρόνησις is found twice, once at Luke 1:17 where the angel tells Zechariah that John will turn "the disobedient to the wisdom of the righteous." In Ephesians 1:8, the author uses both "wisdom" and "insight." ἀνδρεία is not found at all in the New Testament, although words for "endurance" are frequent. Εὐσέβεια, which was so important a virtue for Philo, is found once in Acts (3:12), four times in 2 Peter (1:1, 3, 6, 7; 3:11), and eight times in 1 Timothy. Of course the lists of virtues and vices found in Galatians 5:19–23, and the triad of Christian virtues (faith, hope, and love) listed in 1 Corinthians 13:13, are well known, but neither reference presents any explicit dependence on the cardinal virtues of Greco-Roman philosophical discussion.

While it would be interesting to investigate the language of the New Testament in the light of the present interest in the cardinal virtues, the immediate concern is with the Paul of Acts and how he is described. Considering that ἀρετή is never used in Acts and that σωφροσύνη and φρόνησις are found only one each in Luke-Acts, it would appear, prima facie, that Acts is not making any deliberate claims suggesting that Paul was such a man of ideal social status and virtue. However, just as the reader of Luke–Acts would have recognized that the Paul of Acts was a man of high social status primarily through allusions, so too would they recognize the allusions to Paul's moral virtue and outstanding character. Luke's intention is apparent not simply through the explicit words and phrases, for he was not writing a philosophical or ethical treatise. Luke makes known his intentions by the juxtaposition and implicit comparison of characters and, most importantly, from the way he shows how Paul acted in certain dramatic situations.

Before returning to the text of Acts to present the evidence for this claim, a few words must be said about the fundamental correlation of social status and moral virtue. Although it is true that many of the classical authors believed that true wisdom and virtue could, in theory, be found in anyone, regardless of wealth and pedigree, it is also true that it was assumed that the virtues were the natural attributes of the aristocracy. From the time of Homer it was impossible to dissociate leadership and virtue.

The aristocratic world of early Greece had a definite ideal of human perfection, and it included moral virtue as well as wealth and social position. It is not an accident that, as a class, these powerful, wealthy, and leisured individuals were called the aristocracy. As mentioned at the start of this section, the adjective virtuous and the noun virtue were "powerful words of commendation" and therefore could easily be used to describe those who possessed a position of power, status, and wealth.

Homer displays this usage clearly when, in the *Odyssey* one of the suitors of Penelope states "we are the virtuous ones." These men are virtuous because, as they claim, they have changes of clothing, warm baths, and they are able to enjoy the pleasures of love.[70] Hesiod naturally accepted that the best man (παναρίστος) attained to material success and good reputation.[71] Theognis assumed that aristocratic excellence was fundamental to true virtue, and wealth was naturally a by-product.[72] As was stated in chapter 2, society in the Greek world was essentially aristocratic and, even in the Athenian democracy of the fourth century B.C.E., some were more equal than others. Citizenship was never simply handed out to everyone, and those of wealth and status were expected to maintain their position and prestige through benefactions and liturgies.

Pindar (seventh to sixth century B.C.E.) assumed that the man of virtue started in life with the natural advantages of birth and wealth,[73] although the man of birth and wealth must always be careful of hubris! Wealth and virtue were closely linked by Homer and Hesiod.

Xenophon's testament to Cyrus extols his outstanding leadership. Cyrus is truly a man of virtue. Cyrus, as described in books I–III, was born into a royal family whose wealth and aristocratic character provided him with all the natural advantages that would allow him to develop into an individual of excellence. Likewise, to Aristotle the "great-souled man" was naturally virtuous.[74]

It is true that few would have disagreed with Philo, who affirmed that true virtue was judged by conduct and not descent.[75] Seneca's writings are replete with references to the fact that wealth is a hindrance to happiness and virtue,[76] and Cicero is obviously sensitive to the fact that wealth without decorum is hardly virtue.[77] Yet what was no doubt true in theory perhaps did not find its full realization in practice.

[70] Homer, *Odyssey*, viii, 236.
[71] Ferguson, *Moral Virtue*, p. 20.
[72] Theognis, 315; Adkins, *Merit and Responsibility*, p. 72.
[73] Pindar, *Pythian Odes*, ii, 55; Jaeger, *Paideia*, p. 19, 142; Adkins, *Merit and Responsibility*, p. 160.
[74] Aristotle, *Nichomachean Ethics*, iv, 3, 14.
[75] *Ibid.*, iv, 3, 226–227.
[76] Seneca, *Moral Letters*, xvii, 3, 12.
[77] *Concerning Offices*, 93–95.

There were Cynic philosophers to whom wealth and prestige were hindrances to wisdom and freedom and, in so being, were attributes to be dismissed. However, for the Platonic and Aristotelian tradition, external advantages were not to be cast away. Likewise, for those of the Stoic school, "preferables" were to be accepted and retained if available.[78] Aristotle reflected such an attitude when he wrote: "For it is impossible, or at least not easy, to play a noble part unless furnished with the necessary equipment. For many noble actions require instruments for their performance in the shape of friends or wealth or political advantages, the lack of which sullies supreme felicity, such as good birth."[79]

Cicero believed that the governing class, which was assumed to be the aristocracy, would provide examples of virtue, particularly "self-control." Cicero also believed that decorum (propriety), which should be translated into the vernacular as "breeding," was part of every man of virtue. He was also loath to consider any man who worked with his hands virtuous, particularly butchers, fishermen, and the like.[80]

It is difficult to find specific instances in these aristocratic philosophers, yet one gets the impression that money was to be despised only if one had to work for it. Wealth was a natural advantage that could be the source of leisure for philosophy and also the source of many a benefaction which was also a mark of the virtuous man.

Plutarch's comments in his homily on virtue and vice reflect the ambiguity of the aristocratic philosophers concerning wealth and possessions. It is true that, at the outset of his remarks, Plutarch scorns those who seek glory in great houses, numerous servants, and wealth. However, he does not dismiss wealth entirely as he goes on to write: "and wealth is pleasanter, and repute and power more resplendent, if with them goes the gladness which springs from the heart."[81]

While φρόνησις was the highest virtue and philosophy was the way to achieve it, there were limits to a lay person's involvement in the practice of any one school. For example, Tacitus was concerned that Agricola devoted himself too eagerly to the study of philosophy and was on the verge of going farther than "was befitting to a Roman and a Senator."[82] Perhaps R. Macmullen expresses it best

---

[78] Philo, *On Sobriety*, xii, 61.
[79] *Nicomachean Ethics*, i, 8, 15.
[80] *Concerning Offices*, 150.88.
[81] Plutarch, *Virtue and Vice*, 100d.
[82] *Agricola*, 4.

when he notes that "specialization in one school, even what we would call real competence in any, belonged to pedants, not to gentlemen."[83] Hence, one need not argue that Luke was a philosopher or that his audience would have had to be specialists in philosophical enquiry. Luke's vocabulary reflects the semantic range of his contemporaries and shows his familiarity with these concepts.

Needless to say, the figures who interested the biographers, poets, philosophers, and the common man were those few who combined both wealth and virtue, authority and righteousness. The virtuous man was the one who balanced both the heroic virtues of Homer with the "quiet" virtues of righteousness and wisdom.

Having thus described the virtues, the next task of this chapter will be to show how these issues are important for the proper understanding of the characterization of Paul in the concluding chapters of Acts.

Acts 26

The most important instance in Acts of Luke making an explicit mention of one of the cardinal virtues is 26:26, when Festus cries out: "You are out of your mind Paul!" (v.24 – RSV), Paul responds: "I am not out of my mind, most excellent, Festus, but I am speaking the sober truth (σωφροσύνης)." Not only is this one response of crucial importance as an interpretative key to the reader/hearer of Luke-Acts but indeed the entire chapter resonates with images that would have been obvious to Luke's audience. Paul, who "sees the light" at his conversion is changed into a man of truth and self-control.

Festus' response is full of ironic import, for Festus could not be more incorrect. Paul has been converted not to madness but sanity. In recognizing Christ, Paul has become a man of true virtue corresponding to his natural advantages of good pedigree, wealth, and high social status, as described by Luke. P. W. Walaskay's comment that Festus called Paul mad because he wanted to release him for "reasons of insanity" is hardly an appropriate interpretation.[84] Walaskay not only presses his interest in stressing the fairness of the Roman authorities to the extreme but he also misses the pregnant literary intention of the narrative.

[83] Macmullen, *Enemies of the Roman Order*, p. 47.
[84] P. W. Walaskay, *And So We Came To Rome: The Political Perspective of St. Luke*, p. 57.

Chapter 26 has been of interest to commentators for many reasons. However, most have failed to notice the extent to which the issues raised in this one scene are important to the overall portrait of Paul in Acts and to the theological intention of the work as a whole. Paul, in chapter 26 tells, for the third time, of his conversion. There are a number of differences between this account and the other two. For example, there is no mention of Ananias, who plays such an important role according to the accounts in Acts 9 and 22. There is no explicit mention of Paul's blindness, although the voice of Jesus commissions Paul to open the eyes of both Jew and Gentile from darkness to light. It has been noticed that chapter 26 contains, in the words of one scholar, "a number of stylistic excellences that compare favourably with the preface."[85] Furthermore, every astute scholar notices and comments upon Luke's use of the Greek proverb in v. 14 and mentions the classical juxtaposition of μανία with σωφροσύνη

Concerning the proverb in verse 14, the classical references are commonly noted[86] and the translation of the proverb by O. Bauernfeind, who interprets the proverb to mean that opposition to God is worthless and impossible, is as obvious as it is certainly correct.[87] Yet, for the most part, commentators do not proceed to study this proverb in any more depth; rather, they are satisfied to note the classical parallels and contend that the use of the proverb shows Luke to be well-read and possibly to have been directly influenced by Euripides.[88] However, since the proverb is found in other literature with the same general meaning and the other similarities between the *Bacchae* and Acts are not exclusive to them, it seems best to conclude that this proverb was a fixed saying of common meaning that was known and used by many.[89] It is, of course interesting that this Greek proverb, which, as far as the evidence shows, does not have an equivalent in Hebrew or Aramaic, is put in the mouth of Jesus, who speaks to Paul in "the Hebrew dialect"

[85] *Beginnings*, iv, p. 315; Rackham, *Acts* p. 462; Bruce, *Acts, p. 408;* Haenchen, *Acts*, p. 680.

[86] Aeschylus, *Agamemnon*, 1624; Pindar, *Pythian Odes*, ii, 94; Euripides, *Bacchinalia*, 795; *Iphigenia in Taurus*, 1396; Terence, *Phormio*, 79; A. H. Smith and W. M. Ramsay, "Notes on a Tour in Asia Minor," *Journal of Hellenistic Studies* 8, (1887), 216–267.

[87] Bauernfeind, *Apostelgeschichte*, p. 267; Haenchen, *Acts*, p. 685; G. Lohfink, *Paulus vor Damaskus.*

[88] Dibelius, "Literary Allusions in the Speeches in the Acts," *Studies*, pp. 186–191; Marshall, *Acts*, p. 395; Cadbury, *Book of Acts*, p. 39.

[89] Dibelius, *Studies*, p. 190 n.92, 93.

(v.14). The comments of Dibelius reflect the general critical appraisal of the inclusion of this proverb in verse 14. He wrote that the proverb is out of place in this context and added:

> simply because the author was an educated man, for only a familiarity with such phrases can explain the use of the saying here, where it is not really appropriate ... It is intended to show that Paul is among those who have struggled against God in vain; it is also intended to provide for the educated reader the pleasure he will find in this kind of literary embellishment.[90]

Contrary to Dibelius, this proverb is more than just a literary embellishment. Indeed the imagery of the proverb is fundamental to Paul's third account of his conversion. Before his conversion he was "kicking against the goads" and hence he was ruled by madness, whereas after his conversion he speaks the truth and self-controlled wisdom (v. 25).

As mentioned above, many scholars note the literary parallels to this proverb and agree as to the meaning, but fail to see its significance in light of the chapter as a whole, particularly in connection with the Greek virtues. In *Bacchae* 795, to "kick against the goads" means to "rage against god" which is the opposite of the self-control and self-knowledge that is fundamental to the meaning of σωφροσύνη. Furthermore, "to kick against the goads" is hardly a sign of "righteousness" or "piety." In fact, to "kick against the goads" is a futile attempt to overstep one's position *vis-à-vis* the gods, or God. Hence, it is hubris! The readers of Acts would find the same imagery in an earlier scene where Herod has beheaded James, imprisoned Peter, and is raging against the inhabitants of Tyre and Sidon (Acts 12:1–25). It is Herod who is "kicking against the goads"! It is no accident that after Luke has described Herod's tyrannical madness, Herod is struck down for accepting the accolades that "his is a voice not of a man but of god." Hubris receives its just reward.

This proverb in Acts 26, and the entire scene, must be interpreted in the light of its implications for the larger study of virtue. Evidenced in other classical literature, the proverb is found in discussions concerning the relationship of virtue and nobility. This is made explicit in the two references from Aeschylus and Pindar.

---

[90] Dibelius, *Studies*, p. 188; Cadbury, *The Making of Luke-Acts*, p. 226.

The context in which this proverb appears in Aeschylus' *Agamemnon* is an increasingly vitriolic dialogue between the chorus of elders and Aegisthus who has murdered Agamemnon. The elders have told Aegisthus that the gods will revenge the murder of the king. Aegisthus responds that the elders should be schooled in "self-control" and learn "common sense."[91] In a phrase reminiscent of Matthew 13:9 (and pars.), Aegisthus questions them: "don't you have ears to hear?", and then quotes the proverb "don't kick against the goads."[92] In this context, it is Aegisthus who warns the elders not to oppose his authority and power. This use of the proverb is a clear example of hubris on the part of Aegisthus and the irony of this whole dialogue is plain. It is Aegisthus who has lost all self-control and wisdom in the killing of Agamemnon and it is he who is "kicking against the goads" of fate as the penultimate verse of the play suggests.[93] The apposition of the virtues "self-control" and "knowledge" with the futility of "kicking against the goads" is important to note and can be found in Acts 26.

Pindar, in the *Pythian Odes*, uses this proverb in the context of a warning to the envious who strain after what cannot be theirs and strive, to the point of suicide, to obtain what they desire.[94] As in *Agamemnon*, to "kick against the goads" is contrasted with self-control and the acknowledgment of what can and cannot be yours. It is interesting to note that the speaker identifies that he, in contrast to those who "kick against the goads", wants to "please them that are good men, and to consort with them." The "good" are those who do not "kick against the goads." "Good" also is a descriptive term of nobility and the connection between moral virtue and social status, as has been noted above, is fully within the semantic range of the term.

H. North, in an appendix to her study of σωφροσύνη, has investigated the imagery related to the word in classical literature.[95] According to North, taming the passions was like taming a wild beast.[96] Surely this idea is reflected in Acts 26:11, where Paul describes himself before his conversion as being "furiously enraged," or "raged beyond measure," in his single-minded madness to persecute the Christians.[97]

---

[91] Aeschylus, *Agamemnon*, 1620.
[92] *Agamemnon*, 1624.
[93] *Agamemnon*, 1671.
[94] Pindar, *Pythian Odes*, ii, 64.
[95] North, *Sophrosyne*, pp. 380–386.
[96] North, *Sophrosyne*, p. 380.
[97] Bruce, *Acts*, p. 443.

Although not using the proverb, Luke's account of Stephen's speech, in Acts 7, displays a similar sense. Stephen accuses the Jewish leaders of having obstinate and uncircumcised hearts who are always resisting the Holy Spirit (7:51). In other words, the Jewish leaders are "kicking against the goads." It is appropriate that Paul, although not described in any detail, is reported as being present at this scene (8:1). At this point in Acts, the reader receives not a formal description of the man, but a glimpse of his inner character. Paul is in sympathy with the fury of the crowd.

Furthermore, it is no coincidence that the word for rescuing is used in 26:17 to signify what Jesus has done for Paul by commissioning him to preach the gospel. Paul is not only rescued from the wrath of the Jews and the idolatry of the Gentiles but is further rescued from his own self-destructive ravings against the Holy Spirit. Paul, before his conversion is not a man of σωφροσύνη; hence, he rages not only against the Christians but also against God.[98] The pre-conversion Paul lacks moral virtue, for he resists God. Likewise, those who fail to recognize the power and status of Jesus as Lord do not have φρόνησις and hence, do not possess ἀρετή in the most full sense. Before discussing this claim in more detail, it is important to comment upon verses 24–5 which make the pre-conversion madness and post-conversion sobriety of Paul explicit.

Like the proverb in verse 14, the opposition of madness with self-control or sobriety in verse 25 has not gone unnoticed. Indeed, the explicit juxtaposition of μανία and σωφροσύνη in Xenophon's *Memorabilia* is often noted.[99] Yet, as is often the case what is not noted is the most important. In this particular section of the *Memorabilia*, Xenophon is describing Socrates' teaching about self-control and madness in this context of a larger discussion about the moral virtues in general and how the knowledge of these things makes for a gentleman.[100] Luke seems to be offering a similar argument, although in not quite the same systematic way as Xenophon's description of Socrates' teaching. Before Paul's conversion he is "beside himself" and therefore is not a man of virtue. After Paul's conversion he has self-control and is sober and therefore has become virtuous.

---

[98] Dibelius, *Studies*, p. 190.
[99] *Memorabilia*, i, 1, 16; Plato, *Timaeus*, 71; *Phaedrus*, 245a; *Protagoras*, 323b; Plümacher, *Lukas*, p. 21; Ramsay, *St. Paul the Traveller*, p. 313.
[100] Xenophon, *Memorabilia*, iii, 9.6.

Returning to the text of Acts, there is no small irony in the reaction of Festus who declares that Paul's erudition has turned him to madness. The image of turning is most important in this chapter, for the word "turning" is used to describe what Paul's mission will be: "to open their eyes so that they may turn from darkness to light and from Satan to God, so that they may receive forgiveness of sins and a place among those who are sanctified by faith in me" (26:18).

Likewise Paul is told to preach repentance so that the Gentiles might turn to God (v.20). Paul, because of his acquired knowledge that Jesus is Lord and cannot be resisted, has turned from μανία to σωφροσύνη. Festus, who does not have the same φρόνησις (proper knowledge), assumes just the opposite character. Festus is shown by comparison with Paul to still be in his madness and darkness. The juxtaposition of μανία and σωφροσύνη, like the appearance of the proverb in verse 14, would conjure, for the first readers/hearers, the images and words naturally used in a discussion of virtue.

An intriguing parallel to this scene in Acts is found in the Oxyrhynchus Papyri.[101] Again the words "madness" and "self-control" or "sobriety" are placed side by side. The proceedings recorded in the papyrus take place at Rome before an emperor in connection with an embassy from Alexandria and a sentence of death pronounced upon one of its members, Appianus. Appianus is a rebel who, although the emperor seemingly wants to set him free, is unrepentant and destined for execution. Before Appianus is led away, he asks the emperor if he might be allowed to wear the insignia of his noble birth. As he is taken from the court into the street he cries out to the Romans who are scattered about: "Run hither, Romans, and behold one led off to death who is a gymnasiarch and envoy of the Alexandrians!" This declaration seems to stir up the crowd, for Appianus is recalled inside and the fascinating dialogue between Appianus and the emperor commences:

> Emperor: We too are accustomed to bring to their senses those who are mad or beside themselves. You speak only so long as I allow you to speak.
> Appianus: I swear by your prosperity, I am neither mad nor besides myself, but I appeal on behalf of my nobility and of my rights.
> Emperor: How so?

---

[101] B. P. Grenfell and A. S. Hunt, *The Oxyrhynchus Papyri* (London: Egyptian Exploration Fund, 1898), vol. I, pp. 62–66, col. 4 line 9.

Appianus: Because I am a noble and a gymnasiarch.

Emperor: Do you mean that we are ignoble?

Appianus: As to that I do not know, but I appeal on behalf of my nobility and my rights.

Emperor: Do you not know that we are noble?

Appianus: On this point if you are really ignorant, I will instruct you. In the first place Caesar saved Cleopatra's life when he conquered her kingdom, and as some say ... [the text ends here]

Although there are some major differences, both this scene and the scene in Acts take place in the context of a legal hearing. Each of the hearings is presided over by the Roman authority; the emperor in the case of Appianus and the governor in the case of Paul. The emperor judges with the help of a tribunal, Festus with the help of Agrippa. Appianus attracts the attention of the Romans outside of the courtroom and Paul make his appeal, in Acts 27, to Caesar in front of an audience of high-status individuals who gather to hear him. Despite the emperor's hesitancy, Appianus is condemned to die. Likewise, the account in Acts is explicit – although Festus, like Felix before him, wanted to release Paul he in fact does nothing to keep Paul from being sent to Rome on a capital charge. The question of the "appeal" will be discussed in the next chapter. Both Paul and Appianus are accused of raving and both deny the description. However, Paul comports himself as a man of self-control and declares that he speaks truthful words, while Appianus declares that he is of high status (he was well-born, an elder, and a gymnasiarch). Appianus' declaration that his high status should somehow protect him from death is an interesting point and is germane to the discussion of Paul's appeal. Paul's social status is not made explicit in this scene; however, the reader/hearer would no doubt recall the descriptions of Paul already alluded to in chapters 21 to 23. Furthermore, those who come to hear Paul are individuals who possessed high local status ("prominent men of the city"), high military authority ("military tribunes"), not to mention Festus, Agrippa and Bernice (25:23f). Needless to say, this would hardly be the kind of audience that one would expect if Paul were some simple artisan of low social status. It would be doubtful if there were a formal dependence of one account on the other; yet the context and the dialogue of each scene revolve, to a large extent, around the character and status of the accused. Luke is aware of the connection between social status, moral virtue, and legal innocence.

Hence, in Acts 26 Luke shows that Paul is a man of true moral virtue and right knowledge after his conversion. It is made explicit that Paul exhibits wisdom and self-control and, therefore, should be listened to and imitated. Plutarch's inclusion of the words of Plato in the former's discussion of virtue is important: "Whenever therefore we begin so to love good men, that not only, as Plato puts it, do we regard as blessed the man himself who has self-control but blessed too anyone of the company which hears the words that come from the lips of such a man."[102]

Not only does Paul have true understanding and exhibit self-control; he is, furthermore, declared innocent (16:31–2) and is shown to be in a proper relationship with God. Hence, Paul possesses true virtue. Finally it would not be too far fetched to add that the reader/hearer would remember that Paul had been in prison for over two years (24:27). Hence Paul was a man of endurance which, as has been shown above, was an attribute of courage.[103] That Paul, who is the man of high social status and moral virtue, should declare his allegiance to Jesus, effectively presents Jesus as a man of authority, the giver of true virtue and the one to whom those of true virtue should direct their attention.

That true virtue is dependent upon conversion is not only recognized by Luke in Acts, it is also made explicit in the writings of Philo. In *On the Virtues* Philo wrote:

> For it is excellent and profitable to desert without a backward glance to the ranks of virtue and abandon vice that malignant mistress; and where honor is rendered to the God who is, the whole company of the other virtues must follow in its train as surely as in the sunshine the shadow follows the body. The proselytes become at once temperate, continent, modest, gentle, kind, humane, serious, just, high-minded, truth-lovers, superior to the desire for money and pleasure, just as conversely the rebels from the holy laws are seen to be incontinent, shameless, unjust, frivolous, petty-minded, quarrelsome, friends of falsehood and perjury.[104]

---

[102] Haenchen, *Acts*, pp. 690–691.
[103] Plutarch, *How a Man may Become Aware of His Progress in Virtue*, 84c.
[104] Philo, *On the Virtues*, 181–2.

To convert is to become virtuous and all the virtues, connected as they are, come immediately to the one who repents.[105] Repentance is the first step to virtue.

With Philo's quotation in mind it is important to consider that in Acts in Peter's first sermon to the gathering at Pentecost he declares, "repent" and be baptized in the name of Jesus. Paul, likewise, preaches repentance to the Gentiles who, in response to the gospel, will do works in keeping with repentance. What is implied in Peter's speech and is made clear in this speech of Paul is that repentance, which is the turning of the true source of knowledge, brings true virtue.

In conclusion, in this scene in Acts, Luke emphasizes that Paul the Roman citizen and citizen of a Greek city and Pharisee, is the social equal of those who have gathered to hear him. Yet Luke is not merely claiming that Paul is as good as those to whom he speaks. Rather, Paul is, due to his conversion on the road to Damascus, an example of a virtuous man and an implied comparison of Paul with his audience occurs. Those who do not believe in the name of Jesus are "kicking against the goads" and are not virtuous. Hence, although those who hear Paul may have wealth, good pedigree and power, they do not possess the true moral virtue that comes from God alone. Therefore, there is an evangelistic function to this story. Luke is concerned to tell his readers who include "both the great and the small," that Paul, who is of high social standing and moral virtue, preaches so that all might "become such as I am – except for these chains" (v.29).

This interest in Paul's social status and moral virtue and the implicit comparison of Paul with other characters in the narrative can be found elsewhere in Acts.

Paul and his antagonists

Luke was concerned to show that Paul was a man of high social status and moral virtue. Furthermore, Luke implied that the one who converted and believed in the name of Jesus became an individual of moral virtue as well. Also implicit was that those who did *not* convert also did not possess true virtue or, for that matter, status as a citizen of the Kingdom of God. Hence, Luke is constantly comparing and contrasting Paul with his antagonists.

---

[105] *Ibid.*, 181–2.

Using the common rhetorical practice of σύγκρισις, or comparison, Luke constructs his narrative in order to place Paul in the company of those of high political and social status. In so doing, he makes implicit comparisons and inevitable judgments on the moral virtue of these characters that redound to Paul's glory and lessen the overall status and virtue of the characters with whom Paul is juxtaposed.[106] The first reader/hearers of Acts would have recognized the use of such techniques and been sensitive to the implications of such common rhetorical devices for the meaning of any given pericope and indeed of the text as a whole.[107]

Aristotle, in his book on rhetoric, writes that praise is founded on action,[108] for acting according to moral purpose is characteristic of a worthy man. Since praise is the language setting forth the greatness of virtue, the orator or writer must show that the individual's actions were virtuous.[109] Aristotle then adds that the point of praising anyone is to exhort other individuals to change and to be more like that one who is praised. The nature of praise, according to Aristotle, is to counsel the hearer to imitate the one who is held up for recognition.[110] While Luke was not necessarily directly influenced by the writings of Aristotle, he presents numerous examples of ways of praising Paul in order to exhort his audience to believe and be like him.

Aristotle continued that if there were not enough specific data with which to make a list of the praiseworthy accomplishments of the individual to be praised, then an effective way of highlighting the virtues of the person is to compare him with others. For by comparing the person with known illustrious men, the individual is raised by comparison.[111] Aristotle also added that if there were not illustrious persons with which to make a comparison, the character should be compared with ordinary persons, "since superiority is thought to indicate virtue."

Cicero, too, in his later years, wrote on oratory and rhetorical

---

[106] Philo, *On the Virtues*, 183.

[107] MacKenzie, "Character Description and Socio-Political Apologetic"; W. S. Kurz, "Hellenistic Rhetoric in the Christological Proof of Luke–Acts," *CBQ* 42, (1980), 171–195; Malherbe, *Social Aspects of Early Christianity*, p. 45; H. I. Marrou, *A History of Education in Antiquity* (New York: Sheeds and Ward, 1964), pp. 233–242; M. L. Clarke, *Higher Education in the Ancient World* (London: Routledge & Kegan Paul, 1971)

[108] Aristotle, *Rhetoric*, i, 9, 32.

[109] *Rhetoric*, i, 9, 32.

[110] *Rhetoric*, i, 9, 35.

[111] *Rhetoric*, i, 9, 39.

skill. Although he contended that panegyric is more the art of the Greeks, he does include several comments that are important to this study. While he considered that desirable qualities such as family, good looks, resources, and riches, are not in and of themselves virtuous or to be praised, virtue is, nevertheless, discerned in those individuals who employ and manage these goods of nature.[112] Cicero claimed that praise is appropriate for those of outstanding merit and is especially fit for those individuals who have faced danger to help others, met adversity wisely, or did not lose their dignity in difficult situations.[113]

Cicero, like Aristotle, recognized the important function of comparison.[114] Quintilian also believed that the proper function of panegyric was to praise virtue.[115] Plutarch's "Lives" are a testimony to the importance of comparison in literature. Certainly Acts is not a formal encomium or panegyric. However, much of the last eight chapters of Acts is in praise of Paul bringing to the fore his social status and virtuous character. One of the ways in which Luke accomplished his task was to use the standard and very common literary device of comparison.

In conclusion, comparison of characters and the implicit judgment which followed was commonplace and taken for granted in all types of epideictic and forensic oratory and literature.[116] Hence, this fundamental classical (and modern) technique will be of the utmost importance for a proper understanding of the extent to which Luke portrays Paul as a man of social status and moral virtue.

It has already been shown that the comparison of characters and the implicit judgment that follows is important to Luke. In Acts 26 where Paul is portrayed as a man of "self-control"; in Acts 21:38 where Paul is insulted by the misunderstanding that he is no more than an Egyptian agitator; and in 22:28 where his inherited citizenship is compared to the purchased citizenship of the tribune the comparisons are obvious and intentional. Paul is not only not an Egyptian, he is a Greek citizen. Paul is not only a Roman citizen, he is a Roman by descent, not purchase.

---

112 *On Orations*, i, 141.
113 *On Orations*, ii, 346.
114 *On Orations*, ii, 348.
115 Quintilian, ii, iv, 21.
116 F. Foke, "Synkrisis," *Hermes* 58 (1923), 327–368; C. Forbes, "Comparison, Self-Praise and Irony: Paul's Boasting and the Conventions of Hellenistic Rhetoric," *NTS* 32 (1986), 1–30.

An example of a positive judgment by comparison can be found in the speech of Paul to the Jews of Jerusalem. Trying to impress them by listing his strong Jewish credentials, he recounts the tale of his conversion. In order to indicate that even after conversion he has not turned his back on Judaism, Paul mentions that Ananias was a "devout man" who was respected by all the Jewish inhabitants (22:12). Here, Paul is trying to share the status of Ananias and the respect that Ananias holds.

Acts 27

The account of the storm at sea and the shipwreck in chapter 27 is yet another scene where there is an implied comparison and judgment of characters. Very little need be said on this well-discussed narrative. Few miss the fact that Paul plays, in the words of W. Ramsay, "The part of a true Roman on a Roman ship, looked up to even by the centurion, and in his single self the savior of the lives of all."[117] Furthermore, it is often noted that Paul, despite the presence of the ship owner and the centurion, knows from the outset the dangers that are to come, and assumes command of the ship even though he is a prisoner. Although Ramsay is indeed correct that Paul is portrayed as a "true Roman," he is incorrect to accept the historicity of this portrayal and he fails, as do all others who make comments to that effect, to define what a "true Roman" is.

The journey by ship to Rome follows Paul's interview with Festus and Agrippa. The purpose of the hearing before governor and king was to show that Paul possessed true moral virtue and Festus and Agrippa did not. Now, in this telling of the shipwreck, the readers/ hearers are given an example of how Paul, the man of virtue, responds to adversity. Cicero's words noted above, concerning dignity in times of adversity, are apposite. In this scene, Paul is shown to be brave while the ship, and everyone on it, is overtaken by the total chaos of the storm. Paul does not, like the narrator and the other passengers, lose heart (27:21–6). Furthermore, Paul is the paragon of self-control as he assumes command of the foundering craft (27:21). Paul's piety is illustrated not only in that he has a conversation with an angel (27:23) but also in his ministrations and prayers over the bread (27:35). Here, Paul exemplifies the classical cardinal virtues. He is shown to be brave, wise, self controlled, and

---

[117] Ramsey, *St. Paul the Traveller*, p. 339; Haenchen, *Acts*, p. 711.

pious even though the technical terms are not used. The Roman centurion, and all the others on the ship pale by comparison. They do not accept a warning from Paul who shares his knowledge with them (27:10); they are afraid (27:17) and they give up hope (27:20).

Acts 24:10ff.

In Acts 24, the implicit comparison and judgment of Paul and Felix, that Luke naturally intends the reader to make, works on the level both of moral value and of social status.[118] Paul, after the plot on his life is made known to him, is taken to Caesarea (23:23) and appears before the Governor, Felix, and his wife, Drusilla. In response to their request to speak about faith in Jesus, Paul "discussed justice, self-control and the coming judgment" (24:25). Felix is alarmed by this forceful sermon and sends Paul back to his cell with the promise of future meetings. The scene ends with a report that Paul was in prison for two years, the implication being that Felix was never converted. He called for Paul only in expectation of a bribe.

Marcus Antonius Felix represents an antithesis of the Pauline character. Paul has been described, just two chapters earlier, as a man of good pedigree and wealth. Having all the proper citizen-ships, he is a man of high social status. Felix, on the other hand, although in a position of high political authority that was usually held by one of high social status, did not possess a prestigious pedigree; the brother of Pallas, he was a favorite freedman of the Emperor Claudius and succeeded Ventidius Cumanus as procurator in 54 C.E.[119] Before his rise to the position of procurator, Felix had held office in Syria and Judaea. The promotion of a freedman to a position of authority became increasingly more common in the second century but during the middle decades of the first century it was highly unusual and those of high social status in Rome were scandalized when Claudius appointed Felix to the equestrian order.[120] Felix, who would never have been mistaken as one of the *honestiores*, used his position of intimacy with Claudius to secure his position. His term as procurator was marked by misrule and fierce attacks on insurgents. He caused a great deal of disaffection on the part of the nation and eventually was recalled to Rome.[121] Tacitus

[118] Rackham, *Acts*, p. 449.
[119] Josephus, *Antiquities*, xx, 137–140; Schürer rev., vol. I, pp. 460–466.
[120] Suetonius, *Claudius*, 28, trans. R. Graves.
[121] Josephus, *Jewish Wars*, ii, 253, 270; Schürer rev., vol. I, pp. 462–463.

wrote: "He practiced every kind of cruelty and lust, wielding the power of king with all the instincts of a slave."[122]

Though not describing Felix's prodigality in detail or reporting on the circumstances of his background with the acerbic disdain of Tacitus, Luke, or his source, was, nevertheless, aware of Felix's reputation, as the subjects of Paul's sermon to him show. F. F. Bruce asserts that justice, self-control, and the coming judgment "were the very subjects that Felix and Drusilla most needed to hear about."[123] That Felix and Drusilla needed to hear these words may be true, but in saying only this Bruce misses the importance of these subjects for Luke's larger interest in moral virtue.

"Justice" and "self-control" are cardinal virtues and it is no accident that Paul preaches on these subjects here. For Paul to preach in this way to Felix hardly makes the governor appear in a positive light. Although there is no dependence on Luke's account in Acts, Seneca seems to have an account such as this in mind when he wrote: "The greatest proof of an evil mind is unsteadiness, and continued wavering of virtue and love of vice."[124]

Felix's unsteadiness is made plain from the content of Paul's talk. Moreover, Felix's wavering between patience and vice is highlighted not only in his seeking to listen to Paul but also seeking a bribe (24:26). According to Josephus, Felix was well known for taking bribes, although it was against the law for anyone to take money for either imprisonment or release of a prisoner.[125] The ending of this scene is an ironic reminder of the opening speech of Tertullus (24:2–8) who praised Felix as a benefactor and ended his remarks by asking for Felix's "understanding judgment," an attribute that Felix decidedly does not possess.

The relationship of Drusilla and Felix was not without scandal. Felix had married Drusilla after, so the story goes, calling upon Atomos, a Cyprian magician to conjure Drusilla away from Aziz, king of Emesa.[126] The commentators in *Beginnings of Christianity*, with their usual sensitivity, wrote on this scene: "Luke is probably sensitive to the marital irregularities of the Herods, but he also had

[122] Tacitus, *Histories*, v, 9; *Annals*, xii, 54.
[123] *Letter to Aristeas*, 278; Bruce, *Acts*, p. 416; H. L. Conzelmann, *Apostelgeschichte* (Tübingen: JCB Mohr (P. Siebeck), 1963), p. 135; *Beginnings*, vol. IV, p. 305.
[124] Seneca, *Moral Letters*, cxx, 20.
[125] Josephus, *Jewish Wars*, ii, 271–273; Conzelman, *Apostelgeschichte*, pp. 133.
[126] Josephus, *Antiquities*, xx, 139; 141–143; H. Wendt, *Handbuch über die Apostelgeschichte* (Göttingen: Vandenhoeck and Ruprecht, 1880), pp. 487.

an interest in the sins of money, and he presently intimates that Felix was greedy for a bribe."[127] Haenchen, while noting the dubious character and reputation of Felix, still concludes that Felix was an "able and honourable" man who was almost convinced of the truth of the gospel.[128] To Haenchen, Luke might have known of the scandals but he covered them up in order to present the Roman authorities as friends of Christianity. Haenchen, and the many scholars who hold a similar view about Luke's attitude to Roman authority, have misread the text on several points. There is little, if any, evidence that the text of Acts presents Felix as either "able" or "honorable," as the bribe and Felix's leaving Paul in prison suggest. Haenchen has placed far too much emphasis on Felix's being troubled by Paul's words and is assuming too much to think that Felix was almost converted. Felix accepted Paul's sermon in much the same way as Herod accepted John the Baptist's words (Luke 3:18–20). It is improbable that Luke intended to portray Roman authority in a positive light. Rather, Luke was interested in showing Paul to be the superior of Felix both in social status and in moral virtue. Even if the first reader/hearers of Acts did not know of the numerous scandals related to Felix, this scene in Acts presents Paul as the preacher of justice and self-control, while Felix is hardly the personification of the Roman ideals of justice and fairness! It is no accident that this scene follows closely upon Paul's recital of his pedigree (21:37; 22:25). That Paul is a man of high social status and moral virtue would only add to his overall appeal and call into question Felix's true stature, and, by extension, the stature of Roman authority in general.

It is now important to consider, in brief, several other passages in Acts where Paul and his associates are contrasted and compared with individuals and groups to the glory of Paul and Christianity and to the detriment of those who do not believe.

Acts 16

In chapters 16, 17, and 19 the excellence of Paul is highlighted both by the company he keeps and the company he does not keep. Chapter 16 is a much-studied periscope with a great deal of attention focused on the form and redactional issues involved in the story of the earthquake and the conversion of the prison guard (16:25–

---

[127] *Beginnings*, vol. IV, p. 365.
[128] Haenchen, *Acts*, p. 661; Plümacher, *Lukas*, pp. 80–81.

34).[129] Paul's confession of his Roman citizenship is also noted and a great deal of speculation revolves around the question of why Paul waited until the morning to proclaim his social advantage that would have saved him from a beating.[130] The issue of Paul's alleged Roman citizenship and legal privileges will be discussed in the next two chapters. Of interest at this juncture is the fact that in 16:20–21 an implicit comparison is made between the Roman citizens who, along with the crowd, drag Paul before the magistrates to receive a beating and imprisonment, and Paul and Silas. The two disciples are not only Jews who are disturbing the city; as the reader will find out, they are Roman citizens too. The comparison of Roman citizenships is more subtle but no less forceful in this scene than in Acts 22. The Roman citizens who stir up the crowd and the Roman magistrates are hardly the paragons of Roman justice and order.

Polybius wrote that mob-rule was the lowest grade of democracy and certainly few others would have disagreed.[131] The Roman citizens are guilty by association in that they stir up the crowd. The Roman magistrates are also accessories to this injustice. The crowd (ὄχλος) is often mentioned in Luke-Acts (forty-two times in Luke and twenty-two times in Acts). Although the crowd follows Jesus and is often the main audience for his teaching (Luke 8:4) the crowd is decidedly fickle in Acts as it can hardly be restrained from offering sacrifices to Paul and Barnabas (14:18). Yet, in the next verse, the mob is persuaded by the Jews of Antioch and Iconium to stone Paul (14:19)! The crowd marvels at the miracles of Philip (8:6) but is more often than not the cause of disturbance, unrest, violence, and confusion (16:22; 17:13; 21:34, 35).[132] Paul and Silas, who proudly refuse to leave the prison until a formal apology has been made, are hardly part of or associated with the throng.

Of even greater importance than the legal issues is the comparison that is made between two types of Roman citizens. On the one hand there is the mob; on the other hand, there are Paul and Silas. It is therefore no accident that Paul and Silas, in the following scene, are joined by "devout Greeks and not a few of the leading women" (17:4), while the Jews are described as jealous and are in the company of "the rabble" (17:5). Luke has intentionally set these two groups at odds precisely in terms of social status. First it was the

[129] Haenchen, *Acts*, pp. 499–504.
[130] Haenchen, *Acts*, p. 504; Bruce, *Acts*, p. 322.
[131] Polybius, *Histories*, vi, 4, 6; vi, 57, 59; Plato, *Laws* ii, 670b; *Philo, Moses*, i, 197.
[132] J. B. Tyson, "The Jewish Public in Luke-Acts," *NTS*, 30 (1984), pp. 574–583.

Roman citizens who are unsympathetic to Paul who ally themselves with the rabble, now it is the Jews.

References to the disdain of the classical authors to crowds and the people of the marketplace are common.[133] The rabble consisted of the lower sort who were easily agitated. By definition they were vulgar. K. Lake recognized the implicit comparison and wrote:

> the word ἀγοραῖος is contrasted with well-born, refined and educated, and is associated with the ill-bred coarse class, especially hucksters and artisans. The etymology of the word suits the reference to this working class, and the Greek scorn for the petty trading and labouring class had given the word its unfavourable meaning. Whether Luke himself shared this feeling is uncertain.[134]

In Acts, Luke sets Paul and the Christians above the crowds. The contrast between the market-people who are with the Jews and the leading women and devout Greeks who are with Paul is clear.

Acts 17:11

Another explicit contrast is presented by Luke in chapter 17. What is interesting about this scene is that the contrast is between two groups of Jews. On the one hand there are the Jews of Thessalonica who have just caused a riot and associated themselves with the wicked rabble, while on the other hand Luke writes that the Jews in Beroea were "more noble" (17:11). Luke goes on to add that their nobility is evidenced because they eagerly received the gospel. Luke does not seek to implicate all Jews in the unrest and reported violence against Paul. Neither does it appear that Luke intended to portray, contrary to J. T. Sanders' recent thesis, the early church rejecting a Jewish mission.

It cannot be denied that most Jews in Acts are hostile to the gospel. However, some truly noble Jews are naturally attracted to the gospel and their acceptance of Paul reflects that nobility. Luke's concern is to highlight the matchless eminence of Paul and those who want to be associated with him.

Acts 19:23ff.

At Ephesus (19:23ff.), Luke has no need to make explicit the contrasting status and virtue of the opposing parties. Demetrius, at

---

[133] Plato, *Protagoras*, 347c; Xenophon, *Hellenica*, vi, 2, 23.
[134] *Beginnings*, vol. IV, p. 204; Bruce, *Acts*, p. 367.

first glance, might seem the type of individual who would have had attractive characteristics. He is a devotee of Artemis and he is wealthy. Yet, Luke is swift to point out that his piety is false and self-seeking. Again, as in the other cities which Paul enters, the inhabitants create an uproar. They lose all self-control as they drag Gaius and Aristarchus into the theater. Paul, by contrast, is kept away from the disorderly gathering by his friends the Asiarchs (19:31), who were individuals of status and authority, wealth and prestige.[135] Not only is Paul's social status enhanced by his friendship with the Asiarchs, but he is contrasted with the crowd. Likewise, Paul's faith in Christ, who is the source of σωφροσύνη, is contrasted with the faith of the Ephesians in Artemis which is expressed in hysteria.

Acts 11:24ff.

That so many of the converts and followers of "the way" are of high social status confirms Luke's overriding concern with this issue. This has been noted before by many. What has not always been noticed is Luke's concern to show the moral virtue of Paul and the converts as well. For example, Barnabas is described as an ἀνὴρ ἀγαθός (11:24). F. W. Danker has shown that the title is one of great honor.[136] As noted at the outset of this chapter, to be an ἀνὴρ ἀγαθός was equivalent to being a man of true virtue. What is important and unique about this particular text is that Barnabas is a "good man" because he is full of the Holy Spirit (11:24). That here the Holy Spirit is the vehicle not only of grace but also of true moral virtue recalls Paul's conversion as told to Festus and Agrippa. Furthermore, it is interesting to note that immediately after this description of Barnabas, he travels to Tarsus to find Saul. Saul at this point in the narrative has not yet been portrayed as a man of high social standing and moral virtue. He is still in his Christian infancy and hence is raised in status because of his association with Barnabas. Faith is both the source and the result of true virtue and true status in the eyes of God.

---

[135] L. R. Taylor, "The Asiarchs," *Beginnings*, vol. V, pp. 256–262; E. Magie, *Roman Rule in Asia Minor*, 2 vols. (Princeton: Princeton University Press, 1950), vol. I, pp. 449–450; vol. II, pp. 1,298–1,301; M. Rossner, "Asiarchen und Archiereis Asias," *Studii Classici* 16 (1974), 101–142; Overbeck, *Apostelgeschichte*, p. 174; Haenchen, *Acts*, p. 367.

[136] Danker, "Benefactor," p. 318.

Acts 13:4ff.

Another scene where the comparison of character is crucial to the proper understanding of the text is shown in chapter 13 when Paul and Barnabas convert the proconsul, Sergius Paulus. Sergius Paulus' conversion is often used as evidence of Luke's concern to describe all Romans in a positive manner. However, this can hardly be the case. Not all Romans act in virtuous ways. For Luke, the importance of this scene depends upon the description of Sergius Paulus as a man of discernment. Σύνεσις (wisdom, or understanding) was recognized by Aristotle as one of the intellectual virtues synonymous with σοφία and φρόνησις.[137] Philo too, recognized σύνεσις as one of the cardinal virtues as he shows in his description of Moses who, to Philo, was the man of virtue *par excellence*.[138] That Sergius Paulus is noted as a man of wisdom and is a Roman citizen only adds to his general distinction and makes his comparison with Bar-Jesus even more striking. That Bar-Jesus is a false prophet and a magician does not place him in a highly regarded circle as far as Luke is concerned.[139] The reader is left in little doubt that Sergius Paulus will follow Paul and Barnabas rather than Bar-Jesus because of his intelligence, which allowed him to make a good judgment about the truth of the gospel.

It would be redundant to mention all the individuals of high status who are described in Acts as being associated with the gospel, for they have often been noted.[140] Yet what is regularly overlooked is that in Acts individuals or groups who receive the gospel and are converted or who are sympathetic and supportive of Paul and the Christians, are subsequently recognized as possessing virtuous characteristics and are often characters of high social status. Conversely, those who do not receive the Gospel are either those of low status or associated with them. Those who have certain qualities related to high status (Festus, Felix, Agrippa), are contrasted to Paul, who, as has been shown, is a man of both moral virtue and social status. Luke was concerned to show by implication that the source of true moral virtue was Jesus and the way to reach this level of excellence was through faith and conversion.

[137] *Nichomachean Ethics*, i, 13, 20; Diogenes Laertius, vii, 126.
[138] Philo, *Moses*, i, 154.
[139] See Acts 8:9–11; 19:18, 19.
[140] Haenchen, *Acts*, p. 507; Cadbury, *Book of Acts*, p. 42.

Acts 18:24–6

Before closing this chapter, brief mention must be made of the relationship of Apollos with Aquila and Priscilla in 18:24–6. This relationship not only highlights Luke's interest in comparison and judgment of characters, but is also an explicit presentation of how Christians, no matter what their original objective social status, can hold high status and authority in the Kingdom of God.

Aquila and Priscilla are introduced in 18:3 as tent-makers. Very probably these tents were leather and, although tent-making is not considered the meanest of crafts, it was hardly a profession for those of high social status.[141] That Paul shared this craft does not easily coincide with his high social standing that is so prevalent elsewhere. It is interesting to note that Codex D omits the reference to the tents hence removing the problematic phrase. This raises the possibility that a later editor or scribe noticed that, in Acts, converts were usually those of high status and so removed the name of the craft to lessen the incongruity.

In contrast to W. Ramsay, A. Deissmann emphasized Paul's tent-making and concluded that Paul was from the lower classes.[142] More recently, R. F. Hock has argued that Paul was of high social status and was aware of his considerable loss of status when he became a Christian (1 Cor. 9:19; 2 Cor. 11:7). To Hock, Paul showed an upper-class disdain for work of that nature.[143] Hock's interpretation is ingenious, yet attempts too much in reconciling Acts with Paul's letters. In the passages of the Corinthian epistles to which Hock refers, Paul is more concerned to show his self-sufficiency than his self-sacrifice of high status. The words of Paul are to be seen in the context of comparing himself with other traveling disciples who live off the proceeds of the community – an alternative that Paul chooses not to accept.

Most recently, P. Lampe has concluded that the tents Paul made were probably sewn from the famous linen of Tarsus. These tents were not for military use but were bought by the wealthy who sought protection from the summer heat.[144] Lampe goes on to suggest that if his thesis is correct, then Paul was a linen worker and

141 Strack-Bill., vol. II, p. 476; Jeremias, *Jerusalem*, p. 234.
142 Deissmann, *Paul*, p. 48.
143 Hock, "Paul's Tentmaking," 555–564; "The Workshop," 438–450; *Social Context*.
144 Lampe, "Paulus–Zeltmacher," 256–260.

hence could not have been a citizen of Tarsus, as noted by Dio Chrysostom.[145]

One could argue that Paul's craft is evidence that Luke was here emphasizing Paul's Pharisaic background for, as is well known, the rabbinic tradition expected rabbis to have a craft. This takes on added weight in the light of the fact that Aquila and Priscilla are introduced as Jews (18:2).[146] This understanding of the scene in Acts 18 has its merits. However, the problem remains that, although Priscilla and Aquila are sympathetic to Christianity, Luke does not indicate, as in the case of other converts, that they possess a high status, nor does he use any language which would necessarily suggest that they possess virtue. Priscilla and Aquila were probably not poor but there is nothing in the text that would suggest their high social status.[147] However, it is at this point that the figure of Apollos becomes important for he *is* given a title that suggests education and status.

Luke describes Apollos as an ἀνὴρ λόγιος ("an eloquent man") from Alexandria (18:24). The prestige of the city of Alexandria would be well known to Luke's readers and Apollos' erudition would be clearly implied. Yet despite his eloquence and his bold preaching in the synagogues, Luke writes that Priscilla and Aquila have to correct his teaching (18:26). That Apollos is explicitly placed under the authority of Aquila and Priscilla, who have fuller understanding of the gospel, raises them to a high degree of authority and status based on the principle of comparison expressed above.

Luke does not need to indicate specific status qualifications. He does it by means of his narrative. That Aquila and Priscilla possess proper understanding of the faith puts them in the circle with Paul and their status would rise accordingly.

Conclusion

At this point it is important to summarize before moving on. In this and the preceding chapter, the argument has been advanced that Luke was intentionally portraying Paul in such a way as to highlight his social status and moral virtue. Paul is portrayed as a man of good birth and heritage. He is upright in character, well educated,

[145] Dio Chrysostom, xxxiv, 23.
[146] Applebaum, "Social and Economic Status," 701–727; Livy, v, 2, 7; xxxvii, 39, 2; Schüssler-Fiorenza, *In Memory of Her*, p. 178.
[147] *Beginnings*, vol. IV, p. 233; Haenchen, *Acts*, p. 550.

pious, and wealthy. In addition to all of this, he is a citizen of Tarsus, a citizen of Rome, and the strictest of Pharisees. Luke naturally used the rhetorical practices of his day and his audience would, likewise, intuitively have understood and recognized his objective. In the various scenes in which Paul stands before, and is implicitly compared with, those in authority, Luke's intention is to emphasize that Paul's social credentials and virtuous character place him in élite company. Even if Paul does not possess the official titles of his antagonists, he shows that he is their moral superior. The point of praising Paul, as Luke did, and showing that in his conversion Paul became a man of virtue invites readers to recognize the foolishness of "kicking against the goads" by trying to stem the tide of Christianity. Gamaliel's words to the Council are important in this context: "if this plan or this undertaking is of human origin, it will fail; but if it is of God, you will not be able to overthrow them – in that case you may even be found fighting against God!" (Acts 5:38–9).

In the next chapter, Paul's social status will again be investigated but now in the light of the legal scenes in Acts. Those scenes in which Paul relies upon the legal rights of the citizenship of Rome have always been taken as verification of Paul's citizenship and objective historical evidence for Roman legal procedure in the first century. This claim should not be accepted without further inquiry. Moreover, while it may be true that the scenes in Acts reflect a knowledge of aspects of Roman law, what is omitted is as important as what is reported. Rather, what the trial scenes in Acts reflect is the knowledge that, in the first century, only those of high social status could secure the legal privileges that were, at least on paper, granted to all Roman citizens. Luke, or his source, shaped these scenes to focus attention, once again, on Paul's social status.

Scant attention has been given by New Testament scholars to the relationship of social status and legal privileges in the Greco-Roman world. This aspect of the legal scenes in Acts must be studied in some detail.

5

PAUL ON TRIAL

The success of the thesis expressed in this study relies upon the weight of cumulative evidence. In the earlier chapters it was shown that the traditional portrayal of Paul raises several problems. Luke, it appears, was attempting to portray Paul as a man of high social status and moral virtue at the expense of strict historical accuracy.

The focus of this investigation will now shift to those scenes in Acts in which Paul confronts Roman or provincial legal authority. However, the importance of the perception of Paul's social status will remain primary.

The last eight chapters of Acts are made up of a number of scenes in which Paul has to defend himself and his ministry before the leaders of the Christian community in Jerusalem (21:17ff.), before the Jewish people (22:1ff.), before the council of the Jews (23:1ff.), before Felix in Caesarea (24:1ff.), before Festus and his tribunal (25:1ff.), before Festus, Agrippa, and Bernice (25:13ff.), and before the Jews of Rome (28:17). Some have argued that Paul's trials on the sea are a symbolic hearing before the court of Nature (27:1 to 28:67).[1] Assuming that a final court appearance would occur before Nero, it is undeniable that Paul is on trial for almost the entirety of the last eight chapters of Acts. Considering the legal context of the concluding chapters it is not surprising that forensic terms appear and proper courtroom speeches are delivered.

That the entire narrative of the last eight chapters is intent upon portraying Paul in a certain way in order to display his social status and upright character is entirely appropriate. Highlighting the *persona* of the defendant is one of the techniques used in legal defense.

Many of these forensic aspects of Acts have not gone unnoticed, and the ever-increasing number of studies concerned with the legal

[1] Miles and Trompf, "Luke and Antiphon," 259–267; Ladouceur, "Shipwreck and Pollution," 435–449.

issues of the last eight chapters of Luke's second book have led to a number of impressive and helpful conclusions. In the last twenty years or so, there has been renewed interest in Luke's knowledge and use of classical legal rhetoric, and in the study of the "Gattung" of defense speeches as a literary sub-unit of courtroom scenes.[2] In a recent article, J. Neyrey has shown convincingly that the defense speeches in Acts follow the profile of defense oratory in the forensic handbook as described by Quintilian.[3] Of significant value is the fact that according to the forensic handbook it was of the utmost importance to portray the defendant as a person of moral integrity and high social standing. For example, Cicero instructed orators to develop the "ethos" of the defendant and "to paint their character in words as being upright, stainless, conscientious, modest, etc."[4]. Likewise, Quintilian wrote that if the defendant "is believed to be a good man, this consideration will exercise the strongest influence at every point in the case."[5]

These studies of the forensic speeches in Acts generally conclude that Luke was defending Paul from those who accused him of less than strict adherence to Jewish law. While Luke does describe Paul as a law-abiding Jew, his portrayal of Paul communicates something more than just his religious innocence.

The various courtroom scenes in Acts seem to provide a wealth of information about Roman legal procedure. Many have set out to describe Paul's protest against punishment in 16:37 and 22:25, his trials, and particularly his "appeal" in Acts 25:11 in the light of what is known about the actual historical legal process of the Roman empire in the provinces of the first century.[6] A proper understanding of the historical "facts" is important. However, the elucidation of the historical background of specific legal issues does not necessarily commend the historicity of the narrative as a whole. That Luke, or his sources, described Paul's trial in terms of Roman legal language and procedure is what one would expect of an edu-

---

[2] Long, "The *Paulusbild* in the Trial of Paul in Acts," 87–106; Trites, "The Importance of Legal Scenes And Language," 278–284; Veltmann, "The Defense Speeches of Paul in Acts," 243–256.

[3] Neyrey, "Forensic Defense Speech," 210–224.

[4] Cicero, *On Oration*, ii, 43, 184; Neyrey, "Forensic Defense Speech," p. 211.

[5] Quintilian, *Institutio Oratoria* iv, 1, 7; Neyrey, "Forensic Defense Speech," p. 211.

[6] Cadbury, "Roman Law," *Beginnings*, vol. V, pp. 297–338; Sherwin-White, *Roman Society and Roman Law*; Long, "The Trial of Paul."

cated writer from the first century. How Luke used these legal scenes is an issue worth investigation.

In this final section of Acts, Paul escapes punishment (22:25), his "appeal" to Caesar is heeded (25:12), while under arrest he is allowed off the ship to visit friends (27:3), and he is placed under the lightest of house arrests in Rome (28:16, 23). In fact, as soon as he begins his journey to Rome, the reader could easily forget that Paul is a prisoner at all. He takes control of the ship during the storm (27:21ff.). Paul is treated with great kindness by the first citizen of Malta (28:7). He is met by the Christians of Rome as if he were some kind of dignitary (28:15). Other than the reference to a debatable two-year Caesarean imprisonment (24:27),[7] Acts mentions only an overnight stay in the Philippi prison (16:25). The one occurrence of his being beaten (16:22) is portrayed as an abuse of power and a mistake.

Paul, in Acts, is treated as a man of high status and prestige. This is hardly the picture the epistles give of Paul's experiences. It is true that the "imprisonment letters" do not suggest undue hardship, in that Paul has time to write letters, has people attending him, has access to money (Philemon 18), and looks forward to release.[8] However, Paul, in 2 Corinthians 11:23ff., lists his many imprisonments, lashings from the Jews, and beating with rods from the Romans. While it might be argued that here he is guilty of overstating his case for effect, the picture of Paul in Acts simply does not coincide with Paul's own accounts. These issues will require further investigation below.

Luke does not emphasize the imprisonments, the lashings, or the beatings. Instead, he consistently shows Paul as a man of recognized *dignitas*, one who assumes control of all situations. Therefore, in this and the following chapter, a careful study of Luke's dramatic account of Paul's protest against punishment as ordered by Roman authority and his "appeal" to Nero must be made. In addition, Luke's description of Paul's various incarcerations, the conditions of his transit to Rome, and his light imprisonment while in the capital, will be investigated.

---

[7] Cadbury, "The Chronology of Acts," *Beginnings*, vol. V, p. 435; Haenchen, *Acts*, p. 661.

[8] W. G. Kümmel, *Introduction to the New Testament*, trans. H. C. Kee (London: S.C.M. Press, 1975), p. 250; J. L. Houlden, *Paul's Letters From Prison* (Bath: Chivers-Penguin Library, 1970), pp. 38–41, 134–139, 240–253.

Roman law and social status

Whoever attempts a thorough investigation of Roman legal history of the first century confronts a monumental task. The evidence required to make indisputable claims concerning almost all issues involved is, unfortunately, lacking. This fact comes as a sobering check to anyone who attempts to understand the legal issues behind the several reports in Acts where Paul depends upon Roman legal rights. Sure historical criteria are wanting which would help judge, for example, the accuracy of Luke's account of Paul's "appeal" in Acts 25:11.[9] Luke's description of Paul's calling on Caesar is the only example from the first century of the Common Era of such an appeal on a capital charge from the provinces. Therefore, both those who appeal to the historicity of the report and those who question the accuracy must acknowledge the absence of sufficient source material.

What is known is that Roman law was developing at a fast rate in the first century as the Roman empire continued its transition from the republican to the imperial form of government. The sources that are extant either come from the age of the Republic or from the writing of the *Digest* – a compilation of laws and rescripts published in the sixth century, some of which come from a much earlier period.[10] However, it is still possible to evaluate the material presented in Acts and attempt to understand Luke's purpose in using it. Of critical importance for this task is a proper comprehension of the relationship between social status and legal privileges in the Roman republic and empire.

The consensus of scholars agrees that, throughout the second century C.E., Roman citizenship was increasingly devalued as a mark of distinction due to the increase of free aliens who had assumed the title of *civis Romanus*.[11] The devaluation was complete with the decree of Caracalla in 212 C.E. which declared that all freeborn men within the boundaries of the empire became Roman citizens.[12] What had once been a social and legal distinction between *peregrinus homo* and *civis Romanus* was now all but gone. In its place, a legal system developed which enshrined legal privileges for those of high social status. "Citizen" and "alien" were no

---

[9] Millar, *The Emperor*, p. 511.
[10] Mommsen and Krueger, *The Digest of Justinian*.
[11] Sherwin-White, "The Roman Citizenship," *ANRW*, vol. I, 2, pp. 23–58.
[12] Jones, "Selected Documents."

longer terms as meaningful as they had once been. The old distinction of legal privileges based on citizenship was replaced by a legal system based on social status.

Although 212 C.E. was assumed to be the historical marker of the end of the citizen distinction, since almost everyone then became a citizen, it is agreed that the legal distinction between *honestiores* and *humiliores* began during the reign of the Emperor Hadrian. Such an assumption is credible since the earliest examples of a dual-penalty system based on social status found in the *Digest* comes from the time of Hadrian. Hence, from the time of Hadrian onward, those of higher status, be they citizens or wealthy provincial non-citizens (*honestiores*), could expect legal advantages over those of lower status (*humiliores*). This "dual-penalty" legal system is clearly reflected in the pages of the *Digest*. To give just one example of what is commonplace, the *Digest* reads: "Those guilty of violating tombs, if they remove the bodies or scatter the bones, will suffer the supreme penalty if they be of the lower orders; if they be more respectable, they are deported to an island. Otherwise the latter will be relegated and the former condemned to the mines."[13] The one of low status was given the death penalty while the one of high status was deported.

Callistratus, a jurist of the Severan age (193–235 C.E.), refers to the deified Hadrian's rescript on moving boundary stones. In the following rescript Hadrian differentiates punishment according to the social status of the person guilty of the crime:

> The extent of penalty, however, should be determined in the light of the rank and intent of the offender. If those convicted be of high rank, they have doubtless done it to encroach on someone else's land, and they may be relegated for a period according to their age; thus, if they be young, it will be for a longer period, if they be elderly, shorter. But, if the offenders be acting on behalf of another and performing some service, they are to be beaten and sent to the mines for two years. If they appropriate the stones through ignorance or casually, it is enough that they be thrashed.[14]

Here Hadrian states that exile (*relegatio*) was the proper penalty for those of high rank, while a sentence of two years to a public work (*opus publicum*) and a beating was expected for *alii* (everyone else).

---

[13] *Digest*, 47.12.11.
[14] *Digest*, 47.21.2; Garnsey, ,"Legal Privileges," pp. 156–157.

In another example, Ulpian refers to the rescripts of the Emperors Antoninus (138–161 C.E.) and Hadrian concerning penalties for those who are found guilty of starting fires in the city: "Those who deliberately start a fire in the city, if they be of lower rank, are usually thrown to the beasts; but if they be of some standing, they are subjected to capital punishment or certainly deported to an island."[15] What the evidence seems to show is that from the first decades of the second century, a major factor in determining punishment was the perception of one's social status and not citizenship alone. A. N. Sherwin-White, to whom a vast majority of biblical scholars look for elucidation on legal issues in the New Testament, describes the development in the following way:

> As the Roman citizenship became ever more widely spread, the privileged class of the Empire ceased to be the Roman citizens, as such. Their place was taken by the *honestiores*, that is, the families of moderate substance from whom the municipal magistrates and the municipal councillors were chosen. In the final system the *honestiores* retained in a sharpened form the privileges that had once been the right of all Roman citizens – that only the Roman courts could sentence them on a capital charge. This right, which was at first limited to town councillors, and decurions, became in time the special privilege of the whole class. This system, which first begins to emerge in the time of Hadrian, is unknown to the author of Acts.[16]

While no one would disagree with Sherwin-White's remarks in general, it is necessary to see if he is correct that all Roman citizens of both high and low status had equal access to those legal rights which were, in theory, granted to all citizens. Moreover, Sherwin-White's conclusion that the system based on status privilege was unknown to Acts must be investigated. For it seems that the author of Acts was decidedly aware of status differentiation and purposely shaped his work in the light of such distinctions. In addition, despite the expertise of Sherwin-White, the importance of status distinction in all parts of Greco-Roman life was fundamental to that society long before Hadrian. It would seem likely that what was taken for granted would be reflected in the laws.

[15] *Digest* 47.9.12.1.
[16] Sherwin-White, *Roman Society and Roman Law* pp. 69, 174; Jones, "I Appeal," pp. 56–57.

Peter Garnsey, who has also studied aspects of the Roman legal system in the first centuries of the Common Era, has come to the opposite conclusion: "Despite the far-reaching political changes which marked this period (mid-1st century to early 3rd century C.E.), the structure and ethos of Roman society remained basically unaltered."[17] Garnsey argues that the Roman legal code had always reflected the foundation of Greco-Roman society which was fundamentally shaped by awareness of the inequality of individuals and distinctions of social status.[18] There is little question that he is correct on this point. One need go no farther than the comments of Cicero: "yet the resulting equality itself is inequitable, since it allows no distinction in rank."[19] It is to be noted that Cicero does not articulate any argument to support this view. It is taken for granted that this is traditional practice.

J. M. Kelly perceives what he calls the academic myopia of those who assume that Roman law operated equally and regularly for all persons.[20] He raises the issue of how the practice of law, as distinct from theory, fared in a state whose social and political life was conditioned by enormous differences in power, wealth, and prestige, and asks the question: "Can it be that in the sphere of law alone the great were really made equal with the humble, the powerful with the weak?"[21] Kelly's work is concerned with civil rather than criminal law but his question is no doubt applicable for both as he concludes:

> The picture ... of the personal element in Roman litigation may be briefly summarized as follows: the administration of justice, civil as well as criminal, tended both in the pre-classical, classical, and post-classical periods of jurisprudence to be subject to the influence of powerful men ... The theory of an equal and objective justice was perfectly familiar, but no one reckoned on finding it applied in practice.[22]

These comments are of great importance to this study of Paul's portrayal in Acts. For it seems that whatever the actual legal basis for Paul's appeals was, Luke's portrayal reflects a sensitivity to the relationship between legal privileges and social status.

[17] Garnsey, *Social Status and Legal Privileges*, p. 1.
[18] Garnsey, *Social Status and Legal Privileges*, p. 3.
[19] *The Republic*, i.43.
[20] Kelly, *Roman Litigation*, p. 1.
[21] *Ibid.*, p. 2.
[22] *Ibid.*, p. 61.

What was fundamental to Roman society, namely recognition of status distinction, was likewise basic to Roman law, and the words of Ulpian, although written as late as the sixth century C.E., reflect the accepted norm: "our ancestors, whatever the punishment, penalized slaves more severely than freemen, and notorious persons more than those of unblemished reputation."[23] It is assumed here that there had always been a connection between social position, good reputation, and legal privileges. Furthermore, even though citizenship of Rome was a mark of social distinction, there was also an awareness among Roman citizens that there were different status levels of Roman citizenship. For example, a slave manumitted from a Roman citizen usually became a Roman citizen, however, his slave pedigree was a status indicator that could, at times, be a disadvantage to him. This distinction between citizenships was understood, if unstated, in the first century as well as the sixth, as the conversation between Paul and the tribune in Acts 22:28 suggests.

At this point it is important to comment on the use of the *Digest* for this study. The *Digest* was published in the sixth century and hence one must be careful in using it to prop up an argument concerned with first- or second-century legal procedure. In this respect, the problems are similar to those concerning the use of the Talmud and Mishnah as evidence for Rabbinic Judaism in the first century. Nevertheless, there is much in the *Digest* that specifically names second-century emperors and jurists, and this brings one back to within fifty years of the writing of Acts. Moreover, the codification of the legal distinction beginning in the second century reflects earlier usage. Used with caution, the *Digest* can be a rich source of material.

Sherwin-White, as noted above, has argued that Luke-Acts reflects an historical period when social status was not as important as the legal distinction of citizenship. He assumes that there would be little difference in the legal privileges of a low-status and high-status Roman citizen. He believes that Luke has little concern for status distinction. We must consider these statements in more detail.

In one regard Sherwin-White is correct. The distinction between low- and high-status Roman citizens becomes less meaningful as one travels farther east from Rome. For example, in Judaea in the middle of the first century, it would be safe to assume that the number of individuals with Roman citizenship would be infinitesi-

---

[23] *Digest*, 48.19.28.16.

mally small. The few who had citizenship would include rich Romans traveling abroad on business, the various Roman officials associated with the governing of the province, the legionary soldiers, presumably the highest officers of the auxiliary troops and a few of the provincial social élites who had been granted citizenship as a reward for acts of service to the emperor. Hence, the Roman citizens found in Judaea in the first century would invariably be those of high social status compared to native inhabitants and would, probably, possess the influence to take advantage of their legal privileges. However, while this may be true it does not solve the manifold problems in Acts.

In a number of places doubt has been expressed that Paul was, in actuality, one of the élite of the Eastern provinces as Luke would have his readers believe. The list of Paul's troubles, recounted in 2 Corinthians 11:23f., suggests that if Paul was, in reality, a Roman citizen he did not receive any beneficial treatment. This seems to suggest that not all Roman citizens received the benefits from their alleged legal rights. Hence, the first of Sherwin-White's assertions cannot be accepted without further investigation.

The discrepancy between Paul's account of his tribulations and Luke's highlighting the preferential treatment that Paul received at the hands of Roman soldiers, magistrates, and governors is often explained in terms of Luke's overall positive portrayal of Roman authority. However, Luke's emphasis is less on the leniency of Roman authority and more on Paul's status.

Furthermore, as noted above, Luke does recognize the differing ranks of citizenship. The first reader/hearer of Acts would no doubt have perceived the importance of the conversation between Paul and the tribune, who was probably of equestrian status. Citizenship alone did not make all citizens equal. Hence, Sherwin-White's second point is also debatable.

Paul, as reported by Luke, is not only described as a rank-and-file Roman citizen. He is a citizen of Tarsus with wealth, education, and a good ancestry. Paul is implicitly contrasted with the Roman citizens of Philippi (16:21), who are no better than the rabble despite their citizenship, and he is explicitly associated with Asiarchs (19:31) and men and women of high social standing in the Greek cities who were not necessarily Roman citizens. We shall see whether Paul's alleged status is more a factor of how he is treated than his citizenship alone.

The thesis, which proposes that Roman law and Roman legal

procedure were fundamentally based on the significance of social stratification, is further supported by the evidence of the lawyers. J. Neyrey has written: "As long as there had been law courts (and rhetorical schools) attention had been drawn to the 'persona' of a witness."[24] A person's birth (*genus*), character (*mores*), and his wealth and position in society (*facultas*) were all important factors for establishing his innocence and trustworthiness.[25] Cicero, in *De inventione*, describes the expected content of a defense speech:

> And frequently an argument can be made out of a person's fortune when account is taken of whether he is, or has been, or will be slave or free, wealthy or poor, famous or unknown, successful or a failure, a private citizen or a public official; or finally when inquiry is made about any of the conditions which are understood to be predicated of fortune.[26]

To Cicero, and doubtless all other students of law, anything that detracted from the defendant's honor and repute lessened his chance of a complete defence.[27] Cicero continues: "The counsel for the defence, on the other hand, will have to show first, if he can, that the life of the accused has been upright in the highest degree."[28]

In the last eight chapters of Acts, Paul is portrayed both as a defendant, claiming his innocence against specific charges, and as a witness, proclaiming the gospel. In order to prove his innocence and indicate the trustworthiness of his preaching, Luke has followed the common legal rhetorical device of highlighting the *persona* of Paul.

It has already been shown that Paul, as described in Acts, is one of the *splendidiores personae*. Furthermore, it has been stressed that his character was intimately intertwined with social status, for, in the words of Garnsey, "*boni mores*, good character, were nothing less than the virtues of the higher orders."[29] Callistratus, writing several centuries after the trials of Paul, still reflects the concern to scrutinize the social status and moral virtue of a witness:

---

[24] Neyrey, "Forensic Defense Speech," p. 211.
[25] Quintilian, *Institutio Oratoria*, v, 10, 24; Cicero, *On Invention*, ii, 35, 107; Livy, vi, 34, 11.
[26] Cicero, *On Invention*, ii, 30.
[27] *Ibid.*, ii, 33.
[28] *Ibid.*, ii, 35.
[29] Garnsey, *Social Status and Legal Privileges*, p. 210.

It is especially important to examine the status of each man, to see whether he is a decurion or a commoner; to ask whether his life is virtuous or marred by vice, whether he is rich or poor (for poverty might imply that he is out for gain), and whether he is personally hostile to the man against whom he is witnessing or friendly to the man whose cause he is advocating.[30]

It is interesting to note that Aulus Gellius (123?–169?) recommends to the judge that he should follow the custom that had been handed down and observed by their forefathers: "that if a question at issue between two men could not be proved either by document or witnesses, then the question should be raised before the judge who was trying the case which of the two was the better man."[31] One's character and social status were always determining factors in the courts. Likewise, it was important to discern the character of the accuser as this example from the *Digest* shows: "The judge must choose the accuser, having taken account of the case and assessed the personalities of the accusers, whether by reference to their status, their interest in the matter, their age, their morals, or any other good reason."[32] Paul's accusers, according to Luke, were jealous Jews and rabble who had no social standing. This would no doubt suggest to the readers of Acts that Paul's person and message were trustworthy in contrast to those who accused him.

The *auctoritas* and *existimatio* (personal reputation) of a defendant were potentially capable of influencing the judge and jury in discerning his guilt or innocence. Furthermore, status could determine how the individual, if found guilty, was to be treated. This claim will be studied in more detail below when a careful investigation is made of Luke's account of Paul's imprisonments. For now, suffice it to say that a man of low social status, regardless of his citizenship, would hardly have been allowed to leave the ship while under guard as Paul was reported to have done (27:3), or to have been placed under light house arrest as Paul's custody in Rome suggests (28:16, 31). That Paul, as reported in Acts, was treated in such a respectful manner supports the thesis that Luke's concern was to advertise Paul's alleged high social position.

What Luke's reporting of Paul's trials and the connecting narra-

---

[30] *Digest*, 22.5.3; Garnsey, *Social Status and Legal Privileges*, p. 212.
[31] *The Attic Nights*, xiv, 2, 21.
[32] *Digest*, 48.2.16.

tive between the trial scenes show is that the author was aware of the social norms and expectations upon which the Roman legal system was based. The description of Paul's *persona* must not be forgotten, for it is the description of Paul that was foremost in Luke's mind in the last eight chapters.[33] Paul, to Luke, was a man of *dignitas* and the recognition of *dignitas* was important at least from the days of Cicero to the publication of the *Digest* when status distinctions were codified. To presume that one's social standing apart from citizenship did not influence the courts until the second century is incorrect.

Generally speaking, Roman citizens had privileges over aliens. A freedman stood above a slave and a citizen was favored over a freedman or an alien. Yet the words of E. A. Judge must also be kept in mind: "Roman citizenship may not have been so decisive a status factor in the Greek cities of the first century as has been supposed. It has now been argued that the social class ranking system that applied later was already beginning to cut across the distinction between citizen and alien."[34]

The words of the younger Pliny to Calestrius Tiro, who was about to assume the position of governor of Baetica in Spain, echo the sentiment of Cicero quoted above and suggest that the status distinction did not simply depend on the matter of citizenship. As governor, Tiro would be responsible for the administration of justice in his province. Pliny writes:

> You have done splendidly – and I hope you will not rest on your laurels – in commending your administration of justice to the provincials by your exercise of tact. This you have shown particularly in maintaining consideration for the best men, but, in so doing, winning the respect of the lower classes while holding the affection of their superiors ... but in praising you for the way you tread the middle course, I cannot help sounding as if I were offering you advice: that you maintain the distinctions between ranks and degrees of dignity. Nothing else could be more unequal than that equality which results when those distinctions are confused or broken down.[35]

Social status, upright character, wealth, prestige, education and "connections" could, at times, be more important than citizenship

---

[33] Garnsey, *Social Status and Legal Privileges*, p. 212.
[34] Judge, "St Paul and Classical Society," p. 25.
[35] Pliny, *Letters*, ix. 5, trans. P. Garnsey, "Legal Privileges," pp. 144–145.

alone, and the individual who combined all these characteristics and possessed citizenship would stand in a privileged position indeed. In the Roman provinces where legates, proconsuls, prefects, and procurators wielded a great degree of authority and jurisdiction, recognition of these characteristics was of great value.[36] It has been asserted all along that Luke purposefully portrayed Paul in such a manner.

As the issue of the legal rights of citizens in the provinces and particularly the account of Paul's appeal is studied, it will be important to keep in mind the conclusions of Sherwin-White and Garnsey which have been quoted above. These scholars assume the opposite positions on almost all the issues, and the investigation of the evidence, as it relates to the portrayal of Paul in Acts, will finally lean more towards one than the other. Sherwin-White insists that: "This privilege was by no means limited to men of exalted status – the so-called *honestiores*, for whom many benefits in penal procedure were invented during the second century. Paul of Tarsus was not the only man of moderate station to take advantage of this privilege."[37] Peter Garnsey, on the other hand, concludes:

> At no stage in the period under survey (1st–3rd centuries) was citizenship as such a source of privilege. Citizenship bestowed certain formal rights on its holders as full members of the Roman community, but provided no guarantee of their exercise. In any society, the principal benefits and rewards were available to those groups most advantageously placed in the stratification system by reason of their greater prosperity, power and prestige.[38]

Obviously, with two such disparate conclusions, a further investigation of the Roman legal privileges in the provinces in the first century is needed.

Paul's appeals

Next for consideration are those passages in Acts where Paul claims legal privileges. In Philippi (16:37), where Paul shames the magis-

[36] Sherwin-White, *Roman Society and Roman Law*, chapter 1; T. Mommsen, *Römische Strafrecht*, pp. 35–48; Jones, "Imperial and Senatorial Jurisdiction," 464–488; Millar, "The Development of Jurisdiction," 362–367; Millar, "Emperor, Senate, Provinces," 156–166; Garnsey, "The Criminal Jurisdiction of Governors," 51–59; Haenchen, *Acts*, p. 634.

[37] Sherwin-White, "The Roman Citizenship," p. 54.

[38] Garnsey, *Social Status and Legal Privileges*, pp. 279–280.

trates for beating and imprisoning him; in Jerusalem, (22:25), where Paul halts an impending flogging by Roman soldiers; and in Caesarea (25:11), where Paul declares his right to be heard in a court in Rome, he assumes legal privileges that were allegedly due to him as a Roman citizen. In all three cases, Paul, as described by Luke, appeals against the action of a Roman authority. However, while in the first two instances (16:37 and 22:25) Paul appeals to the laws which were intended to protect a citizen from summary beating, tortures, and imprisonment without trial, in the third account (25:11) Paul rejects Festus' request to move the court to Jerusalem.

There has been no little debate concerning the actual historical background of Paul's "appeal" to Caesar and for that reason comments concerning that scene will be saved for the next chapter. Legal scholars have noted that these settings suggest that Luke was familiar with the Roman laws protecting the ancient custom of *provocatio ad populum* which was, it is generally agreed, a call to the people for protection from the *coercitio* of a Roman magistrate.

It is true that these scenes in Acts demonstrate a knowledge of Roman law and the privileges that were, *de jure*, accorded to Roman citizens. However, this does not necessarily prove that the scenes in Acts are accurate historical reports of Paul's encounters with Roman authorities. Indeed, as will be shown, there were important exceptions to these laws. Therefore, it cannot simply be acknowledged that all Roman citizens everywhere were equally protected. In addition, the evidence indicates that these laws favored those of high social status; in other words, only those of standing and reputation could expect to assume the legal privileges provided. The events recorded in Acts might testify to Luke's recognition of the reality of the social expectations upon which these laws were based. Hence even the courtroom scenes might have been shaped by Luke in order to suggest Paul's authority and control which had implications for his comprehensive portrayal as an individual of high social status.

Magisterial 'coercitio'

The laws designated to protect Roman citizens from the *coercitio* of a Roman official or magistrate are well known, and have been discussed in detail by many Roman legal scholars and some students of the New Testament.[39] It is generally taken for granted, as noted above, that the laws of the Roman empire were equally enforced for all; therefore any exceptions to the enforcement of the laws must be explained in terms of aberrations from the norm. However, the evidence shows that, in the provinces, deviation from these laws was the norm.

Of immediate concern is an investigation of the laws which purportedly protected the Roman citizen, to see how effective and extensive they were. It is of great importance to this overall study to ascertain whether or not these laws favored those of high social status.

The discussion of the legal issues in Acts should be grounded on an understanding of the legal jurisdiction and political authority of the governor and local Roman magistrates in the provinces. Since so much has been written on this subject, a full discussion of the differences between those governors appointed by the Senate and those by the emperor will not be necessary. Exact distinctions are not important at this point. What is important is that proconsuls (senatorial status) and procurators (equestrian status) were administrative officials who held *imperium* (authority). The authority of the governor over ordinary provincials was limited only by certain statute laws pertaining to extortion and the law of treason. Few would dispute the view that in the Julio-Claudian period those holding this authority had few limits set on the free use of it.[40]

During the imperial period the princeps could if he so desired, become involved in the administration of a province, as is suggested by the edicts to Cyrene issued by Augustus.[41] However, generally speaking, it was not until the reign of Domitian that imperial control over the provinces was practiced in earnest.[42] Unless the governor offended the wealthy magnates of his province, or consistently abused his position, he was unlikely to be called to account at Rome for abuse of power when his term was over. Governors were under no compulsion to consult the Senate or the princeps.[43] The proconsul and procurator, having *imperium*, were relatively un-

---

[39] Mommsen, "Die Rechtsverhältnisse," 81–96; Sherwin-White, *Roman Society and Roman Law*, pp. 48–70; Garnsey, "Lex Julia," 167–189; A. W. Lintott, "Provocatio," pp. 226–267.

[40] Sherwin-White, *Roman Society and Roman Law*, p. 1.

[41] *Ibid.*, p. 2.

[42] J. G. C. Anderson, "Augustan Edicts from Cyrene," *JRS* 17, (1927), 33–48; Ehrenberg and Jones, *Documents*, p. 139, note 311.

[43] Sherwin-White, *Roman Society and Roman Law* p. 2.

restrained in their administrative and judicial authority over the locality of which they were in control. Maintenance of public order was by far the most important duty and, as long as order was maintained, there would have been little reason for supervision from Rome.

For all practical purposes, the governor was unchecked in his authority over provincials who were not Roman citizens – with the exception of wealthy and powerful provincials who would assume a privileged position. However, it is generally accepted by experts that the governor's wide-ranging authority did not include as extensive a legal jurisdiction over Roman citizens. Yet governors and lesser Roman magistrates in the provinces did possess the authority to judge and punish Roman citizens for minor offenses. The exact nature of the punishment and the rights of the citizen in these cases will be discussed in more detail below; they have important implications for a proper understanding of Acts 16:37 and 22:25.

What the governor and local magistrates did not legally possess, it is commonly asserted, was the authority to punish Roman citizens accused of capital crimes, unless specifically authorized to do so by the emperor. Citizens accused of capital crimes, which would have included murder, treason, and adultery, would probably have been sent to Rome either to appear before the emperor or in one of the unappealable courts established to handle such capital cases.[44]

The "lex Valeria," "leges Porciae," and "lex Julia de vi Publica"

The earliest references to the laws which purportedly protected Roman citizens are found in Livy and Cicero. Cicero proudly recalls the introduction of the law proposed by Publius Valerius in 509 B.C.E., which protected the Roman citizen from the *coercitio* of the magistrate by appealing to the people (*provocatio ad populum*).[45] To Cicero, P. Valerius' law was merely a re-statement of the right to appeal which was recognized against a king's sentence and was recorded in the *Records of the Pontiff*.[46] Few present-day Roman legal historians would accept Cicero's dating of the *lex Valeria*. W. R. Long has recently summarized the accepted position: "The

---

[44] Sherwin-White, *Roman Society and Roman Law*, p. 2; Lintott, "Provocatio," p. 252; Millar, "Emperor, Senate, Provinces," 51–53.

[45] Jolowicz and Nicholas, *Historical Introduction*, pp. 49, 329.

[46] Cicero, *The Republic*, ii, 31, 54.

projection of the Valerian law back to 509 can be recognized as a product of annalistic legitimation which desired to show that *provocatio*, considered by Livy and Cicero to be the palladium of Republican freedom, really originated from the exclusion of the kings of Rome."[47] Despite the scholarly skepticism concerning the date of the "first" *lex Valeria*, Cicero's description of the actual force of the law is accepted as historical and is, therefore, quoted in full:

> It was the same man who, by an act whereby he shows himself in the highest sense "the people's friend," proposed to the citizens that first law passed by the centuriate assembly, which forbade any magistrate to execute or scourge a Roman citizen in the face of an appeal. The records of the pontiffs, however, state that the right of appeal, even against a king's sentence, had been previously recognized, and our augural books confirm the statement. Besides, many laws of the Twelve Tables show that an appeal from any judgment or sentence was allowed.[48]

According to Cicero, the Valerian law forbade magistrates to execute or scourge a Roman citizen in the face of an appeal. One of the many important issues contained in this law, and in the laws which followed it, is the nature of the appeal. Did such an appeal force the magistrate to hand over the case to a court of second instance or was the appeal only a cry of protection against the magistrate? This question has been hotly debated and an understanding of the matter will be important to the discussion of Paul's appeal in Acts 25:11.

Livy mentions a "third" Valerian law which was enacted in 299 B.C.E. Livy's account is as follows:

> In the same year Marcus Valerius the consul proposed a law of appeal with stricter sanction. This was the third time since the expulsion of the kings that such a law had been introduced, by the same family in every instance. The reason for renewing it more than once was, I think, simply this, that the wealth of a few carried more power than the liberty of the plebs ... The Valerian law, having forbidden that he who appealed should be scourged with rods or

[47] Long, "The Trial of Paul," p. 107.
[48] Cicero, *The Republic*, ii, 31, 54.

beheaded, merely proved that if anyone should disregard these injunctions it should be deemed a wicked act. This seemed, I suppose, a sufficiently strong sanction of the law, so modest were men in those days; at the present time one would hardly utter such a threat in earnest.[49]

Of particular interest is Livy's off-hand editorial comment: "The reason for renewing it more than once was, I think, simply this, that the wealth of a few carried more power than the liberty of the plebs." That *provocatio* was a privilege serving the interests of the wealthy should be duly noted. Implied in this comment is the assertion that the law was never effective in protecting the rights of the plebs. Livy and Cicero agree that the Valerian law(s) protected Roman citizens from being scourged with rods or beheaded. Yet Livy goes on to say, with no little sarcasm, that the penalty for those who broke this Valerian law was remarkably lenient and that those of Livy's day would hardly have taken it seriously.

The Porcian laws, of which there were three, provided stricter sanctions against those magistrates who failed to uphold the Valerian law. The fact that stricter sanctions had to be imposed is evidence of the fact that the Valerian law was not always followed by magistrates. The actual dates of the enactments of the Porcian laws are unknown. It is agreed that the first of the laws was named after P. Porcius Laeca, authorized by the elder Cato, and should be dated 199 or 195 B.C.E.[50]

Numismatic evidence seems to indicate that the third Porcian law extended the right of protection and appeal for the Roman citizen outside Roman city limits and throughout the military districts. Up to this time, it is assumed, the provincial authorities had unappealable *coercitio*.

In 104 B.C.E., or thereabouts, a coin was minted in commemoration of P. Porcius Laeca whose name is affixed to the Porcian law. On the reverse of the coin is a standing figure clothed in a toga with his right hand held out in protest. In the center is a taller figure dressed in military clothing, whose right hand is pointing at the protesting figure. A third person, on the right, is carrying a lictor's rods. Under the scene is the word "PROVOCO." Although there is some disagreement among scholars concerning the exact interpreta-

---

[49] Livy x, 9.
[50] Jolowicz and Nicholas, *Historical Introduction*, p. 307.

tion of the depiction on the coin, the standard explanation is that the togate figure must be a Roman citizen who is appealing against the punishment of the military governor in the provinces.[51]

The last of the specific laws which were intended to protect the citizen from severe punishment at the hands of governors and magistrates is the *lex Julia de vi publica*. Most date the passing of this law to 50 B.C.E., although some suggest a later date. Ulpian's mention of the law, as recorded in the *Digest*, makes plain the prohibition against execution, flogging, torture, or imprisonment of a Roman citizen in the light of an appeal:

> Also liable under the *lex Julia* on *vis publica* is anyone who, while holding *imperium* or office, puts to death or flogs a Roman citizen contrary to his (right of) appeal or orders any of the aforementioned things to be done, or puts (a yoke) on his neck so that he may be tortured. Again, so far as relates to ambassadors, pleaders, or those who accompany them anyone who is proved to have beaten or done them an injury.[52]

Placed immediately following Ulpian's comments is a fragment of a work by the mid second-century jurist Maecian which reads: "It is provided in the *lex Julia* on *vis publica* that no one is to bind or hinder an accused so as to prevent his attending Rome within the fixed period."[53] What exactly is meant by "fixed period" is unknown.

There can be little doubt that laws protecting Roman citizens were known in some form from the days of the Republic to the days of the *Digest*. Yet, that the *lex Julia de vi publica* is, for all practical purposes, merely a restatement of the earlier laws on appeal again suggests that the Valerian law and the Porcian laws were far from effective.

---

[51] G. F. Hill, *Historical Roman Coins: From the Earliest Times to the Reign of Augustus* (London: Constable and Co., 1909), p. 67 no. 36, plate 10; E. A. Sydenham, *The Coinage of the Roman Republic* (London: Spinks and Sons, 1952), p. 78; M. H. Cranford, *Roman Republican Coins*, 2 vols, (Cambridge: Cambridge University Press, 1974), vol. I, pp. 313–314; J. P. C. Kent, *Roman Coins* (London: Thames and Hudson, 1978), plate 12, no. 41, p. 268; Keaveney, "Civis Romanus Sum," 345–372.

[52] *Digest*, 48.6.7.

[53] *Digest*, 48.6.8.

Exceptions to the laws

Having thus described those laws which protected Roman citizens, it is necessary to turn to some classical sources which will help to discern the extent and force of the laws and then to evaluate Acts 16:37 and 22:25.

Even Sherwin-White, who supports the traditional view that Roman legal privileges were equally administered to every Roman citizen regardless of the social status up to the middle of the second century, finds it "remarkable" that, "There were certain exceptions to the rules which forbade the capital sentence and execution of a Roman citizen by a provincial court."[54] It is indeed remarkable that the evidence used to support the claim that Roman citizens were protected in the provinces suggests the opposite. High-ranking Roman officials, and even some lesser magistrates, do not appear to have been unduly bound by these laws. These exceptions have continually confounded the experts. Yet the exceptions seem to show that magistrates were held accountable for forgetting social distinctions, rather than solely for abusing citizen's rights.

Cicero's masterful prosecution of Verres is often cited as a proof-text for the efficacy of the Valerian law and Porcian laws.[55] G. Verres, who was governor of Sicily (73–70 B.C.E.), was tried before the senators in Rome on charges of extortion, which was, formally, a civil case. Yet above and beyond this specific crime, Verres had so oppressed and alienated the people of Sicily that, in effect, it was a criminal prosecution for general misgovernment. Verres was especially cruel to a number of Roman citizens whom he had herded into the mines and killed. Cicero recounts one particularly horrific scene. He describes the humiliation, torture, and death of Gavius of Consa who, having escaped from prison, was betrayed to Verres who, in turn, charged Gavius with spying. Gavius was flogged, beaten with rods in the open marketplace, and finally crucified within sight of the coastline of Italy. All this took place despite Gavius' cry "civis Romanus sum!" Cicero claims that Verres has ignored the *lex Porcia*, and it is in this context that Cicero speaks the often-quoted words: "To bind a Roman citizen is a crime. To flog him is an abomination. To slay him is almost an act of murder. To crucify him is – what? There is no fitting word that

---

[54] Sherwin-White, *Roman Society and Roman Law*, p. 16.
[55] Cicero, *Against Verres* II, 5, 149–151.

can possible describe so horrible a deed."[56] Although Cicero's remarks suggest that there were binding laws to protect the Roman citizen outside of Rome, it is interesting to note that Cicero described Gavius as not only a citizen of Rome but also as a gentleman, and a burgess of Consa who served with the distinguished Roman equestrian Lucius Raecius. In other words, it was not an obscure, ordinary citizen who was crucified. Cicero is stressing the credentials and status of Gavius before the senators in Rome, who would be particularly horrified at such disrespect for status. Verres had, it is true, been abusing Roman citizens, whose status is unknown, for some time. However, it is also true that Cicero is particularly appalled because Verres flogged and crucified Gavius, a man of distinction and social standing. The issue, apparently, was not merely one of killing a Roman citizen but of killing a Roman citizen of reputation.

A. H. J. Greenridge long ago argued that: "he [Cicero] invokes the guarantee furnished by the restored tribunate, whose *auxilium* was not valid outside the walls, but he makes no mention of any law which extended the *provocatio* to the provinces – obviously because there was no such law to quote."[57] Cadbury too recognized that there is no unambiguous written evidence to suggest an extension of these laws outside of Rome.[58]

A. H. M. Jones disagrees. He contends that Cicero would not have had "to give chapter and verse for so obvious a fact, ... it would have marred the rhetorical effect of the passage."[59] Jones' remark has a logical weight but it does not diminish the force of the contention that individuals of high status would have been able to call upon this law with more effect than a rank-and-file citizen. There is more specific evidence to support Jones' claim that Roman citizens were protected beyond the city. However, that such laws exist do not prove their efficacy.

Mention is made of Flaccus' abortive bill of 125 B.C.E. that proposed to give certain allies the option of citizenship or the right of *provocatio*.[60] *Provocatio* was also offered as a reward for noncitizens according to the epigraphic *lex Acilia*. H. B. Mattingly

---

[56] Cicero, *Against Verres* II, 5, 170.
[57] Greenridge, *Legal Procedure*, p. 413.
[58] Cadbury, *Roman Law*, p. 314; Jolowicz and Nicholas, *Historical Introduction*, p. 307.
[59] Jones, "I Appeal," p. 54.
[60] Jones, "I Appeal," p. 53; Lintott, "Provocatio," p. 251.

points out that only the higher Latin magistrates acquired it.[61] A. Lintott assumes that this provision of the extension of the right of appeal to certain non-citizens "would only be of real value to them if it applied outside Rome."[62] Lintott also refers to a law proposed by Livius Drusus in 122 B.C.E. forbidding the flogging of Latins, even on military service.[63] If Latin soldiers were exempt from flogging, certain citizen soldiers would likewise have been exempt. However, Lintott admits that soldiers were never fully free from corporal punishment; at best the Porcian laws mitigated the severity of a military flogging. Furthermore, Lintott concedes that it is uncertain if Drusus' law was indeed passed or, if passed, remained on the statute books.[64]

The case of T. Turpilius Silanus provides even stronger evidence that if laws existed to protect both citizen soldiers and non-military citizens outside of Rome, they were of dubious value in practice. T. Turpilius Silanus was a citizen, but of Latin extraction, who held the post of *praefectus fabrum*.[65] During the war with the Numidian Jugurtha, Turpilius apparently conspired with the rebel forces against Mettelus, the Roman to whom Numidia had been assigned by the senate. While the Numidians of the city of Varga turned on and massacred the Roman centurions and tribunes, who had defected to their side, Turpilius escaped. He was then summoned by Metellus before a court martial, was condemned to be scourged and put to death. Sallust's disgust with Turpilius is clearly reflected in the words, "he seems to be a wretch utterly detestable."[66] Yet Plutarch believes that Turpilius was innocent.[67] In any event, he was executed and his citizenship did not make any significant difference to Metellus. A. Lintott believed that he was executed because "his Latin origins made reprisals for this unlikely."[68] Nevertheless, if a citizen of Latin extraction, one who held a position of authority, could not depend on the protection of the Porcian laws, one can

---

[61] H. B. Mattingly, "The Extortion Law of the Tabula Bembina," *JRS* 60 (1970), 154–168; H. B. Mattingly, "The Two Republican Laws of the Tabula Bembina," *JRS* 59 (1969), 129–143; E. Badian, "Lex Acilia Repetundarum" *AJP* 75, (9154), 374–384.
[62] Lintott, "Provocatio," p. 251.
[63] Plutarch, *Tiberius and Gracchus*, 9; Lintott, "Provocatio," p. 251.
[64] Lintott, "Provocatio," p. 251.
[65] Sallust, *The War with Jugurtha*, 69.4.
[66] Sallust, *The War with Jugurtha*, 69.3.
[67] Plutarch, *Marius*, 8.
[68] Lintott, "Provocatio," p. 252.

only wonder if a certain citizen of Tarsian extraction would have automatically received protection several generations later.

By far the most important evidence which suggests that the Porcian laws extended the right of *provocatio* outside the city limits is the Laecean coin which has been mentioned above. Most agree that the figure on the left is appealing against the figure in the center who represents the military authority. Others propose that the figure on the left is appealing *to* the military figure for protection.[69] Very few find this second option convincing. However, even if the coin was minted to commemorate the law that extended the right of *provocatio* into the military districts, it does not prove its effectiveness in restraining the coercive options of the governor, nor does it prove that protection for rank-and-file Roman citizens against Roman provincial authority was ever guaranteed.

But, if the laws were not always effective, or perhaps were never intended to extend outside of Rome, why did Romans in the provinces appeal and, more to our interest, why would Luke describe Paul relying on the protection of these laws? Furthermore, if the laws were not effective, why would Luke emphasize that the magistrates of Philippi (16:38) and the tribune and centurion in Jerusalem (22:29) were frightened when it was discovered that they had mistreated a Roman citizen? It can safely be assumed that both Luke and his audience were aware of the social and legal customs of the day and would have understood the implications of the accounts. What, then, was Luke attempting to portray? What Greenridge, states, Cadbury implies, and Kunkel and Garnsey assume, is that any protection that a Roman citizen received in the provinces was a matter of custom rather than of law. A Roman citizen in the provinces was a privileged person. His citizenship could, at times, save him from non-Roman provincial justice. Yet only those citizens who also possessed wealth and prestige as well as the citizenship were in the position to procure any certain legal advantages.

Sherwin-White has placed great importance on the second edict of Augustus to Cyrene which, he claims, shows that the Julian law was being applied in the provinces. He writes:

> A certain Sextius Scaeva, who appears to be a private citizen rather than a magistrate, had caused three Roman citizens to be sent in chains from the province to Rome for a

[69] Bleicken, "Provocatio," p. 2,448.

judicial inquiry. Augustus declares that: "no blame or ill-feeling should attach to Scaeva for this act ... which was in order and proper." Augustus was protecting Scaeva in advance against any charge made against him under the clause of the *lex Julia* ... which forbade anyone to bind a Roman citizen.[70]

Yet the evidence of Augustus' edict is hardly as clear as Sherwin-White would have it. There is no specific mention of the Julian law in the edict. Augustus was not necessarily referring to the law that allegedly extended into the provinces. Furthermore, it is not entirely clear what infringement Sextius Scaeva had committed which needed protection. Was it that he chained and sent Roman citizens to Rome, or was it that he was a private citizen doing what was assumed to be only permitted to the Roman magistrate? Acts mentions that Paul was in chains or at least handcuffed during his light imprisonment in Rome (28:20) and there is no mention of any law being broken. Finally, the three Roman citizens were sent to Rome because they possessed knowledge pertaining to the welfare of the emperor! Therefore this edict indicates, if nothing else, that if certain laws were binding in the provinces, exceptions for special cases could be made, and if any specific laws are implied in the words of Augustus, this edict points to the fluidity of their interpretation.

Josephus reports that G. Florus (66 C.E.) flogged and then crucified a number of Jewish Roman citizens who were of equestrian rank.[71] Jones contends that "it was clear from his [Josephus'] comment that this action was illegal."[72] However while Josephus is indeed appalled, he does not mention that Florus broke any law. Instead, he appears shocked that Florus would treat equestrians in a manner usually reserved for slaves. Treating equestrians in this way was, to Josephus, without precedent and hence notable.[73]

Suetonius reports that Galba, while governor of Spain, crucified a Roman citizen.[74] When the man cried out his protest, Galba, pretending to lighten the punishment, ordered a new, larger, whitewashed cross and ordered the man to be crucified again. There is no mention that Galba broke any law. It can be argued that the

[70] Sherwin-White, *Roman Society and Roman Law*, p. 60.
[71] Josephus, *Jewish Wars*, ii, 305–308.
[72] Jones, "I Appeal," p. 56.
[73] Josephus, *Jewish Wars*, ii.308.
[74] Suetonius, *Galba*, 9.1.

Roman citizen was appealing not against the sentence but against the means of execution: crucifixion was usually reserved for slaves and provincials of low status. However, it must be noted that Galba did not automatically send the citizen to Rome, as he felt competent to judge the case, deliver the sentence, and punish the prisoner. Furthermore, this act did little to harm Galba's future imperial position.

Pliny writes that Marius Priscus, who had been the pro-consul of Africa, accepted bribes to condemn and to execute innocent persons and to allow Roman equestrians to be condemned to various tortures. Marius Priscus was impeached not on charge of breaking the Valerian law but for accepting bribes.[75]

The evidence does not indicate that Roman provincial authority felt unduly bound by laws which explicitly forbade flogging and crucifixion of Roman citizens. The evidence does show that where specific mention is made of abuses of power, it is always connected with cruelty to individuals of high social status: those who would normally have expected protection due to their rank. This fact is important for a proper understanding of the report of Paul's "appeals" in Acts 16, 22, and 25.

A. H. M. Jones and A. N. Sherwin-White have attempted to circumvent the apparent difficulties of the noted exceptions by arguing that there was a distinction in matters of appeal "between two classes of crime – those of the *ordo* defined by statute laws, and those that fell *extra ordinem*."[76] Certain capital crimes defined by the statute laws (*ordo*) fell under the jurisdiction of specific courts in Rome, to which Roman citizens would be referred.[77] Those crimes which were defined by the *ordo* included murder, adultery, forgery, and treason. However, both Jones and Sherwin-White believe that for "reasons of practical utility" exceptions were made. Sherwin-White rightly perceives that sending every Roman citizen to Rome "could lead to great inconvenience, or even to a breakdown of jurisdiction."[78] To Jones and Sherwin-White, provincial authorities could sentence and punish those citizens found guilty of crimes which were defined by the statute laws. The citizen's right of appeal was no longer allowed in such cases. However, those citizens

---

75 Dio Cassius, 64.2.3.
76 Jones, "I Appeal," p. 57; Sherwin-White, *Roman Society and Roman Law*, p. 61.
77 Jolowicz and Nicholas, *Historical Introduction*, pp. 305–397.
78 Sherwin-White, *Roman Society and Roman Law*, p. 61.

involved in crimes which were not so defined (*extra ordinem*) could appeal. While Jones' and Sherwin-White's contention does offer a possible explanation, it founders on several accounts. Primarily, these exceptions seem to dilute the force of the laws and give the provincial governors extensive freedom in their *coercitio*. This counts against Sherwin-White's insistence that the Roman laws were binding and effective throughout the empire for all Roman citizens. Furthermore, Sherwin-White appears to be forcing an incorrect interpretation of *extra ordinem*. As P. Garnsey asserts:

> The whole theory leans on a false interpretation of *cognitio extra ordinem*. *Extra ordinem,* does not mean "off the list." The whole phrase describes a form of magisterial action which might be employed in the trial of one accused of any criminal offence, irrespective of whether or not it fell under a *lex publica*.[79]

It seems as if the governors in the provinces had wide jurisdiction, their options were not severely limited. W. Kunkel has claimed that the governors were never legally bound to follow the procedure laid down by the statute laws.[80]

Acts 16 and 22

A short recapitulation will facilitate the transition from the discussion of Roman legal history to more specific comments on the particular scenes in Acts. In chapter 16, and again in chapter 22, Paul makes explicit use of his alleged Roman citizenship. In Philippi, Paul and Silas shame the magistrates who had them beaten and thrown into prison. Likewise, in Jerusalem, Paul halts an imminent beating by the Roman soldiers. These two accounts, with the report of Paul's "appeal" in Acts 25:11, have traditionally been used to support the historicity of Paul's Roman citizenship. The crucial query is raised; why doubt that these events occurred as Luke reported?

As we have shown, there were laws that were intended to protect Roman citizens from summary beatings, torture, chaining, imprisonment, and death at the hands of a Roman magistrate. Admittedly, if one looks at these specific scenes alone, and does not judge them in the light of the crucial relationship between social

---

[79] Jolowicz and Nicholas, *Historical Introduction*, pp. 397–400.
[80] Kunkel, *Introduction* p. 67.

status, legal privilege, and the overall picture of Paul in Acts, one is apt to conclude that there is little to be gained in questioning the historicity of Paul's Roman citizenship or in suggesting that Luke shaped these scenes to highlight Paul's status.

However, in an earlier chapter, it was shown that Paul's troubles in Philippi and Jerusalem were shaped by Luke in order to compare and contrast Paul with those who have arrested him. In both cases Paul is placed before individuals who are of Roman status and implicit comparisons are made which would have been recognized by Luke's audience. On the one hand, the magistrates of Philippi are compared with the rabble (a Roman rabble – 16:21) which drags Paul and Silas before the *duoviri*. On the other hand, the Roman magistrate and the Roman rabble are contrasted with Paul and Silas who are also, it is reported, Roman citizens. Similarly, in Acts 22, the status of the tribune stationed in Jerusalem, is diminished because his citizenship was purchased and not inherited. This explicit comparison of status is of special interest because tribunes were usually Roman citizens of equestrian rank.[81] Paul, by contrast, shows himself to be of higher inherited status than the tribune. Likewise, in Philippi, Paul, despite his night in prison, is portrayed as a man of *dignitas* who commands the magistrates to escort him personally from the prison. Therefore, on one level, the purpose of these stories is to highlight Paul's social standing by contrasting him with others.

Furthermore, there is reason to question the details of Paul's Roman citizenship in the light of the ambiguities raised in Luke's statement that Paul was also a Pharisee and a citizen of Tarsus. Yet, assuming for the moment that Luke has accurately recorded the particulars of the events at Philippi and Jerusalem, a problem arises. If Paul could have saved himself from a beating, as happened in 22:25, why did he wait to make his citizenship known only after a night spent in prison? This is, of course, a question which has often been asked.

Most commentators rely on one of two explanations. Either Paul did cry out his protest but it was not heard,[82] or he chose not to make his citizenship known. In the words of Haenchen, "it was wise for him not to appeal to his Roman right of citizenship. It would indeed have spared him from the lashing, but the appeal would have entangled him in a protracted trial with an uncertain outcome, and

---

[81] "Tribuni Militum," *The Oxford Classical Dictionary*, 2nd edn, pp. 1,901–1,092.
[82] Marshall, *Acts*, p. 274; Bruce, *Acts*, p. 322.

during this time the possibility for a mission would be as good as gone."[83] Haenchen's comments, as they stand, are hardly helpful. If Paul had been a Roman citizen who could rely on the various laws of protection which were, it is argued, binding, his appeal would not necessarily have led to a "protracted trial." His appeal, had it been heard, would have stopped the punishment and, probably, have led to his immediate release. As indicated in the story, the magistrates, without knowledge of Paul's citizenship, were going to release him after only one night in the prison. In any event, Haenchen's explanation is no doubt based upon his insistence that Luke always portrayed Roman officials in a positive light. If Paul withheld, by not appealing, the vital information about his citizenship, the magistrate could not be held accountable for the oversight.

While Haenchen has missed the significance of the scene, there is something in his comment worth remembering. It appears that the onus was on the individual for making his citizenship known. If a Roman citizen did not reveal his citizenship, then the magistrate or governor could not be held responsible for the punishment which followed. The precise wording of the various laws does not suggest otherwise. It is interesting to note that Cicero's specific accusation against Verres, which was alluded to above, is not simply that he beat and crucified a Roman citizen, but that Verres punished and sentenced Gavius to death despite Gavius' assertion that he was a Roman citizen. Cicero finds it inexcusable that Verres did not even stop the punishment in order to investigate Gavius' claim.[84]

With regard to Acts 16, if it is the case that Paul would have been responsible for making his citizenship known, then the "fear" of the magistrate, reported by Luke, is interesting – for why should the magistrates have been afraid?

The first alternative, that Paul appealed to his citizenship but was ignored, is the better of the two. Considering the potentially riotous consequences of the uproar of the crowd, it is logical to assume that any cries of protest would have been ignored or unheard. Yet if Paul's appeal had been ignored, then there is no reason why the magistrates would have been afraid the next morning. That leaves the alternative that, in Luke's account, Paul did cry out but was not heard. However, even this explanation is unsatisfactory for it is not so stated in the text.

Besides the potential internal incompatibility of Acts 16 and 22,

83 Haenchen, *Acts*, p. 504.
84 Cicero, *Against Verres* II, 65,168.

there is the potential external inconsistency between the reports in Acts and Paul's explicit statement that he was thrice beaten with rods (2 Cor. 11:25) and also thrown to the wild beasts (1 Cor. 5:31–2). These specific punishments do not easily square with Luke's account in Acts that Paul was a Roman citizen nor, needless to say, that he was a Roman citizen of high status.

In his second letter to the Corinthian community, Paul describes his many tribulations. The list begins in the following manner: "Five times I have received from the Jews the forty lashes minus one. Three times I was beaten with rods. Once I received a stoning. Three times I was shipwrecked; for a night and a day I was adrift at sea" (2 Cor. 11:24–25). There have been many attempts to reconcile the list in Corinthians with the description of Paul's punishments in Acts, in order to harmonize the accounts.[85] Luke does not describe any of the five times that Paul received the forty lashes minus one. But Luke does report a stoning (Acts 14:19), and the shipwreck reported in Acts 27:13ff. might coincide with one of the three shipwrecks noted by Paul. However, the precise coincidence of the shipwreck in Acts and one of the three listed by Paul in 2 Corinthians falters on the fact that the historical context of the epistle corresponds to Acts 20:1 not Acts 27. While the account of the shipwreck in Acts was probably shaped by the traditions about Paul's three sea disasters, little more can be said.

Furthermore, Acts makes no mention of Paul being thrown to the beasts. While there has been a lively debate concerning the literal, as opposed to the symbolic, importance of Paul's words in 1 Corinthians 15, the fact remains that it was highly unlikely for a Roman citizen to be condemned "to the beasts."[86] C. K. Barrett and H. Conzelmann have noticed a rescript in the *Digest* which suggests that there were some crimes for which persons could lose their rights of citizenship and, thereby, be liable for punishments not usually associated with Roman citizens.[87] However, as Barrett points out, Acts 22:25 assumes that Paul was still a citizen. It is hardly likely that Paul would have lost his citizenship and then had it restored so that he could call upon its privileges! Without doubt, Luke, or his

[85] Marshall, *Acts*, p. 271.
[86] H. Conzelmann, *A Commentary on the First Epistle to the Corinthians*, trans. J. W. Leitch (Philadelphia: Fortress Press, 1975), pp. 277–278; C. K. Barrett, *The First Epistle to the Corinthians*, 2nd edn (London: Adam and Charles Black, 1971), p. 366.
[87] *Digest*, 28.1.8.4.

source, was highly selective with the material, or only knew some of the items, which were to be included in Acts.

Of particular interest is Paul's claim that he was beaten with rods three times. Rods were held by the lictor who was under the authority of the magistrate or the governor.[88] Being beaten with rods or being whipped with a leather quirt were Roman punishments that Roman citizens would, it is traditionally argued, have legally been able to void under the Valerian, Porcian, and Julian laws. Attempts at harmonization have usually rested on the assumption that magistrates confronted by a potential riot were not always careful or concerned about specific laws.[89] As Plummer noted long ago, "the fact that St. Paul was thrice treated in this way is evidence that being a Roman citizen was an imperfect protection when magistrates were disposed to be brutal."[90] Most commentators today would agree with Plummer's remarks. Yet the admission that there were exceptions at three different places on Paul's itinerary seems to support my contention that the *lex Julia* was not applied consistently or extensively throughout the empire. Furthermore, if exceptions were commonplace, why would the magistrates of Philippi be afraid? Apparently what Luke seems to imply is that Paul had the "connections" to get revenge if he so desired. It is interesting to note that "fear" is, of course, the same reaction expressed by the tribune when he discovered that he was about to flog a Roman citizen (22:29).

Sherwin-White has presented another alternative.[91] His interpretation rests upon his reconstruction of three distinct developmental stages in Roman law concerning protection of citizens. The first stage prohibited the punishing of any Roman citizen on any charge, the second stage accepted certain exceptions to the strict interpretation of the laws, and the third stage formalized the distinction between the *honestiores* and *humiliores*.

Sherwin-White suggests that a more careful reading of the Lucan account of Paul's difficulties in Philippi reveals that Paul was not just protesting against the fact that he was beaten but that he had been beaten although "uncondemned" or "untried" (16:37; 22:25). To Sherwin-White, such terms imply that provincial authorities

[88] Sherwin-White, *Roman Society and Roman Law*, p. 74.

[89] *Beginnings*, vol. III, p. 201.

[90] A. Plummer, *A Critical and Exegetical Commentary on the Second Epistle of St. Paul to the Corinthians* (Edinburgh: T. & T. Clark, 1915), p. 324.

[91] Sherwin-White, *Roman Society and Roman Law*, pp. 71–75.

might administer a flogging after sentence if the Roman citizen did not appeal or, in special cases, which are recognized by the *lex Julia*, recorded in the *Sententiae Pauli*, which allowed magistrates certain police powers.[92] Hence, that Paul, in the Corinthian correspondence, acknowledges that he was beaten with rods three times suggests, to Sherwin-White, that in these three cases Paul was condemned by the Roman authorities and was properly beaten. Hence, these legal punishments fit into Sherwin-White's second stage.

While this might remove the difficulty, one must be careful not to follow Sherwin-White's reconstruction uncritically. Despite his proven expertise in many areas of Roman law, in many places he seems to shape his understanding of Roman law by an uncritical acceptance that Acts is historical. Therefore, where Acts does not easily coincide with the laws, Sherwin-White seems to assume that changes must have taken place in Roman law so that the testimony of Acts can be accommodated.

Sherwin-White is correct that provincial governors and local magistrates did possess *coercitio*. Local magistrates of Roman colonies were allowed two lictors apiece and could, presumably, use them in certain situations.[93] Furthermore, Josephus reports that the non-Roman magistrates of Caesarea, a city which did not possess a privileged status were not reprimanded for punishing rioters with stripes and bonds.[94] Paul's thirty-nine lashes at the hands of the Diaspora Jews and the prohibition against non-Jews in the Temple seem to suggest that non-Roman officials could punish their own prisoners. If non-Roman magistrates had *coercitio*, it seems to follow *a fortiori* that Roman magistrates in Roman colonies possessed a like *coercitio* over citizens. This contention is also supported by the evidence which was provided in the preceding section.

Of course non-Roman magistrates and free cities, like Rhodes and Cyzicus, could be punished for ill-treating Roman citizens.[95] That Rome protected her citizens from non-Roman law seems certain. However, the evidence does not show that a Roman magistrate, claiming to maintain law and order, would be punished for use of his police privilege. This is particularly so if the citizen, like Paul, had not revealed his citizenship.

---

92 *Ibid.*, p. 71.
93 *Ibid.*, p. 74.
94 Josephus, *Jewish Wars*, ii, 13.7.
95 Dio Cassius 60.24.4.; Suetonius, *Tiberius*, trans. R. Graves, 37.3.

Sherwin-White concludes his discussion of the events at Philippi with the following summary: "The narrative agrees with the evidence of the earlier period that a Roman citizen of any social class was protected against a casual beating (without trial) whereas the *humiliores* of the late empire had lost this protection."[96] Although Sherwin-White presents a plausible explanation for the scenes in Acts 16 and 25, his comments do not exclude another interpretation. First, there is ample evidence to challenge Sherwin-White's claim that a Roman citizen "of any social class" was protected. A distinction between citizens was always recognized, even if not so stated in specific legislation. Second, Sherwin-White assumes that there is nothing particularly special about the Lucan portrayal of Paul. In a later publication Sherwin-White describes Paul as a "rank-and-file" Roman citizen.[97] A "rank-and-file" Roman citizen Paul, in actuality, might have been. However, the Lucan portrayal of Paul indicates that the author of Acts was not satisfied with the description of Paul as such. On the contrary, Luke again and again portrays Paul as a citizen of high social standing.

The narrative in Acts addresses throughout the fundamental importance of social status in the Greco-Roman world. If Roman magistrates in Roman colonies could, under certain circumstances, use force and punishment for minor offenses, then it seems likely that the magistrate of Philippi would have had little concern unless the one who was punished was of sufficient status to be in the position of complaining to the governor or seeking to revenge his humiliation.

Again, in Acts 16, Paul is contrasted with the Roman rabble. This suggests that a subtle, but obvious, status claim is being made about Paul. The mistake of the magistrate was not in beating a citizen but in treating a citizen of high station with contempt.

Paul and Silas are going to be released in any event by the magistrates of Philippi and, at first reading, the insertion of the claims for citizenship seems redundant. The introduction of the Roman citizenship at this point serves primarily an important dramatic function. Luke can hardly recount a scene in which his hero is beaten up by Roman authorities with no response. It would not coincide with the overall portrayal of Paul as a man in control of every situation, of high social status and moral virtue. That Paul is beaten emphasizes the brutality of the Roman magistrates and

96 Sherwin-White, *Roman Society and Roman Law*, p. 76.
97 Sherwin-White, "The Roman Citizenship," p. 55.

draws special attention to the low status of the crowd which initiated the proceedings against Paul. This scene emphasizes Paul's control and his reputation.

Since many of the issues raised in Luke's account of Paul's arrest in Jerusalem (Acts 22) coincide with the issues raised in Acts 16, a lengthy discussion is not required. Like Acts 16, the emphasis of the account in Acts 22 is placed upon the dramatic revelation of Paul's citizenship, the comparison of Paul's inherited status with the purchased citizenship of the tribune and the mention of the tribune's fear (22:29).

The mention of the leather whip is interesting. The *Digest* records that the *flagellum* was an appropriate punishment for slaves in certain circumstances.[98] Cicero notes that being beaten with the *flagella* was a more severe punishment than being beaten with rods.[99]

There has always been, as indicated at the outset of this chapter, a correspondence between the severity of the punishment and the social status of the one who was punished. That here, in Acts 22, Paul was about to be treated as a slave makes his appeal to his citizenship all the more dramatic. No wonder the tribune was so afraid: he had almost treated Paul, who possessed a superior status, in a manner usually reserved for those who held no legal status at all. The fact that Paul had been tied up and was about to be tortured was not, in itself, a breach of Roman law. As mentioned above with regard to Paul's confrontation with the magistrates of Philippi, if Paul had not appealed to his citizenship, the tribune in Jerusalem would not have been held responsible for the beating. As described in Acts, Paul claimed his citizenship rights, his appeal was accepted by the tribune, and he was released. There would have been no reason for the tribune to be afraid.

The events in Philippi and Jerusalem have much in common that is important. In both accounts, Luke has emphasized the fear of those individuals who were in authority. Yet as the narratives stand, there appears to be no legal reason why the magistrates and the tribune would have been afraid. In Philippi, as retold in Acts, Paul never formally appealed and so the magistrates would not have been held accountable. In Jerusalem, Luke reports that Paul did appeal for protection and, after a personal interview, the tribune accepted Paul's claim and halted the proceedings which could have led to

---

[98] *Digest*, 48.19.10.28.
[99] Cicero, *On Behalf of Rabirio*, iv, 12.

torture, a punishment which was usually reserved for slaves. The tribune, like the magistrates, had no reason to be afraid of breaking any law. Therefore, there is not sufficient evidence that would suggest that Roman authorities were unduly restrained in their maintenance of law and order. In fact, Sherwin-White's evidence that provincial Roman authorities did posses *coercitio* over citizens, indicates just the reverse.

In the light of this evidence, it seems clear that the fear expressed by the magistrates and the tribune was not caused by a legal infraction but rather by a severe breach of social convention. They realized that Paul was no ordinary citizen and Luke, in shaping these accounts as he did, wanted to give this impression to his reading audience.

Conclusion

This chapter set out to investigate two scenes (Acts 16 and Acts 22) where Luke reports that Paul "appealed" to his Roman citizenship in order to protect himself from the *coercitio* of Roman officials. These two scenes have traditionally been accepted as, at the very least, relying upon sources which described historical occurrences in the life of the historical Paul. Hence, while most critical commentators recognize a certain amount of dramatic intention on the part of Luke, there is little in the way of a full discussion of the problematic issues involved. However, through the study of the actual Roman laws which Paul supposedly used to protect himself, it was discovered that the laws were not always effective in stopping provincial authorities from punishing and even killing Roman citizens. By the middle decades of the first century, Roman law was not uniformly followed in all places of the empire. Furthermore, it appears certain that those individuals of high social standing and reputation were more likely to receive the protection which these laws intended to provide than were those citizens of low social status. Therefore, while recognizing that these scenes raise many difficult questions, it must be concluded that Luke, or his source, dramatically shaped these scenes in order to highlight Paul's status and stature. That Luke, in both accounts, emphasized the fear of the Roman authorities suggests that Paul was no mere "rank-and-file" citizen, but was an individual one could not dismiss lightly or punish without regret.

6

PAUL'S "APPEAL"

The case against Paul seems straightforward as he comes before
Festus. Luke reports that the Jews from Jerusalem have accused
Paul of "many serious charges" (25:7). Luke, at this juncture, does
not specify the charges although Paul, in verse 8, denies the unstated
accusations that he has broken the law of the Jews, brought a
non-Jew into the Temple, or preached against Caesar. That Paul
had broken the law of Moses had been raised previously even by the
Jewish Christians in Jerusalem (21:21). Furthermore, the allegation
that Paul had brought a Gentile into the Temple led to the uproar by
the Jews which, in turn, brought out the Roman soldiers who then
arrested Paul (21:33). Although serious charges, breaking the religious laws of the Jews did not fall within the legal competence of the
Roman authorities. This is clearly expressed by Gallio's response to
the Jews of Corinth (18:14–15). The more serious charge against
Paul, which would be of great interest to the Roman authorities,
was the matter of riotous behavior caused by Paul's preaching and
the potential for political rebellion. Paul is, after all, called a "pesti-
lent fellow," an "agitator" and a "ringleader of the sect of the
Nazarenes" (24:5). Potential political insurrection and provincial
unrest were causes of considerable concern to Rome, particularly in
Judaea in the middle decades of the first century of the Common
Era. It is, therefore, interesting to note that Luke stressed the religious charges and all but ignored the political accusations against
Paul during the formal trial.

Of present concern is Festus' question to Paul, depicted as a favor
to the Jews, that the trial be moved to Jerusalem. It is at this point
that the narrative becomes particularly interesting and particularly
confusing. Paul declares: "Now if I am in the wrong and have
committed something for which I deserve to die, I am not trying to
escape death; but if there is nothing to their charges against me, no
one can turn me over to them. I appeal to the emperor" (25:11). It is

accepted that Paul, as recorded by Luke, was worried that Festus would be influenced by Jewish pressure if the trial were moved to Jerusalem. Hence, Paul appealed to the court of the emperor in Rome. Scholars generally agree that, since Paul was a Roman citizen, Festus had no choice, having checked the details with his *consilium*, but to grant his appeal and send him to the capital, even though Paul is declared innocent on three occasions. Since the evidence against Paul confused Festus, he called in King Agrippa as an assessor to help him draft an explanation of the charges which would accompany Paul to Rome.[1]

At first sight, the scene does not appear to be problematic. However, when one looks more closely at the legal issues involved and considers how Luke's audience would have perceived what was presented, it is probable that Luke had a particular intention in mind when he included and shaped this account of Paul's trial before Festus. In order to understand better what is presented, two questions must be raised: (1) did Luke accurately report the detail of the "appeal" and (2) how would the readers of the first century have understood the narrative? A proper understanding of the legal and historical milieu will help uncover the way in which Luke shaped the narrative.

In the preceding chapter it was shown that in a number of cases provincial authorities ignored appeals of Roman citizens and felt competent to judge, sentence, and execute. Some provincial governors, and even a few magistrates, took police powers and legal jurisdiction over Roman citizens not specifically granted to them in the various laws of the empire. It seems certain that only those of wealth, authority, and prestige could assume the legal privileges that were, at least on paper, granted to all Roman citizens.

Hence, as Luke's account of Paul's "appeal" to Caesar and the details of his treatment at the hands of the Romans are studied, the relationship of social status and legal privileges must be kept in mind. As in chapters 16 and 22, so in chapter 25 and to the end of the narrative Luke has shaped the material he received from his sources in order to give prominence to Paul's authority, his control over the situation, and his exceptional social standing.

---

[1] Sherwin-White, *Roman Society and Roman Law*, p. 48.

Paul's appeal in Acts: some preliminary considerations

The issues raised in Acts which are related to the development and efficacy of the right of the Roman citizen to appeal against the decision of a provincial magistrate are complicated and many have attempted to explain them. From the magisterial work of T. Mommsen[2] to the more recent works of F. Millar[3] and W. R. Long[4], the conclusions reached have been disparate due to the confusing nature of the primary evidence and the problematic issue of the historicity of the account in Acts. In short, Paul's "appeal" to Nero's tribunal (Acts 25:11), which has often been explained simply in terms of Paul's status as a Roman citizen and as a case study of the *provocatio* procedure in the first century, raises more questions than it answers.

For example, some questions are raised by the account in Acts. Since Paul's "appeal" was not expressed in response to a sentence, can it be said that Paul's declaration was a formal appeal? What seems to be the important issue is the matter of rejecting the location of the court and demanding a new venue for the court of first instance. In the account given in Acts, Paul rejected Festus' intention to move the court to Jerusalem and declared his desire to be tried in Rome by the emperor. Did every citizen have the same right to this change of court? Would the governor have been obliged to accept the demands of the one who protested and send the one who "appealed" to Rome? Did the governor have the authority to judge, condemn, and execute an individual charged with a serious crime, or would he have been expected to send the case of a Roman citizen directly to the capital? If the governor were convinced of the defendant's innocence, could he have acquitted the individual? Could the governor have acquitted the defendant even after an appeal? Who paid for the appeal and journey to Rome? Did one's social status have anything to do with any of these decisions? What actually happened to Paul?[5]

In the last fifty years most New Testament discussions of the legal issues contained in Acts have depended upon the works of H. J. Cadbury[6] and A. N. Sherwin-White.[7] These scholars, in turn,

2 Mommsen, "Die Rechtsverhältnisse," 81–96.
3 Millar, *The Emperor*.
4 Long, "The Trial of Paul."
5 Cadbury, "Roman Law," p. 316; Conzelmann, *Acts*, pp. 203–204.
6 Cadbury, "Roman Law," pp. 297–338.
7 Sherwin-White, *Roman Society*, pp. 48–70.

owe much to the earlier work of T. Mommsen.[8] Cadbury's study was written in 1933 as part of the massive and still excellent commentary edited by F. Jackson and K. Lake. Sherwin-White's series of Sarum lectures was published in 1963. Although both studies are old, as evidenced by recent articles and commentaries they are still influential.[9] Cadbury was skeptical that Luke had accurately reported the details of Paul's trial and "appeal." He wondered if Festus would have been obliged to accept Paul's appeal if, in fact, Paul actually appealed. A. N. Sherwin-White, however, argued that Luke's legal account, for the most part, presented a highly accurate report of the legal procedure of the first century and showed detailed knowledge of specific legal intricacies. To Sherwin-White, Paul relied upon the right which was given to all citizens regardless of their social status and Festus was merely doing his duty.

While Sherwin-White's expertise in matters of Roman legal history is duly recognized, Cadbury's honest skepticism should not be overlooked. Furthermore, although the study of Sherwin-White has received much acclaim from conservative New Testament scholars, it has failed to convince many Roman historians and critical students of the New Testament. For example, A. H. M. Jones confesses his skepticism about the accuracy of Luke's report: "The only account we possess of a *provocatio*, that of Paul before Festus, is unfortunately very confused ... and one is led to suspect that neither Paul nor his biographer understood the legal position."[10] Today, most critical New Testament scholars would agree and therefore offer little more than an acknowledgment of their confusion.[11] Hence, due to the problematic nature of the legal issues involved, most have emphasized the rhetorical, literary, and theological aspects of the narrative.

M. Dibelius contended that Luke was limited by his source and unconcerned about offering the reader a full description of the events.[12] E. Haenchen believed that "this appeal to Caesar raises many problems." Yet he concluded that "to the author the details of

---

[8] Mommsen, "Die Rechtsverhältnisse," 87.
[9] Marshall, *Acts*, p. 385 note 1; F. F. Bruce, *New Testament History* (London: Nelson and Sons, 1971), pp. 339–340; Walaskay, *And So We Came to Rome*, p. 77 note 22.
[10] Jones, *The Criminal Courts*, p. 101.
[11] Schneider, *Apostelgeschichte*, vol. II, p. 356; Schürer rev., vol. II, p. 369 note 76.
[12] Dibelius, "The Speeches in Acts and Ancient Historiography," in *Studies*, p. 149.

the juristic problems are completely irrelevant."[13] To Haenchen, Luke has fashioned a "suspense-laden narrative."[14] J. Roloff concurred and suggested that the point of the narrative was theological: Luke intended to show that Paul was loyal to and had accepted Roman protection and, in so doing, had rejected Jerusalem and, by extension, Judaism.[15]

General agreement exists among critical scholars that Luke was not interested in the minutiae of Roman legal procedure. Therefore, these scenes in Acts are studied with regard to their dramatic, literary, and theological import. In other words, some scholars, while they recognize the problems of this passage and the difficulties of the legal issues involved, dismiss the specific legal issues as unimportant and use their critical acumen merely to discuss the narrative.

There is no doubt that Luke shaped a narrative laden with suspense. Yet to suggest that Luke was insensitive to specific historical legal issues needs further investigation. What seems to be the case is that while Luke did not necessarily present actual historical details of the events of Paul's trials, he did provide a great deal of accurate evidence about the social expectations of his age.

Appeals to the emperor

Suetonius reports that Augustus referred appeals from cases involving citizens to the city praetor and those of foreigners to ex-consuls.[16] According to Dio, Tiberius always referred appeals to Marcus Sulianus.[17] Gaius, as described by Suetonius, allowed magistrates unappealable power, but Dio goes on to remark that Caligula took on many appeals from the Senate.[18] Claudius was known for his involvement in the court system and for not always following the letter of the law.[19] Nero, to whom Paul's "appeal" was made, seems to have been, at first, as conscientious as Claudius in matters of legal hearings and appeals, but his interest soon all but disappeared.[20]

[13] Haenchen, *Acts*, p. 667.
[14] Haenchen, *Acts*, p. 667; Schille, *Apostelgeschichte*, p. 442.
[15] Roloff, "Die Paulus-Darstellung," 525.
[16] Suetonius, *Augustus*, trans. R. Graves, 33.3.
[17] Dio Cassius, 59.8.5.
[18] Suetonius, *Gaius*, trans. Graves, 16.2; Dio Cassius, 59.18.2.
[19] Suetonius, *Claudius*, trans. Graves, 14.
[20] Suetonius, *Nero*, trans. Graves, 15.

Emperors throughout this period also heard appeals of delegations from the provinces, of which the Jewish delegation from Alexandria is perhaps the best known.[21] Yet as W. Kunkel remarks:

> Although many emperors devoted a great deal of time to jurisdiction still at no stage can more than a small fraction of all cases have come before their court, and we may assume that, when they did, it was because they were of special legal, social, or political significance. In particular, criminal prosecutions of senators and high equestrian officials were regularly brought before the emperor after the disappearance of the Senate's own jurisdiction.[22]

It appears certain, as Kunkel implies, that only those who were of high social status could assume they would be heard by Caesar in Rome. Kunkel's summary is hardly controversial but few studying the case of Paul in Acts 25 appear to keep this fact in mind. It is usually assumed that Paul's appeal must have been heeded simply because he was a Roman citizen. The evidence used to support this claim simply cannot command the confidence that so many scholars want to place upon it.

Paul's appeals: "provocatio" or "reiectio"?

A full discussion of the history of *provocatio* would be beyond the scope of this work. This chapter is specifically interested in how the various laws of the Roman Empire favored individuals of high social status. However, since so many scholars interpret Paul's "appeal" in terms of the *provocatio* procedure, as recorded in the *lex Julia*, a few comments are in order.

Sherwin-White, representing traditional scholarship from the time of T. Mommsen's famous work, has argued that the description of the events of Paul's appeal in Acts was not only an example of *provocatio* in the first century but also "sufficiently accurate in all its details."[23] More recently, however, Roman legal historians have begun to re-evaluate the evidence.

The strength of the recent re-evaluation depends upon the fact that, according to the account in Acts, Paul's "appeal" to Caesar was not made after a sentence handed down by Festus, nor was it

---

21 Philo, *Legatio ad Gaium*, trans. E. M. Smallwood.
22 Kunkel, *Introduction*, p. 69.
23 Sherwin-White, *Roman Society and Roman Law*, p. 68.

declared in response to imminent punishment. Rather, Paul's declaration was expressed in reaction to Festus' proposal to move the hearing to Jerusalem.[24] Sherwin-White, among others, has attempted to circumvent this difficulty by suggesting that the first century was a period of transition for Roman law. Accepted legal procedure from the time of the Republic, for example, *provocatio ad populum*, was undergoing significant development and transition. Therefore, to Sherwin-White, Paul's "appeal" was an example of a first-century form of *provocatio* that allowed a citizen to appeal before sentence.[25] This early first-century *provocatio* then became obsolete in the second century when, according to Sherwin-White, provincial governors were required to send Roman citizens to Rome. Furthermore, at some time in the same century, *provocatio*, which had been recognized since the beginning of the Republic, was subsumed under the formal *appellatio* procedure.

It is true that potentially *provocatio* and *appellatio* were two ways of achieving a court of second instance. *Provocatio*, as described in the previous chapter, was an appeal against the *coercitio* of the magistrate which would, if accepted by the magistrate, lead to a hearing before a public court. *Appellatio*, known from the Republic, was an appeal used in civil cases made against the judgment of a lower to a higher magistrate. Yet, from the time of Augustus, *provocatio* and *appellatio* became almost synonymous and an exact distinction between the two, as Sherwin-White would require, is extremely difficult to make.[26] Furthermore, it is not correct that *provocatio* became obsolete, because the procedure was still recognized in the *Digest*. Regardless of the similarities, distinctions and the development of a variety of appeal procedures in the first century, the fact remains that in the case of Paul, as described by Luke, Paul neither appealed against Festus' abuse of his *coercitio* nor did he appeal against a formal sentence of the court.

While Sherwin-White's reconstruction is ingenious and many have been persuaded by it, it is problematic on several counts. Primarily, Sherwin-White offers no evidence, except this account in Acts, that such a first-century *provocatio*, as distinct from the republican *provocatio*, ever, in fact, existed. There is not enough documentation to prove that provincial governors were required, in all cases, to send Roman citizens to Rome even in the second

²⁴ Cadbury, "Roman Law," p. 317; Millar, *The Emperor*, p. 511.
²⁵ Sherwin-White, *Roman Society and Roman Law*, p. 57.
²⁶ Livy, viii. 33.8; viii. 56.5; Lintott, "Provocatio," p. 234.

century. The provincial governors had a wide-ranging jurisdiction throughout this period, either legal or assumed. Governors could choose to send individuals to Rome. The fact of Roman citizenship might be an influential factor in the decision, as it was for Pliny when confronted by the Christians of Bithynia. However, there is nothing to prove that the governor was obliged to do so.[27]

Yet, if Paul's "appeal", as reported by Luke in Acts 25, was neither a formal protest against the abusive authority of Festus nor an "appeal" against a sentence, what was it? P. Garnsey has argued that St. Paul's case can be compared with Pliny's handling of the Bithynian Christians, Eusebius' account of the Christians at Lyons, and the not-so-well-known instances of Trebonius Rufinus, Claudius Ariston, and others. To Garnsey these belong to a special class of cases which were referred to a higher or lower jurisdiction at the prerogative of the one judging but *not* because of an appeal by the defendant.[28] Garnsey's distinction is an important one when considering the account in Acts. However, a further distinction – one that Garnsey himself does not make explicit – must be made among the examples he offers.

The Christians of Bithynia and Lyons had no choice in the matter of what happened to them. However, in the case of Paul, Trebonius Rufinus, Claudius Ariston, and others who are sent to Rome, the transfer of the case is initiated by the individual, not the governor. What is important to stress is that those cases where the accused initiates the procedure involve individuals of high status.

In a later work, Garnsey presses his point even further and his comments are again illuminating:

> There is no sign that any governor was ever purchased by an ordinary provincial plaintiff to send a case out of his jurisdiction to a higher tribunal. As for provincial defendants of low status, when they did appear before the Emperor's judgment seat, it was hardly by choice, and hardly in circumstances favorable to them.[29]

Pliny, as indicated in his letter to the Emperor Trajan, is confronted by Christians of all classes and professions, some of whom are Roman citizens.[30] Those who are Christian citizens Pliny pre-

---

[27] Kunkel, *Untersuchungen*, p. 24.

[28] Dio Cassius 52.33; Garnsey, "Lex Julia," p. 181.

[29] Garnsey, *Social Status and Legal Privileges*, p. 72; Jones, "Imperial and Senatorial Jurisdiction," 464–488.

[30] Pliny, *Letters*, x. 96.

pares to send to Rome. More will be said below concerning this important evidence; for the account in Pliny offers clues for understanding what might actually have happened to Paul.

The point to be made here is that in the account of Paul's "appeal" in Acts, and what makes it different from Pliny's report, it is Paul himself who initiates the process of moving the hearing from Caesarea to Rome. In fact, Festus asks Paul: "Do you wish to go up to Jerusalem and be tried there before me on these charges?" (25:9) – a very peculiar query. What is obvious is that Luke here, as in other places throughout the narrative, demonstrates that those who are in authority do not have complete control of the situation and so look to Paul for advice. Luke wishes to emphasize that the Roman magistrates, governors, and soldiers recognize the authority of Paul.

In comparison, Bithynian Christians had no such privileges. There is no indication in the letter of Pliny that he asked the Christian Roman citizens of Bithynia where they wanted to be tried. If a governor needed clarification, as Pliny did, the question was directed to the emperor, not, as in the case of Festus, to the accused.

Likewise, Eusebius' account of the Christians of Lyons is interesting for the same reason.[31] It is true that Attalus was saved from the humiliation of being paraded around the amphitheater and was rescued from being thrown to the beasts because of his Roman citizenship. However, an important detail is not often noted: Attalus was a "person of distinction."[32] Because of his reputation, as well as his citizenship, Attalus was removed from the humiliating parade around the amphitheater and saved, for the time being, from execution.

What is interesting about Eusebius' account is not only that a sensitivity to status is expressed but that the governor did not automatically send his Romans to the capital. Rather, he wrote to the emperor for clarification. Nor, in the end, were the Christians sent to Rome for execution. The Christian Roman citizens were killed in front of Verus the governor. The point is that these Christians did not have any control over the matter of where the court was to be held and there is no question of an appeal. Furthermore, in both Bithynia and Lyons, the governor did not hesitate to hold a trial or pronounce guilt. Paul's "appeal", as described by Luke, does not easily correspond to either of the accounts of the Christians of Lyons or Bithynia.

[31] Eusebius, *The Church History*, trans. A. C. McGiffert, v.1.1–63.
[32] Eusebius, *The Church History*, v.1.43.

In the provinces, non-Roman citizens of free cities could either choose the laws and courts of the locality or select those courts administered by Roman officials.[33] Roman citizens, too, at least on paper, had choices. Citizens were not, except in a few specific cases, subject to local laws and could choose to be heard by Roman authority. There were other options allowed to the Roman citizen as well. A defendant was able to select a number of *iudices* for the *consilium* and reject others.[34] The *lex Vatinia* (59 B.C.E.), according to Cicero, allowed a citizen the right to reject an entire *consilium*.[35]

Garnsey claimed that Roman citizens could also "reject" an entire court, although the evidence he provides does not indicate a technical legal procedure for such an option. He offers as evidence the case of a Senator, C. Antonius, who rejects the court after the decree had been issued.[36] C. Antonius' request was refused and, it is reported, he was dismissed from the Senate. One can only wonder if an individual who was not of senatorial rank could have made such a request.

Cicero sought a more favorable council for L. Mescinius Rufus, desiring to move the trial from the jurisdiction of the governor of Achaia to Rome.[37] However, Mescinius had been Cicero's quaestor and, hence, was of relatively high rank. Furthermore, having Cicero as a mentor presented quite an advantage.

Dio records an instance where the accuser in a murder trial is concerned that he might lose his case because Germanicus, who was perceived as a popular advocate, might intimidate the jury.[38] Therefore, the accuser wished to move the court so that the case could be tried before Augustus. It is difficult to discern from the account whether the accuser got his wish. In any event, he lost his case! It is important to note, in this instance, that the prosecuting attorney, not the defendant, applied for a new venue. It is also significant that both of these examples took place in the capital.

It does not always follow that what occurred in Rome happened with equal effectiveness in the provinces. It is no doubt true that a defendant might wish to be judged by the court of the emperor, and it is also correct that emperors might assume the legal jurisdiction

---

[33] F. F. Abbott and A. C. Johnson, *Municipal Administration in the Roman Empire* (Princeton: Princeton University Press, 1926), pp. 272–276.

[34] Garnsey, "Lex Julia," p. 183.

[35] Cicero, *Philippicae*, xii.18; *In Vatinium*, xi.27.

[36] Garnsey, "Lex Julia," p. 182.

[37] Cicero, *Letters*, xiii, 26, 3; 28.1–3; xvi, 4.3.

[38] Dio Cassius 56.24.7.

that was usually reserved for the provincial governors. However, the fact remains that it was extremely difficult to bypass the governor. An individual who wished to be heard by the emperor would have had to present his request in person, or have a powerful benefactor who had the ear of the emperor to present it for him, or let the emperor find out about the case by some other means. For example, it seems as if Augustus inadvertently discovered a miscarriage of justice and so appointed Asinius Gallus to investigate the case against Euboulos and Tryphera of Cnidus. Tryphera, it seems, had escaped from the local authorities and had somehow made her request to Augustus.[39]

Cicero reports that Sthenius, who fled to Rome before the notorious Verres could bring a case against him, received a sympathetic hearing from the Senate.[40] The envoy from Cyrene to Augustus complained of unfair courts.[41] Later in Cicero's oration against Verres, he describes the ignominious conduct of the governor in his handling of the case which Publius Scandilius brought before him.[42]

Verres, it seems, was illegally receiving a portion of the taxes gathered by one of the collectors. The collector involved, Apronius P. Scandilius, who was an *eques Romanus*, sought to bring this injustice to court. However, his application for a court or for a single judge to try the case had to be presented to none other than Verres. Cicero reports that Verres should have appointed a court from the local Roman citizens, but, in order to protect himself, Verres selected three of his cronies to hear the case. P. Scandilius "rejects" the selection and Verres, in turn, rejects the rejection. P. Scandilius requests that the case be sent to Rome and Verres dismisses that appeal as well.

Several points in this case are interesting. First, it must be noted that P. Scandilius was an equestrian. Although his requests were not granted, it is not improper to assume that he would have had much more opportunity to press his claim than one of low status. Cicero implies as much.[43] Second, Scandilius "rejects" first Verres' selection of his cronies and then the entire court. Third, although Verres' conduct showed no respect for either custom or Scandilius' status, and one can assume that a more scrupulous governor (e.g. Pliny)

---

[39] Ehrenberg and Jones, *Documents*, no. 312.
[40] Cicero, *Against Verres*, II, 2, 90.
[41] Ehrenberg and Jones, *Documents*, no. 311.
[42] Cicero, *Against Verres* II, 2, 90.
[43] Cicero, *Against Verres* II, 3, 135–141.

would have complied with the demands, there is nothing to suggest that he was obliged to accept Scandilius' request. Fourth, it is unclear why P. Scandilius did not simply travel to Rome himself and seek to have the case heard in the capital. The evidence has led A. Lintott to conclude: "If a trial laid down by either a magistrate or a governor was rejected it would have to have the support of the governor which was not automatic."[44]

Paul's request for a change of venue appears to have much in common with the examples just provided. One could argue that Festus would have been more like Pliny than Verres and be open to sending Paul to Rome. Perhaps he was. However, Luke makes it clear that Festus was more concerned to please the Jews than he was to see that justice was done (25:9).

Pliny provides several excellent examples of the types of individuals who could have expected to have their cases heard by the emperor. In his letter to Sempronius Rufus, he presents the qualifications of the defendant, Trebonius Rufinus.[45] Rufinus was one of the *duoviri* in Gallia Norbonensis and Pliny describes him as "my worthy friend." In addition, Pliny praises Rufinus for his ability to deliver his speech with "deliberate gravity, proper to a true Roman and a good citizen." Rufinus was no rank-and-file Roman citizen!

Also of great importance is Pliny's letter written to Cornelianus. In it he describes his experience serving on the emperor's privy council.[46] Pliny gives a report of the three cases that he heard.

First was the case of Claudius Ariston. The details of the charges brought against Claudius are difficult to discern, but what is important is that Claudius Ariston is an individual of high social standing and reputation. Pliny writes that Ariston is "an Ephesian nobleman, of great munificence and unambitious popularity." What is particularly interesting is that Pliny does not identify Ariston as a Roman citizen. If Ariston were not a citizen, this account provides evidence that non-citizens could appear before the emperor. However, what is important is Ariston's status. In comparison with Ariston, those bringing the accusations are "persons opposite in character." Pliny, like Luke, is aware of the importance of comparing his protagonist with those who bring charges against him.

The next day, according to Pliny, the emperor heard the cases against Gallitta who was charged with adultery. The details of the

44 Lintott, "Provocatio," p. 262.
45 Pliny, *Letters*, iv.22.1.
46 Pliny, *Letters*, vi.31.

charges are unimportant. What is important is that Gallitta's husband was a military tribune and was about to stand for office. Gallitta was condemned and given up to the punishment directed by the Julian law, which was a forfeiture of half her dowry, and one-third of her property, and banishment to an island!

The third case concerned the will of Julius Tiro, part of which was genuine and part of which was forged. The two individuals charged with forgery were Sempronius Senecio, an *eques Romanus*, and Eurythmus, Caesar's freedman and procurator. Again, the defendants were not ordinary individuals.

What is common to all the individuals mentioned above is either high social status and reputation, or personal ties with the emperor. In the light of these examples, Garnsey's conclusions are even more compelling:

> It is risky to attempt a generalization on the basis of so few examples; but it would seem that if a governor transferred a case to Rome it was not because he lacked the competence to try it himself. Furthermore, the Rufus affair raises doubts as to whether a citizen could expect to win *reiectio* if he were not a man of rank and influence himself, or a man with powerful supporters.[47]

As the report stands in Acts, Paul's "appeal", whatever its formal description, is more like those cases in which individuals of high status are involved than it is like the description of the Christians who appeared before Pliny. The *raison d'être* of the discussion of Paul's "appeal" in Acts seems to be to illustrate that Paul was a man of such status that he could have presumed to influence the governor's decision concerning where he was to be tried.

Another important issue concerns Festus' obligation in the matter of Paul's "appeal." Sherwin-White, Haenchen, Bruce, and others have become convinced that once Paul appealed the case was out of Festus' hands.[48] He had no other options. In other words, even if Festus thought Paul innocent (as he did) he could not release him.

There are several problems with these conclusions. Festus' words themselves suggest a decision on his part (25:11 and 25:25). Even though Paul is innocent Festus *decides* to send him to Rome. A legal

[47] Garnsey, *Social Status and Legal Privileges*, p. 56; "Lex Julia," p. 182.

[48] Sherwin-White, *Roman Society and Roman Law*, p. 64; Haenchen, *Acts*, p. 690; Bruce, *Acts*, p. 450.

obligation is not made explicit. It is only the supportive words of
Agrippa which suggest that the decision was out of Festus' control
("This man could have been set free if he had not appealed to the
emperor" – 26:32). However, it is important to note that the
relationship between Roman governor and client king was not one
of equals. Agrippa, concerned to stay in Rome's good graces, would
hardly contradict the decision of the governor unless it was in his
own self-interest. Sherwin-White himself admits: " no sensible man
with hopes of promotion would dream of short circuiting the appeal
to Caesar unless he had specific authority to do so."[49] Non-consti-
tutional custom played its part in the legal process. Roman law, like
Roman life, was impressed by status and authority. The relationship
between Agrippa and Festus had to be carefully nurtured. Agrippa
would hardly have questioned Festus' decision.

Furthermore, the *Digest* is explicit: "No one who can condemn is
unable to acquit"![50] As the events are recorded by Luke, it appears
as if Festus had no hesitation about holding the court of first
instance nor was he at first reluctant to pass the sentence that was
appropriate for the crime. It seems clear that if Festus had so desired
he could have set Paul free. He was not restricted by the law. He
must have had other reasons.

Festus was only too glad to "wash his hands" of Paul's case.
However, that Festus, as described by Luke, asked Paul for his
preference of court (25:9) and then accepted his "appeal", shows
that he was aware of Paul's social status and *auctoritas*. The case
was not legally out of his hands, it was socially out of his jurisdiction.

Far from its being a case study of *provocatio*, the description of
Paul's appeal to Caesar highlights the Paul of Acts as a man deemed
worthy to stand before Nero. Moreover, this scene attests to the fact
that Paul is a man in control in the law court as well as on the high
seas. In addition, Luke's account indicates that Festus was a man
who gave in to the mob, despite the innocence of the accused. Luke
shaped the account of Paul's "appeal" in order to make a status
claim about Paul.

By way of summary, it is hardly conceivable that every Roman
citizen, regardless of status, from throughout the provinces, could
have expected his appeal to be heard or have expected to influence
the governor and be sent to Rome. The court system could hardly

[49] Sherwin-White, *Roman Society and Roman Law*, p. 65.
[50] *Digest*, 50.17.37.

have withstood the strain. The logical conclusion is that only those who were of sufficient influence to gain the favor of the governor could expect any privileges.

Through the last eight chapters of Acts, Paul is portrayed as just such a man of influence and this scene in which Paul "appeals", when properly understood, confirms such a judgment. Luke did not have eyewitness reports of the trial and either he, or his source, shaped the account in order to emphasize Paul's status and authority.

In the conclusion of the section of an article concerned with Paul's appeal, Garnsey writes:

> If, as I hold, Festus was under no obligation to grant Paul his request, then a complex of causes must be acknowledged to lie behind his decision. Festus' personality and attitudes, his uncertainty about the basis of the allegations against Paul, and the strain of Jewish pressure – as well as Paul's status – were probably relevant factors.[51]

Indeed, of all of the factors which would have influenced Festus, Luke has placed most importance on the last – Paul's status. Luke has not merely emphasized Paul's Roman status, but goes on to portray Paul as one who would be at ease with the élite of the empire.

Travel expenses

From the investigation of the evidence, it appears certain that only those individuals of high social status who also possessed wealth and reputation could have depended upon legal privileges that were, at least on paper, granted to all Roman citizens. For the fact remains that, if an appeal to Rome were accepted, the one who appealed was responsible for all costs of the journey, housing, and legal fees. There is no evidence of any kind of legal aid.

Ramsay, long ago, described the process of an appeal:

> An appeal to the supreme court could not be made by everybody that chose. Such an appeal had to be permitted and sent forward by the provincial governor; and only a serious case would be entertained. But the case of a very poor man is never esteemed as serious; and there is little

---

[51] Garnsey, *Social Status and Legal Privileges*, p. 76.

doubt that the citizen's right of appeal to the Emperor was hedged in by fees and pledges. There is always one law for the rich man and another for the poor; at least, to this extent, that many claims can be successfully pushed by a rich man in which a poor man would have no chance of success.[52]

The truth of Ramsay's insights has not been convincingly challenged, although few who have studied the account of Paul's appeal in Acts have appropriated them.

Garnsey, writing seventy years after Ramsay, agrees: "It was plainly more difficult and expensive for a provincial than for an Italian or a Roman, and a poor provincial than for a rich one, to bring his grievance in person to the Emperor."[53] Attempts to explain how Paul paid for his travel and appeal are varied. Ramsay, who believed that the Paul of Acts was the historical Paul, assumed that Paul was a man of high social standing who would have his family's wealth on which to reply.[54] While Ramsay's description of the Lucan Paul of Acts is to be commended, his reliance upon Acts as an accurate biographical sketch is far from certain.

Cadbury, who disagreed with Ramsay, sought to explain the journey to Rome in terms of Paul's other journeys around the Mediterranean.[55] In other words, Paul need not have had much wealth to get to the capital. While under normal circumstances this might be true, the current circumstances were not normal.

J. Munck believed that Paul used the collection that he was bringing to the church in Jerusalem for his journey to Rome.[56] Munck's conjecture is possible. Yet there is no mention of any collection for the church in Jerusalem at this point in Acts (although see 11:29–30), and one should not necessarily assume that the readers would have knowledge of it.

Whatever the actual scenario behind the account in Acts, it is impossible to know what Paul's travel arrangements were. But, in the light of the portrayal of Paul in Acts which has been constructed

[52] Ramsay, *St. Paul the Traveller*, p. 311.
[53] Garnsey, *Social Status and Legal Privileges*, p. 65; Jones, "Imperial and Senatorial Jurisdiction," pp. 464–488.
[54] Ramsay, *St. Paul the Traveller*, p. 312.
[55] Cadbury, "Roman Law," p. 320; G. Horsley, *New Docs I*, p. 36; S. Mitchell, "Requisitioned Transport in the Roman Empire: A New Inscription from Pisidia," *JRS* 66 (1976), 107–131.
[56] J. Munck, *The Acts of the Apostles* (New York; Doubleday, 1967), p. 231.

so far, it is hard not to imagine that Luke's audience would have considered that Paul traveled any way other than first class![57]

Other possible reconstructions

The historical account which lies behind the re-telling in Acts of Paul's transport to Rome is difficult to discern. What is important is that, for Luke, Festus' concern to receive confirmation from Paul about the location of the trial, Paul's "appeal" to Caesar's tribunal in Rome, and Festus' acceptance of the appeal, all suggest that Paul was a man not only of reputation but also of wealth who was able to afford the travel from Caesarea to Rome, and maintain private lodgings in the capital. Pliny's descriptions of Claudius Ariston and Trebonius Rufinus, which were mentioned above, provide possible parallels to the Lucan portrayal of the Paul of Acts. Both Claudius Ariston and Trebonius Rufinus were men of wealth and reputation who could afford to bring their cases to the emperor. But few would have been able to bypass the governor and those who did would most probably be members of the higher orders of society. Luke intended his readers to perceive Paul in just such a manner.

In the previous chapter it was argued that Luke, or his source, had taken accounts of Paul before the Roman authorities in Philippi and Jerusalem and had shaped them in order to suggest an implicit comparison between Paul and the magistrates and tribune. In so doing, Luke attempted to draw attention to Paul's control and social standing. A similar intention is revealed in this scene with Paul and Festus.

Festus, shown to be in two minds on the matter and influenced by the Jewish leaders, would have been associated with the mob. Paul, in contrast, demands to be heard by Caesar and will not put up with the lesser court of Festus in Caesarea. Yet, if it is correct that Luke, or his source, has shaped this scene and the report in Acts is not factual in all its details, then how did Paul get to Rome? If it is true that Festus would not have been required to send Paul to Rome then why did he do so?

It has been shown that *Festus* would not have been required to send Paul to Rome although he could have sent anyone he liked to the capital if he felt that it was a particularly vexing case. Of particular interest would have been cases against potential revolution-

---

[57] Casson, *Travel in the Ancient World* (London: G. Allen and Unwin Ltd., 1974), pp. 149–162.

ary leaders. For example, Josephus reports that Felix had the brigand Eleazar arrested and sent to Rome.[58] Eleazar, as far as can be determined, was not a Roman citizen. However, his notorious reputation and the possibility of provincial unrest on a large scale no doubt influenced Felix's decision.

Paul, who was called the ringleader of the Nazarenes and who had also been associated with a number of riots throughout the eastern empire, might also have been perceived by the successor of Felix as being a sufficiently dangerous character who, under the interrogation of the emperor, might provide helpful information for further policy. Although Luke placed the religious charges of the Jews against Paul in the foreground, the more serious political charges – whether or not he was in fact involved in political intrigue – were obviously attached to Paul. In other words, Paul need not have been a Roman citizen to be sent to Rome.

Another alternative should be offered which recognizes the tradition of Paul's Roman citizenship. Particularly interesting is the account of Pliny's handling of the Christians of Bithynia. Pliny, who writes to Trajan that he had never taken part in trials involving Christians, admits that he is ignorant about the proper handling of the case: "Having never been present at any trials of the Christians, I am unacquainted with the methods and limits to be observed either in examining or punishing them."[59] That he sends the Roman Christians is his choice alone. He is neither required to send them nor does he ask the prisoners their preference of court. Pliny was unsure of what to do with the Roman Christians, and needed clarification.

Similarly in Acts, Festus had recently come to his province and was confronted by a confusing case. As the text of Acts indicates, Paul was innocent of political charges, and the evidence of the epistles seems to confirm this. Furthermore, as expressed in the narrative, Festus was confused by the religious charges, and under considerable pressure from the Jewish leaders. Unsure of how to continue, and wishing to "wash his hands" of the affair, Festus sent Paul to Rome. Like the Christians of Bithynia, Paul, in fact, would have had little control over the decision.

However, whether Paul was a Roman citizen or not, it is precisely the matter of control which was of such importance to Luke. Throughout this study, it has been stressed that the Paul of Acts was

[58]   Josephus, *Jewish Wars*, iii, 253.
[59]   Pliny, *Letters*, x.96.1.

a man who was in control, was never at a loss for words, and showed himself to be an individual who was at home among the élite of the empire. Here, in Luke's account of the trial before Festus, Paul's control over the proceedings is once again highlighted.

Paul's imprisonment and journey to Rome

It is also important to investigate how Luke described the way in which Paul was treated both before his formal trial, and subsequently on his journey to Rome. It must be granted that there is not an abundance of descriptive material concerning the imprisonment of Paul in the last eight chapters. As was indicated, far more attention has been given to the account of Paul's trial and interaction with the Roman authorities. However, what has been presented indicates that Paul was given certain freedoms while under arrest.

Furthermore, it is significant to note that the final picture the reader receives of Paul is one which conveys his independence in Rome. In fact, after the dramatic and hair-raising episode on the stormy seas, one can almost forget that Paul is a prisoner at all. As Paul arrives in Italy, greeted by the Christians who come to welcome him, the reader receives the impression that the Roman soldiers are there to escort an arriving dignitary, not to guard a prisoner!

It has traditionally been assumed that Luke presented the material in this way in order to highlight the kindness of Roman protection and to suggest to the Christians of his community that they must respect the authority of Rome and look to her for justice. This traditional interpretation is hardly convincing. What is alluded to in the description of Paul's various imprisonments is that he is being treated in a manner corresponding to his alleged high status.

Since the accounts of Paul's treatment in Philippi and Jerusalem (Acts 16:37–39 and 22:25–29) have already been discussed, it is hardly necessary to repeat the full discussion of these texts here. In short, the importance of those scenes was three-fold. First, Paul, who was of higher status than either of the Roman authorities, suffered punishment usually reserved for slaves and others of little or no social standing. Second, the Roman authorities are not portrayed, as is traditionally argued, as being kind or just. Third, Luke emphasizes the fear of the magistrates and tribune when they discover the identity of their prisoner. That these are the only two accounts in Acts where Paul is about to receive harsh treatment does not easily correspond to the evidence of Paul's own letters, and Clement's description of Paul's endurance. In Acts, Paul is only once physically punished by Roman authority, and, on that one occasion, Paul humiliates the magistrates who punished him. The author of Acts either did not know of these incidents or considered it inappropriate to his overall concern to present more than he did. What Luke did emphasize was Paul's status and, with the two noted exceptions, the lenient punishment which was given to him.

In the previous chapter, mention was made of the correspondence between social status and how prisoners were sentenced and treated. Many scholars think that execution was rare for offenders of high status.[60] An individual found guilty of a capital crime might face deportation, which meant banishment, loss of property, and loss of citizenship; or relegation, which was a temporary exile and did not involve loss of citizenship; or expulsion from the Senate if a senator or from the council if a decurion. Yet, an individual of low status, for the same crime, might face the wild beasts, crucifixion, or be burned alive. He might also be condemned to a life in the mines, or be sentenced to public works.[61] It should be noted that the list of punishments which Paul received, gathered from outside the narrative of Acts, corresponds to those penalties usually saved for individuals of low status.

The *Digest* offers a very interesting passage that concerns the duties of the proconsul with regard to the means by which prisoners were to be handled. Ulpian wrote:

> The proconsul normally determines the custody of the accused persons, whether someone is to be lodged in prison, handed over to the military, entrusted to sureties, or even on his own recognizance. He normally does this by reference to the nature of the charge brought, the honorable status, or the great wealth, or by the harmlessness, or the rank of the accused.[62]

It is true that in Acts Luke emphasized Paul's innocence, and this might have been a factor in the description of his light imprisonment. However, the other factors which influenced a Roman proconsul were: honorable status, great wealth, and rank. It has been

[60] Garnsey, *Social Status and Legal Privileges*, p. 103; Millar, "Condemnation to Hard Labour," pp. 124–147.

[61] *Digest* 48.19.15; 48.28.9; 48.22.6; 47.17.1; 47.20.3.2.

[62] *Digest* 48.3.1.

demonstrated throughout this work that these three qualities were among the many that Luke emphasized as he formed his portrait of Paul. Paul's custody, as described in Acts, is lenient by any standards and the social implications of such treatment would not have been missed by Luke's audience.

Imprisonment was properly regarded as a means of detention rather than as a means of punishment. However, as is made evident in the *Digest*, some governors did not recognize such a formal distinction.[63] There is not enough evidence to allow for a full description of the prison conditions of the first century. Reports from the fourth century suggest that prisons were inhospitable and dangerous places to be.[64] It is assumed that there was little change from one century to the next as the evidence from Sallust, Philostratus, and Josephus suggests.

In Sallust's account of the trial of those who were indicted in Catiline's rebellion, he takes special interest in describing the trial and character of Publius Lentulus Sura. Sallust reports that while the trial was in session, Publius Lentulus Sura, who had been one of the followers of Catiline and who was himself of senatorial rank, was to resign his office and be held, along with the other leading conspirators, in free custody.[65] What is meant by "free custody" is that Lentulus remained under the supervision of a senator who was to be responsible for his appearance at the next court hearing. Lentulus' guilt was recognized by all from the moment of his arrest and the debate in the Senate was not concerned with deciding his guilt or innocence. Rather, the senators were divided on the matter of his punishment. Hence, the lenient custody afforded him during the trial was neither given on account of his innocence nor on account of the nature of the crime. It seems certain that Lentulus' "free custody" was given to him because of his standing and his past reputation.

At the conclusion of the trial, the Senate called for the execution of Lentulus, which was recommended by Marcus Porcius Cato. The Senate had rejected Gaius Caesar's plea for a more lenient punishment consisting of exile and imprisonment. The speech of Gaius Caesar is important because he alluded to one of the Porcian laws which stated that a Roman citizen should not lose his life but rather

---

[63] *Digest* 48.19.8.9.
[64] Garnsey, *Social Status and Legal Privileges*, p. 151 note 4.
[65] Sallust, *War*, 48.2; Garnsey, *Social Status and Legal Privileges*, p. 147.

be sent into exile.[66] Cato's response is significant, for it shows that he, and ultimately the Senate, did not feel constrained to follow the Porcian law since the conspirators were executed.

Of further interest is the description of the prison into which Lentulus was thrown and where he was strangled. Sallust's description of the prison is chilling in its details:

> In the prison, when you have gone up a little way towards the left, there is a place called the Tullianum, about twelve feet below the surface of the ground. It is enclosed on all sides by walls, and above it is a chamber with a vaulted roof of stone. Neglect, darkness, and stench make it hideous and fearsome to behold.[67]

Sallust concludes his account of Lentulus' fate with an important description which includes a serious moral lesson: "Thus that patrician of the illustrious stock of the Corneli, who had held consular authority at Rome, ended his life in a manner befitting his character and crime."[68]

The extremes of his imprisonment are important. As a man of status, one was allowed relative freedom and was guarded by one's equal, a fellow senator. However, when guilt was declared, Lentulus lost not only his status as a senator but also his Roman citizenship. When he was stripped of all social and legal status, he was removed to the prison of a common criminal. The lesson to be learned in Sallust's account is plain: although one would expect good pedigree to produce virtuous action, past nobility does not guarantee *dignitas*.

Philostratus, in his biography of Apollonius, depicts the prison into which Apollonius and his fellow prisoners were thrown.[69] It is described as a "free" prison where the captives were not bound. That Philostratus would describe a prison in which the prisoners were not chained implies that a prison in which prisoners were chained existed. It is impossible to be certain that men of high status were always placed in a "free" prison and men of low status were segregated in the "unfree" prison. However, it is interesting to note that those who were in the unbound prison with Apollonius included a wealthy Cilician, an office holder from Tarentum, and a

---

[66] Sallust, *War*, 51.22.40; Plutarch, *Cicero*, 21.3.
[67] Sallust, *War*, 55.3–4.
[68] Sallust, *War*, 55.6.
[69] Philostratus, *The Life of Apollonius*, vii.22.

property and ship owner from Acarnania, near the mouth of the Achelous.[70] In all, about fifty prisoners were together who were, it can be assumed, men of substance and status. Apollonius too, despite his outward appearance, was born into an exceedingly wealthy family whose descendants were among the first settlers of Tyana.[71] One can assume with a high degree of probability that those who lacked status in the way of wealth or prestige would not have been placed with the men who were with Apollonius.

Perhaps the most revealing evidence concerning the diverse types of imprisonments into which an individual could be placed is found in Josephus' description of the various incarcerations suffered by Agrippa at the hands of Tiberius.[72] What is interesting and important to note is that Agrippa, as is well known, was a friend of Gaius and Claudius, and was among the most notable of Jews in the empire. Despite his lack of discipline with money, Agrippa was accustomed to a lifestyle shared by only a few of the wealthiest citizens, Jew or non-Jew, in the known world. Josephus' account is enlightening in that it presents evidence that is important for a proper understanding of Luke's description of Paul's imprisonments. Luke's and Josephus' separate accounts reflect contemporary descriptions and converging assumptions on how individuals were treated while under arrest.

Either during a carriage ride or around a dinner table, Agrippa openly prayed that he might live to see Gaius as "ruler of the world."[73] Josephus' account in *The Jewish Wars* does not offer much in the way of descriptive material concerning what happened to Agrippa. Josephus, in this earlier account, reports only that when Tiberius heard of Agrippa's words, he threw him into prison, where Agrippa was mistreated.[74] Josephus' subsequent description in *Antiquities* is more colorful in detail.

When Tiberius heard of Agrippa's remarks he orders Macro to arrest him, although "handcuff" or "bind" are possible translations as well.[75] Macro, not believing that Tiberius would treat Agrippa in such a manner because of his status and his relationship to the imperial family, hesitates until Tiberius orders him a second time. Agrippa is then arrested and Josephus describes Agrippa being led

70 *Ibid.*, vii.23,24,25,26.
71 *Ibid.*, i.4.
72 Josephus, *Antiquities*, xviii, 188–237; *Jewish Wars*, ii.178–180
73 *Jewish Wars*, ii.178; *Antiquities*, xviii, 168, 187.
74 *Jewish Wars*, ii.180.
75 *Antiquities*, xviii, 189.

away as a prisoner still wearing the crimson robes.[76] Crimson robes were a mark of high status. There is no lack of irony intended here in the contrast between the royal stature of the prisoner and his less-than-royal treatment. Josephus notes that Agrippa's feelings are divided between those of distress and those of dishonor.

Still in his crimson robes and chained to a guard, Agrippa stands in front of the palace until he is thrown into prison.[77] Agrippa's exact conditions are unknown. Yet the concessions that Antonia requests from Macro give some indication of the initial harshness of Agrippa's quarters. The concessions acquired were: that the centurion to whom Agrippa was chained would be a moderate man; that Agrippa should be permitted to bathe every day; that he should be permitted to receive visits from his freedmen and friends; and that he should have other bodily comforts such as scraps of clothing used to make a bed.[78] This new, "lighter" imprisonment was certainly more in keeping with Agrippa's social status.

When Agrippa's freedman Marsyas heard the news that Tiberius had died, he rushed to tell Agrippa who, in turn, passed on the news to the centurion with whom he had formed a friendship. Agrippa and the centurion were feasting and drinking when they discovered that the report concerning Tiberius had been premature. Incensed and frightened that he might be accused of rejoicing at the news of the death of the emperor, the centurion ordered that Agrippa again be put in chains, although he had previously taken them off.[79] When Gaius at last became Emperor, he sent Piso, the prefect of the city, to remove Agrippa from the camp to the house where he had lived before his imprisonment.[80]

Josephus' description of this final house arrest suggests an interesting parallel to Paul's accommodation in Caesarea and Rome: "After that he had no hardship to fear, for though he was still guarded and watched, yet the watch on his daily activities was relaxed."[81] The important facts to remember are that because of Agrippa's status and relationship to Antonia he could gain several concessions that would have been impossible for one of lesser status or one who did not possess his connections. Furthermore, Agrippa is watched over by a centurion. Important prisoners were guarded

[76] *Antiquities*, xviii, 192.
[77] *Antiquities*, xviii, 195.
[78] *Antiquities*, xviii, 203.
[79] *Antiquities*, xviii, 233.
[80] *Antiquities*, xviii, 235.
[81] *Antiquities*, xviii, 235.

by soldiers of high rank. Finally, even after Tiberius' death, Gaius believes that it would be unwise simply to release Agrippa at once. Hence, Agrippa is placed under the lightest of house arrests and assumes a lifestyle similar to that which he had before his initial trouble with Tiberius.

From the writings of Sallust, Philostratus, and Josephus, it is apparent that those of differing status could be held in various forms of custody. Furthermore, it can be assumed that those of high status consistently would have received lighter custody than those of low social status. The rescript in the *Digest*, presented above, only confirms that this practice was not limited to the late Roman Empire but was accepted from, at the very least, the first century, if not long before.

It is undeniable that from Acts 21 until the conclusion of Luke's two volumes, Paul is held in some form of custody. Mention has been made of Paul's and Silas' treatment in Philippi. It is only necessary to add a description of their imprisonment: "Following these instructions, he put them in the innermost cell and fastened their feet in the stocks" (16:24). This is hardly the prison of Apollonius and the other men of status and might well be closer to that of the final cell of Lentulus, or the first cell of Agrippa mentioned above. It is no wonder that the magistrates would be so embarrassed by Paul's declaration of his Roman citizenship. They had not simply held a Roman citizen in custody; rather, they had placed Paul in a prison normally reserved for those of low status.

After his presentation to the crowd and his statement before the chief priests and the council, Paul was taken and held in the barracks of the Roman garrison. Since he had already acknowledged that he was a Roman citizen by birth and was, furthermore, proud of his citizenship of the Greek city of Tarsus, he was held alone under the protection of a centurion. According to Luke, Paul's nephew visited him with no reported interference. This suggests that Paul was held in light custody more for his protection than for punishment (23:16). That Paul ordered the centurion who was guarding him to take his nephew to the tribune is just one more instance, of which there are many, of Paul's assuming control and ordering Roman officers to follow his directions. Although not explicitly stated, the portrait created by Luke shows that Paul was waited on by the Roman soldiers rather than guarded by them.

After the plans of the Jews who wished to kill Paul were disclosed to the tribune, Luke reported that Paul was then moved to

Caesarea. According to Luke, 200 soldiers, 70 horsemen, and 200 spearmen were required to guard Paul on his journey to Caesarea. It is inconceivable that Paul would need that much protection against a band of Jews. Again, this indicates the author's concern to emphasize Paul's importance (23:23).

Luke's understanding of Paul's custody upon arrival in Caesarea is unknown, but the description of his imprisonment after the trial is reminiscent of Josephus' description of Agrippa's final custody: "Then he ordered the centurion to keep him in custody but to let him have some liberty and not to prevent any of his friends from taking care of his needs" (24:23).

Luke used the word ἄνεσις to describe Paul's relaxation of custody. This is the same word used by Josephus to describe Agrippa's light imprisonment after Caligula had allowed him to return to the house where he had lived before his arrest. Implied in this scene in Acts is that Paul could not only receive visitors but was, for all practical purposes, free under the recognizance of a centurion.[82]

It is mentioned that Paul was guarded by a centurion. This implies that he was a prisoner of status and importance. In the absence of contrary evidence, one can assume that Paul remained in this light custody until his journey to Rome.

Julius and the Augustan cohort

After the "appeal", Paul was sent to Rome. Luke reports that Paul was guarded by Julius, a centurion of the Augustan cohort. Ramsay, many years ago, argued that σπεῖρα Σεβαστή was not a Greek translation of any specific Latin military cohort but was intended to be translated "troop of the emperor."[83] Hence, the intention was to portray Paul as a prisoner worthy of such a guard. T. S. Broughton, and more recently R. W. Davies, have argued that σπεῖρα Σεβαστή referred to the Cohors I Augusta, known to have been an auxiliary troop stationed in Syria in the first century.[84]

---

[82] *Beginnings*, vol. IV, p. 304.

[83] Ramsay, *St. Paul the Traveller*, p. 315.

[84] *Beginnings*, vol. V, pp. 427–445; G. L. Cheesman, *The Auxilia of the Roman Imperial Army* (Oxford: Clarendon Press, 1914), pp. 45–48; R. W. Davies, "The Daily Life of the Roman Soldier under the Principate," *ANRW* vol. II.1, pp. 299–338; J. B. Campbell, *The Emperor and the Roman Army 31 B.C.-A.D. 235* (Oxford: Clarendon Press, 1984); L. Keppie, *The Making of the Roman Army from Republic to Empire* (London: B. T. Batsford, 1984); G. Webster, *The Roman Imperial Army of the First and Second Centuries A.D.*, 3rd edn (London: Adam and Charles Black, 1985).

According to Broughton, the Cohors Augusta did not possess any significant status and Julius, while being a centurion, would not have possessed the status of a legionary centurion and, despite his name, would probably not even have been a Roman citizen. However, Broughton confesses to some confusion: "It is perhaps surprising that a centurion of a Syrian auxiliary Cohors Augusta should have been given charge of an important prisoner on the road to Rome, for we should expect at least a legionary centurion ... In the absence, however, of evidence ... the question must be left open."[85] Although Broughton's and Davies' expertise should not be dismissed, on this point Ramsay's more sensitive reading of the text has allowed him to perceive the importance of the Lucan intention behind this scene. Neither Luke, who would be following his sources, nor his audience would have been experts in military terminology. One can only wonder if the name of Julius, who was a centurion in a cohors named after Augustus, would not have echoed sufficient prestige to serve Luke's purpose. Broughton might have identified the true historical background behind Luke's source, but, in this instance, finding the historical referent does not necessarily uncover the true intention of Luke.

Luke was more concerned with impressions than historical precision. Here the reader is left with the impression that Paul, as would be expected of a man of high social status, was guarded by one corresponding to the status given to the prisoner.

Other status indicators

Luke reports that Julius allowed Paul to leave the ship at Sidon to visit friends and be cared for. While this is, as the text indicates, an act of kindness, it also indicates Paul's freedom of movement which would be naturally associated with one of high social standing. Given that most of Paul's friends mentioned by Luke in Acts are among the élite of the provinces, this scene presents implications which go far beyond the mere reporting of an event. Furthermore, it is at this point in the narrative that Paul's custody fades into the background and what is emphasized is his control, his courage, his leadership, and his piety. These are characteristic virtues which would have had important overtones to the reader of the first century.

---

[85] Broughton, *Beginnings*, vol. V, p. 433.

There are several other smaller details in Luke's account of Paul's journey to Rome which would have been meaningful for Luke's first audience. Paul is entertained by Publius who, it is often noted, is the Roman official of Malta. In Acts 28:11 Luke describes the departure from Malta at the end of the hazardous winter season. The ship, upon which Paul traveled to Rome originated in Alexandria and sailed under the figurehead of the "heavenly twins" Castor and Pollux, who were "sons of Zeus" and the patron deities of navigators.[86] Of great importance, considering this scene in Acts, is that these heavenly twins were also the patron deities of the innocent, guardians of the truth, and punishers of perjurers. Furthermore, D. Ladouceur mentions that Castor and Pollux were also patrons of the equestrian order.[87]

This one small detail, whether part of a source or intentionally inserted by Luke, would inspire a number of important associations in the mind of the Greco-Roman reader. Paul had been declared not guilty on a number of occasions and the reader would, by now, be assured of Paul's innocence. The mention of Castor and Pollux would only emphasize this fact once again. In addition, that Luke is conscious of highlighting Paul's social status is also reflected by the mention of the "heavenly twins."

Another small detail, not formally connected with the technical legal issues of Acts but which would have indicated to the first reader/hearer that Paul was no ordinary man, is found in Acts 28:15 where Luke writes: "The believers from there, when they heard of us, came as far as the Forum of Appius and Three Taverns to meet us." Luke, or his source, uses the word ἀπάντησις to describe the meeting of those Christians who had come such a long way to welcome Paul as he landed in Italy. F. F. Bruce suggested that this word was used in a technical sense as a term applied for an official welcome of a newly arrived dignitary.[88] In a more recent discussion of the semantic range of the word, F. W. Danker noticed Acts 28:15 and believed that the noun was so employed in order to impress Luke's audience with "the prestige enjoyed by the Pauline entourage."[89] The term is also found in the inscription describing the meeting between the envoys and Eumenes II.[90]

---

[86] Horace, *Odes*, i.3.2; iii 29.64; *Beginnings*, vol. IV, pp. 343–344; R. Harris, *Cult of the Heavenly Twins* (Cambridge: Cambridge University Press, 1906).
[87] Ladouceur, "Shipwreck and Pollution," 445.
[88] Bruce, *Acts*, p. 475.
[89] Danker, "Benefactor," p. 415 note 62;
[90] Dittenberger, *OGIS*, 763.4, vol. II, pp. 505–506.

Furthermore, the first-person narration in Acts 28 has striking similarities with Caesar Augustus' account of the greeting he received from the consul, Q. Lucretius, and other prominent individuals:

> At the same time, by decree of the Senate, a portion of the praetors and tribunes of the plebs, together with the consul Q. Lucretius, and the men of note, were sent as far as Campania to meet my arrival, an honour which up to this day, has been decreed to none other by myself.[91]

These are, it is granted, small points. But they seem to indicate that Luke was aware of the nuances of the words he used and sensitive to the scenes that his construction of the scenes in Acts would give to his audience. If it is correct that in these last eight chapters Luke has intentionally described Paul as a man of *dignitas* deserving the advantages due his status, then the word ἀπάντησις, at this point in the narrative, is likewise meaningful.

A full description of Paul's custody in Rome is not provided in the text except at 28:16. T. Mommsen argued that Paul's custody was indeed lenient.[92] Although much of Mommsen's work has recently been re-evaluated, on this point there is no dissension. Garnsey favorably compares Lentulus' custody, noted above, with Paul's: "both were held under *libera custodia* which ... was a mild form of detention one reserved (in Imperial times, at any rate) for men of high status."[93]

Debate continues over the precise meaning of the various references to Paul's dwelling in Rome.[94] However, Paul's privacy and freedom are assured and the final picture the reader/hearer receives of Paul is one of financial independence and social worth. According to Luke, Paul has been allowed this degree of freedom because he is a man who deserves such treatment.

In conclusion, it is no mere coincidence that Paul's imprisonment and treatment are lenient by any standards. Luke was concerned to show that even during his trials, Paul was treated as one would expect a defendant of high social status to be treated. From the perspective of a twentieth-century reader, such subtlety on the part

---

[91] *Res Gestae Divi Augusti* 12, trans. C. K. Barrett *The New Testament Background: Selected Documents*, p. 1.
[92] Mommsen, *Römische Strafrecht*, p. 317 note 5.
[93] Garnsey, *Social Status and Legal Privileges*, p. 147.
[94] Pliny, *Letters*, x,57; Haenchen, *Acts*, p. 718.

of Luke might seem farfetched. Nevertheless, what seems subtle today was clearly understood in the first century. In addition, even today there exists a relationship between one's social status and one's treatment in the courts and in prison. Luke's sensitivity in Acts is not so farfetched after all.

Conclusion

In these last two chapters specific scenes in Acts have been evaluated in terms of what can be known about the Roman law and legal procedure in the first century of the Common Era. The initial task was to investigate not only specific laws and rescripts, but also to understand the fundamental presuppositions behind these laws. Although Roman citizens had both social and legal advantages over those who were not Roman citizens, it is also apparent that there were recognized social and legal distinctions between citizens themselves. Those of wealth, prestige, and high social status could take advantage of the legal privileges which, at least on paper, were given to all Roman citizens.

A defense attorney emphasized the *dignitas* of the individual he was defending and pleaded the case with due stress on the character of the accused. Courts were more likely to be lenient in sentencing those who could establish their pedigree and *auctoritas* than those who could not.

Moreover, it appears that judges took account of the status of the prisoner before declaring punishment and considering the type of custody in which the prisoner was to be held. Those of low social status were more likely to face severe punishment than those of high social status. It is true that it was not until the time of Hadrian that explicit mention was made in the laws themselves of a legal distinction between individuals of high and low status. However, the formalization of status distinction was a final articulation of what was always taken for granted. In other words, it seems that it was always the case that those individuals who were poor, who did not have a wealthy benefactor, who were not of the upwardly mobile, or who were not from the best families, could not assume the full benefits of the legal privileges that were, *de jure*, not denied them.

In addition, after the investigation of the primary evidence, it was discovered that provincial magistrates and governors wielded a great degree of authority and jurisdiction. They often assumed legal police powers or abused their responsibilities in punishing Roman citizens. The sources indicate that these "exceptions" – if they were indeed exceptions – were so common that it would be difficult to establish without doubt that the laws were, in all cases, binding or extensively followed. Citizens might cry out "*provoco!*" but this did not always halt the proceedings, nor did it automatically lead to a court of second instance.

Likewise an individual might exclaim "*civis Romanus sum!*," yet this was not a guarantee that the one who declared his citizenship would be sent to Rome or protected from harsh punishment. The evidence indicated that although governors could send prisoners to Rome, and often did so, it was usually not to the advantage of the one being sent. Only those wealthy and prestigious provincial Romans could influence a court or governor to send their case to Rome with hopes of a more favorable hearing.

In the light of this understanding of Roman law in the provinces, and our claim that the portrayal of Paul in Acts was deliberately shaped by the author to emphasize Paul's social status and moral virtue, it was necessary to study those accounts where according to Luke, Paul was confronted by Roman authorities. In Acts 16, Paul was beaten and thrown into the inner prison in Philippi. When Paul and Silas were released the next day, Paul declared his citizenship and the magistrates became afraid. It has usually been assumed that Paul would have automatically been protected from beatings and imprisonments on the strength of the *lex Porcia* and *lex Julia*. Yet, from the investigation of the various legal issues involved, there would have been no reason for the fear of the magistrates unless they discovered that the citizen who was before them was also one who would have influence with the governor, or could exact revenge. The declaration of citizenship is a dramatic insertion in order to make a distinctive contrast between Paul and the magistrates and Roman citizens of Philippi.

Likewise, in Acts 22, the tribune had not broken any law. He was fearful when he discovered that Paul was not only a citizen, but a citizen of inherited status from Tarsus. That the tribune was about to treat a citizen of such standing in a manner usually reserved for slaves was a serious breach of social convention.

Admittedly, it is difficult to discern how much of these narratives is based on factual reports and how much is editorial insertion. However, judged in terms of Paul's own account in his letters, and compared with the traditions saved in other early Christian writers of his various tribulations, it seems certain that Luke did not know about, or more likely chose not to include, information of Paul's harsh treatments.

The actual legal issues involved in Paul's appeal to Nero, as reported in Acts 25, are somewhat different from those mentioned by Luke in Acts 16 and 22. In Luke's account of Paul's hearing before Festus it is not a matter of magisterial *coercitio* that is at stake, but rather the citizen's right to have his case moved to Rome in order to be heard before the emperor. However, the evidence does not suggest that the provincial authority was obligated to transfer a case to Rome. It appears that only those individuals of prestige and importance could influence the governor in the matter of where the court was to be heard.

The first readers/hearers of Acts would have recognized and understood both the explicit and implicit status indicators given to them by Luke. They also would have realized that the Paul of Acts was a man of such status and prestige that he could presume to influence the governor and arrange for his case to be heard by Nero in Rome. Luke emphasized Paul's control by showing that the Roman authority deferred to him. Roman deference does not mean that Roman authority was just or lenient. Rather, what it indicates is that Paul, as described by Luke, was recognized as a man of social status.

H. B. Rackham, who often shows a perceptive insight into the literary and rhetorical issues that belies his generally conservative commentary, had this to say about Paul's appeal to Caesar: "The appeal to Caesar shows the vast strides Christianity has made. In thirty years it takes us from the Galilean company in the upper chamber to the imperial palace at Rome ... to the highest tribunal in the Empire, Caesar."[95] What Rackham is aware of is the sense of movement in Luke-Acts from rural Galilee to imperial Rome and the social consequences of such a move. This sense of upward mobility and movement towards the center of the empire is what Luke wanted to stress above all else.

[95] Rackham, *Acts*, p. 403.

CONCLUSION

The purpose of this work was to investigate the Lucan portrayal of Paul. The evidence suggests that Luke was highlighting, if not creating, Paul's high social status and moral virtue. By the end of Acts, the Paul who has been described is, quite frankly, too good to be true.

Two questions remain: why would Luke have done this? To whom was Luke writing? It would presume too much to seek complete answers here. However, our study suggests a certain direction in which to go to resolve these crucial queries.

The majority of present day scholars are convinced that Luke-Acts was written for a specific Christian community. Furthermore, there is a growing consensus which describes Luke as a pastor writing to assuage the anxiety of his congregation in the time in between Jesus' ascension and his return. Issues such as the Church's relationship to Judaism and the individual Christian's relationship to Roman authority, among others, are at the forefront of this supposed Lucan community.

However, the very style and substance of Acts does not fit this hypothesis. From the opening dedicatory preface to Theophilus in Luke to the close of Acts where Paul is preaching unhindered in the capital of the empire, the mood of Luke's work is expansive and evangelistic, not introspective and defensive. Luke-Acts was written as much for the non-believer as the believer.

E. Schüssler-Fiorenza believes that not enough attention has been paid to what she calls the "public-societal dimension of Christian literature."[1] Schüssler-Fiorenza understands the early Christian movement and its literature as rooted in the attempt to attract and convince persons of the Hellenistic world be they Christian, Jew

[1] E. Schüssler-Fiorenza, "Miracles, Mission and Apologetics: An Introduction," in Schüssler-Fiorenza, *Aspects*, p. 1.

or Pagan. The evidence about Paul from Acts would confirm Schüssler-Fiorenza's insights.

Luke himself identifies the audience to whom the work is addressed. Luke does not dismiss individual Jews, although he no longer believes that all Jews will convert. The number of Greeks and Romans who are mentioned, particularly those of high standing, suggests that Luke intended his writing for the larger Greco-Roman world. Moreover, the numerous instances in the narrative of God-fearers and other Gentiles who are worshiping in the synagogue indicate that Luke recognized this important mission field. However, he does not forget those who are on the fringes of society, as the Magnificat and the Lucan Beatitudes show. There is a universality to Luke's gospel that is inclusive of everyone.

Luke, above all, wished to present Christianity as a vibrant, universal, and unstoppable faith. Jesus, despite his humble origin, was the authoritative Son of God who was the giver of true status and virtue. Paul, who had the social credentials, was not finally a man of ἀρετή until he recognized the status of Jesus.

Christianity could no longer be perceived only as the faith of the uneducated masses. To Luke, Paul was the one character who could be held up as an example to those of high social status to imitate and for those of low social status to claim. From now on Christians could be found in the upper circles of the Hellenistic world and belief was now a mark of social distinction.

However, Luke must be defended from simply accepting the structures of the secular social hierarchy and merely assimilating the faith to it. For in Acts the various characters are confronted by the power of the risen Jesus in word and in action and forced to respond to it. One's social status is of little consequence unless one recognizes the ultimate status of Jesus.

SELECT BIBLIOGRAPHY

Achtemeier, P. J. "An Elusive Unity: Paul, Acts and the Early Church," *CBQ* 48 (1986), 1–26
"Gospel Miracle and the Divine Man," *Interpretation* 26 (1972), 174–197
Adkins, A. W. H. *Merit and Responsibility: A Study in Greek Values* (Oxford: Clarendon Press, 1960)
Alexander, L. "Luke's Preface in the Context of Greek Preface Writing," *NovT* 28 (1986), 48–74
Alon, G. *Jews, Judaism and The Classical World*, trans. I. Abrahams (Jerusalem: The Hebrew University, 1977)
Applebaum, S. *Jews and Greeks in Ancient Cyrene* (Leiden: E. J. Brill, 1979)
"The Legal Status of The Jewish Communities in The Diaspora," in Safrai, Stern, Flusser and van Unnik *The Jewish People* vol. I, pp. 420–463
"The Organization of The Jewish Community in The Diaspora," in Safrai, Stern, Flusser, and van Unnik, *The Jewish People*, vol. I, pp. 464–503
"The Social and Economic Status of Jews in The Diaspora," in Safrai, Stern, Flusser, and van Unnik, *The Jewish People*, vol. II, pp. 701–727
Baeck, L. *The Pharisees and Other Essays* (New York: Schocken Books, 1947)
Barber, B. *Social Stratification: A Comparative Analysis of Structure and Process* (New York: Harcourt, Brace and World, Inc., 1957)
Barnes, T. D. "An Apostle on Trial," *JTS* 20 (1969), pp. 407–419
Baron, S. W. *A Social and Religious History of the Jews* (New York: Columbia University Press, 1966)
Barrett, C. K. "Acts and The Pauline Corpus," *ET* 88 (1976–1977), 2–5
Luke The Historian in Recent Study (London: Epworth Press, 1961)
The New Testament Background: Selected Documents (rev. and ed.) (London: S.P.C.K., 1987)
"Pauline Controversies in the Post-Pauline Period," *NTS* 20 (1974), 229–245
"Paul Shipwrecked," in B. P. Thompson (ed.) *Scripture; Meaning and Method. Essays Presented to Anthony Tyrrell Hanson* (Hull: The Hull University Press, 1987)
Bartchy, S. S. *First Century Slavery and 1st Corinthians 7:21, SBLDS* 11 (Missoula, Mont.: Scholars Press, 1972)

Bauman, R. A. "The Leges Iudiciorum Publicorum and Their Interpretation in the Republic and Later Empire," *ANRW* vol. II, 13 pp. 103–233

Baur, F. C. *Paul The Apostle of Jesus Christ, His Life and Work, His Epistles and His Doctrine*, rev. E. Zeller, trans. A. Menzies (Edinburgh: Williams and Norgate 1876)

Becker, J. C. *Paul the Apostle: The Triumph of God in Life and Thought* (Edinburgh: T. & T. Clark, 1980)

Belkin, J. "The Problem of Paul's Background," *JBL* 54 (1935), 41–60

Bendix, R. and S. M. Lipset. *Class, Status and Power: Social Stratification in Comparative Perspective* (London: The Macmillan Co., 1966)

Benko, S. and J. J. O'Rourke. *The Catacombs and The Colosseum: The Roman Empire as the Setting of Primitive Christianity* (Valley Forge: Judson Press, 2nd Printing, 1977)

Benoit, A., K. Philonenko, and C. Vogel. *Paganisme, Judaïsme, Christianisme: Influences et affrontements dans le monde antique, Mélanges offerts à Marcel Simon* (Paris: Editions E. De Boccard, 1978)

Betz, H. D. (ed.) *Plutarch's Ethical Writings and Early Christian Literature* (Leiden: E. J. Brill, 1978)

Black, M. "Paul and Roman Law in Acts," *Restoration Quarterly* 24 (1981) 209–218

Bleicken, J., "Provocatio," *PRE* vol. XXIII.2, pp. 2,444–2,463

"Ursprung und Bedeutung der Provocation," *Zeitschrift für Rechsgeschichte* 76 (1959), 324–377

Böhlig, H. *Die Geisteskultur von Tarsos in augusteischen Zeitalter mit Berücksichtigung der paulinischen Schriften* (Göttingen: Vandenhoeck and Ruprecht, 1913)

Boer, M. C. de. "Images of Paul in the Post-Apostolic Age," *CBQ* 42 (1980), 359–380

Boer, W. P. de. *The Imitation of Paul: An Exegetical Study* (Kampen: J. H. Kok, 1962)

Borgen, P. "From Paul to Luke," *CBQ* 31 (1969) 168–182

Bornkamm, G. *Paul*, trans. D. M. G. Stalker (reprinted London: Hodder and Stoughton, 1975)

Brawley, R. L. *Luke-Acts and the Jews: Conflict, Apology and Conciliation* (SBL Monograph Series 33, Atlanta: Scholars Press, 1987)

"Paul in Acts: Lucan Apology and Conciliation," *New Perspectives*, pp. 129–147

Brecht, C. H. "Zum römischen Komitalverfahren," *Zeitschrift für Rechtsgeschichte* 59, 1939, 261–314

Brewer, E. "Roman Citizenship and its Bearing on the Book of Acts," *Restoration Quarterly* 3 (1961), 205–219

Brown, S. "The Role of The Prologues in Determining The Purpose of Luke-Acts," *Perspectives*, pp. 99–111

Bruce, F. F. *The Acts of the Apostles* (London: The Tyndale Press, 1951)

"The Acts of the Apostles: Historical Record or Theological Reconstruction," *ANRW*, vol. II, 25.3, pp. 2,569–2,603

"Is the Paul of Acts the Real Paul?," *BJRL* 58 (1976), 282–305

Paul: Apostle of the Free Spirit (London: Paternoster Press, 1978)

"St. Paul in Rome," *BJRL* 46 (1964), 326–345

Budesheim, T. "Paul's Abschiedsrede in the Acts of the Apostles," *HTR* 69 (1976), 9–30

Burchard, C. *Der dreizehnte Zeuge: Traditions-und Kompositions- geschichtliche Untersuchungen zu Lukas' Darstellung der Frühzeit des Paulus* (Göttingen: Vandenhoeck and Ruprecht, 1970)

"Paulus in der Apostelgeschichte," *TL* 12 (1975), 881–895

Buss, S. *Roman Law and History in The New Testament* (London: Rivington's, 1901)

Cadbury, H. J. *The Book of Acts in History* (London: The Macmillan Co., 1927)

The Making of Luke-Acts (London: The Macmillan Co., 1927)

"Roman Law and the Trial of Paul," *Beginnings*, vol. V, pp. 297–338

Callistratus, *The Digest of Justinian* ed. T. Mommsen, trans. A. Watson, 4 vols. (Philadelphia: The University of Pennsylvania Press, 1985)

Campbell, J. B. *The Emperor and The Roman Army 31 B.C.-A.D. 225* (Oxford: Clarendon Press, 1984)

Carcopino, J. *Daily Life in Ancient Rome: The People and The City at the Height of The Empire*, trans. E. O. Lorimoer (New Haven: Yale University Press, 1941)

Carrez, M. "L'appel de Paul à César (Ac 25,11)," in *De la Torah au Messie*, ed. M. Carrez, J. Doré, and P. Grelot (Paris: Descleé, 1981), pp. 503–510

Cassidy, R. J. and P. J. Scharper, *Political Issues in Luke-Acts* (Maryknoll: Orbis Books, 1983)

Casson, L. *Travel in the Ancient World* (London: Allen and Unwin Ltd., 1974)

Clark, G. "The Social Status of Paul," *ET* 96 (1984–1985), 110–111

Conzelmann, H. L. *The Acts of the Apostles* (Hermeneia), rev. and trans. J. Limburg, J. T. Kraabel, D. H. Juel, edited E. T. Epp, and C. R. Matthews (Philadelphia: Fortress Press, 1987)

"Luke's Place in the Development of Early Christianity," *SLA*, pp. 289–309

The Theology of St. Luke, trans. G. Boswell (London: Faber and Faber, 1960)

Corley, B. C. (ed.) *Colloquy on New Testament Studies: A Time for Reappraisal and Fresh Approaches* (Atlanta: Mercer University Press, 1983)

Craft, R. A. "Judaism on the World Scene," in Benko and O'Rourke, *The Catacombs and the Colosseum*, pp. 81–98

Cranfield, C. E. B. *A Critical and Exegetical Commentary on St. Paul's Letter to the Romans*, ICC (Edinburgh: T. & T. Clark, 1975)

Crehan, J. H. "The Purpose of Luke in Acts," *Studia Evangelica* 2 (1964), 354–368

Daniélou, J. *Gospel Message and Hellenistic Culture* (Philadelphia: Westminster, 1973)

Danker, F. W. "The Endangered Benefactor in Luke-Acts," in *SBL Sem Pap* (1981), pp. 39–48

"Graeco-Roman Cultural Accommodation in the Christology of Luke-Acts," *SBL Sem Pap* (1983), pp. 391–414

"Reciprocity in The Ancient World and in Acts 15:23–29," *PLA*, pp. 49–58

Davies, P. "The Ending of Acts," *ET* 94 (1983), 334–5

Davies, W. D. *Paul and Rabbinic Judaism* (London: S.P.C.K., 1962)

Deissmann, A. *Paul: A Study in Social and Religious History* trans. W. E. Wilson (London: Hodder and Stoughton, 1926)

Delling, G. "Das letzte Wort der Apostelgeschichte," *NovT* 15 (1973), pp. 193–204

Derrett, J. D. M. *Law in the New Testament* (London: Darton, Longman and Todd, 1970)

"Luke's Perspective on Tribute to Caesar," *PLA*, pp. 38–48

Dibelius, M. "The Speeches in Acts and Ancient Historiography," *Studies*, pp. 138–185

Dibelius, M. and W. G. Kümmel, *Paul*, trans. F. Clarke (London: Longmans Green and Co., 1953)

Dillon, R. J. "Previewing Luke's Project From His Prologue (Lk. 1:1–4), *CBQ* 43 (1981), 205–227

Dodd, C. H. "The Mind of Paul: A Psychological Approach," *BJRL* 17 (1933)

"The Mind of Paul: Change and Development," *BJRL* 18, 1934

Dodds, E. R. *Pagan and Christian in an Age of Anxiety: Some Aspects of Religious Experience from Marcus Aurelius to Constantine* (Cambridge: Cambridge University Press, 1965)

Conelson, L. R. "Cult Histories and The Sources of Acts," *Biblica* 68 (1987), pp. 1–27

Downey, G. *Ancient Antioch* (Princeton: Princeton University Press, 1963)

A History of Antioch in Syria: From Seleucus to the Arab Conquest (Princeton: Princeton University Press, 1961)

Duff, A. M. *Freedmen in the Early Roman Empire* (Cambridge: W. Heffer and Sons Ltd., 1958)

Dupont, J. *The Sources of Acts*, trans. K. Pond (London: Darton, Longmann, and Todd, 1964)

Earl, D. "Prologue in Ancient Historiography," *ANRW*, vol. I, 2, pp. 842–856

Easton, B. S. "The Purpose of Acts," *Theology Occasional Papers* 6 (London: S.P.C.K., 1936)

Ehrenberg, V. and Jones, A. H. M. *Documents Illustrating the Reigns of Augustus and Tiberius*, 2nd edn (Oxford: Clarendon Press, 1955)

Enslin, M. S. "Paul and Gamaliel," *JR* 7 (1927), 360–375

Fascher, E. "Paulus," *PRE* vol. VIII, pp. 431–466

Feldman, L. H. "The Orthodoxy of the Jews in Hellenistic Egypt," *JJS* 22 (1960), 215–237

Ferguson, J. *Moral Values in The Ancient World* (London: Methuen and Co., Ltd., 1958)

The Religions of the Roman Empire

Finkelstein, L. *The Pharisees: The Sociological Background of Their Faith*, 2 vols. (Philadelphia: The Jewish Publication Society of America, 1938)

Fisher, N. R. E. "Hybris and Dishonour: II," *Greece and Rome* 26 (1979), 32–47

Frey, J. B. (ed.) *Corpus Inscriptionum Iudaicarum* (Rome: Pontificio Instituto Do Archeologia Cristiana, 1952)

Freyne, S. *Galilee from Alexander the Great to Hadrian 325 B.C.E. to 135 C.E.: A study of 2nd Temple Judaism*

Funk, A. *Status und Rollen in den Paulusbriefen: Eine inhaltsanalytische Untersuchung zur Religionssoziologie* (Vienna: Tyrolia-Verlag, 1981)

Gager, J. G. "Jews, Gentiles and Synagogues in the Book of Acts," *HTR* 79 (1986), 91–99

　　Kingdom and Community: The Social World of Early Christianity (Englewood Cliffs, N.J.: Prentice Hall, 1975)

　　The Origins of Anti-Semitism: Attitudes Towards Judaism in Pagan and Christian Antiquity (Oxford: Oxford University Press, 1983)

　　"Religion and Social Class in the Early Roman Empire," *Catacombs and the Colosseum*, pp. 99–120

Garnsey, P. "The Criminal Jurisdiction of Governors," *JRS* 58 (1968), 51–59

　　"Legal Privileges in the Roman Empire," in M. I. Finey, *Studies in Ancient Society*, pp. 141–165

　　"The Lex Julia and Appeal Under the Empire," *JRS* 56 (1966), 167–189

　　Non-Slave Labour in the Greco-Roman World (Cambridge: Philological Society, 1980)

　　Social Status and Legal Privileges in The Roman Empire (Oxford: Clarendon Press, 1970)

Gasque, W. W. "A Fruitful Field: Recent Study of The Acts of the Apostles," *Interpretation* 42 (1988), 117–131

　　A History of Criticism of the Acts of the Apostles (Grand Rapids: Eerdmans, 1975)

Georgi, D. "Socioeconomic Reasons for the 'Divine Man' as a Propagandistic Pattern," in Schüssler-Fiorenza, *Aspects of Religious Propaganda*, pp. 27–42

Ginzberg, L. *The Legends of the Jews*, 7 vols. (Philadelphia: The Jewish Publication Society of America, 5th imprint, 1974)

Glotz, G. *The Greek City and Its Institutions* (London: Routledge & Kegan Paul, reprinted 1969)

Goldstein, J. "Jewish Acceptance and Rejection of Hellenism," in Sanders, Baumgarten, and Mendelson, *Jewish and Christian Self-Definition* vol. II: *Aspects of Judaism in the Graeco-Roman Period* (London: S.C.M. Press, 1981), pp. 64–87

Goodenough, E. R. *Jewish Symbols in the Greco-Roman Period*, 12 vols. (New York: Bollingen Foundation, 1965)

　　"The Perspective of Acts," *SLA*, pp. 51–59

Goodfellow, C. E. "Roman Citizenship: A Study of its Territorial and Numerical Expansion from the Earliest Times to the Death of Augustus," unpublished dissertation, Bryn Mawr, Pa., Bryn Mawr College, 1935

Grant, R. M. "The Social Setting of Second Century Christianity," in Sanders, Baumgarten, and Mendelson, *Jewish and Christian Self-Definition*, vol. I, pp. 16–29

Green, W. S. *Approaches to Ancient Judaism: Studies in Judaism and its*

Greco-Roman Context vol. II, Brown Judaic Studies 9 (Chico, Calif.: Scholars Press, 1980)

Greenridge, A. H. J. *The Legal Procedure of Cicero's Time* (Oxford: Clarendon Press, 1901)

"The Porcian Coins and the Porcian Law," *Classical Review* 11, 1897, 434–440

Grenfell, B. P. and A. S. Hunt (eds.) *The Oxyrhynchus Papyri* (London Egyptian Exploration Fund, 1898–)

Gutmann, J. *Ancient Synagogues, The State of Research*, Brown Judaic Studies 22 (Chico, Calif.: Scholars Press, 1982)

Hadas, M. and M. Smith, *Hellenistic Culture: Fusion and Diffusion* (New York: Columbia University Press, 1959)

Haenchen, E. *The Acts of the Apostles*, trans. R. McL. Wilson (Oxford: Basil Blackwell, 1971)

Apostelgeschichte, Meyers Kommentar (Göttingen: Vandenhoeck and Ruprecht, 1959)

"The Book of Acts as Source Material for the History of Early Christianity," *SLA*, 258–279

Hands, A. R. *Charities and Social Aid in Greece and Rome* (London Thames and Hudson, 1968)

Hanfmann, G. M. A. *Sardis, From Prehistoric to Roman Times: Results of the Archaeological Exploration of Sardis, 1958–1975* (Cambridge, Mass.: Harvard University Press, 1983)

Hansack, E. "Er lebt ... von seinem eigenen Einkommen (*Apostelgeschichte*, 28, 30)," *BZ* 19 (1975), 249–253

Harrer, G. A., "Saul Who is Also Called Paul," *HTR* 33 (1940), 19–33

Harris, H. A. *Greek Athletics and the Jews* (Cardiff: The University of Wales Press, 1983)

Hedrick, C. "Paul's Conversion/Call: A Comparative Analysis of the Three Reports in Acts," *JBL* 100 (1981), 415–432

Hemer, C. J. "The Name of Paul," *Tyndale Bulletin* 36 (1985), 179–183

Hengel, M. *Acts and the History of Earliest Christianity*, trans. J. Bowden (London: S.C.M. Press, 1979)

Jews, Greeks and Barbarians: Aspects of the Hellenization of Judaism in the Pre-Christian Period (Philadelphia: Fortress Press, 1980)

Judaism and Hellenism: Studies in Their Encounter in Palestine During the Early Hellenistic Period 2 vols., trans. J. Bowden (London: S.C.M. Press, 1973)

Hock, R. F. "Paul's Tentmaking and The Problem of His Social Class," *JBL* 97 (1978), 555–564

The Social Context of Paul's Ministry: Tentmaking and Apostleship (Philadelphia: Fortress Press, 1980)

"The Workshop as a Social Setting for Paul's Missionary Preaching," *CBQ* 41 (1979), 438–450

Hollander, H. W. and M. de Jonge. *The Testament of the Twelve Patriarchs: A Commentary* (Leiden: E. J. Brill, 1985)

Holtheide, B. *Römische Burgerrechtpolitik und römische Neubürger in der Province Asia* (Düsseldorf: Hochschul-Sammlung Philosophie Politikwissen-schaft, 1983)

Horsley, G. H. R. *New Documents Illustrating Early Christianity: A Review of Greek Inscriptions and Papyri 1976–1980* (North Ryde: Macquarie University, The Ancient History Document Research Centre, 1981–1987)

Jacobson, G. R. "Paul in Luke-Acts: The Savior who is Present," *SBL Sem Pap* 1983, pp. 131–146

Jaeger, W. *Early Christianity and Greek Paideia* (Cambridge: Belknap Press, 1961)
  Paideia: The Ideals of Greek Culture. 3 vols. (Oxford: Basil Blackwell, 1939–45)

Jeremias, J. *Jerusalem in the Time of Jesus: An Investigation into Economic and Social Conditions During the New Testament Period*, trans. F. H. and C. H. Cave (London: S.C.M. Press, 1969)

Jervell, J. *God's Christ and His People* (Oslo: Universitetsforlaget, 1978)
  Luke and The People of God: A New Look at Luke-Acts (Minneapolis: Augsburg Publishing House, 1972)
  "Paulus in der Apostelgeschichte und die Geschichte des Urchristentum's, *NTS* 32 (1986), 378–392
  "Paul in the Acts of the Apostles: Tradition, History and Theology," in J. Kremer (ed.) *Les actes des Apôtres: Tradition rédaction, théologie (BETL 48)* (Louvain University Press, 1979) 297–305
  The Unknown Paul: Essays on Luke-Acts and Early Christian History (Minneapolis: Augsburg Publishing House, 1984)

Jeske, R. L. "Luke and Paul on the Apostle Paul," *Currents in Theology and Mission* 4 (1977), 28–38

Jewett, R. *A Chronology of Paul's Life* (Philadelphia: Fortress Press, 1979)

Jolowicz, H. F. and B. Nicholas, *Historical Introduction to Roman Law* (Cambridge: Cambridge University Press, 1972)

Jones, A. H. M. and M. Avi-Yonah (ed.) *Cities of the Eastern Roman Provinces* (Oxford: Clarendon Press, 1971)
  "Claudius and the Jewish Question at Alexandria," *JRS* 16 (1926) 17–35
  The Criminal Courts of the Roman Republic and Principate (Oxford: Basil Blackwell, 1972)
  The Greek City From Alexander to Justinian (Oxford, Clarendon Press, 1940)
  History of Rome Through the Fifth Century, vol. II: The Empire: Selected Documents (London: Macmillan and Co., 1970)
  "I Appeal to Caesar," *Studies in Roman Government and Law*, 51–65
  "Imperial and Senatorial Jurisdiction in the Early Principate," *Historia* 3 (1954–1955), 464–488
  Studies in Roman Government and Law (Oxford: Basil Blackwell, 1960)

Jonge, M. de. *The Testament of the Twelve Patriarchs: A Critical Edition of the Greek Text* (Leiden: E. J. Brill, 1985)

Judge, E. A. *Rank and Status in The World of The Caesars and St. Paul*, The Broadhead Memorial Lectures, 1981, University of Canterbury
  "St. Paul and Classical Society," *JAC* 15 (1972) 19–36
  The Social Pattern of Christian Groups in the First Century: Some Prolegomena to the Study of New Testament Ideas of Social Obligation (London: Tyndale Press, 1960)

Juel, D. *Luke-Acts* (London: SCM Press, 1983)

Karris, R. J. *Invitation to Acts: A Commentary on the Acts of the Apostles*, with complete text from the Jerusalem Bible (Garden City: Doubleday and Co., 1978)

"Missionary Community: A New Paradigm for the Study of Luke-Acts," *CBQ* 41 (1979), 80–97

"Poor and Rich: The Lukan Sitz im Leben," in *Perspectives*, 112–125

Kasher, A. *The Jews in Hellenistic and Roman Egypt: The Struggle for Equal Rights* (Tübingen: JCB Mohr (P. Siebeck) 1986)

Katzaoff, R. "Sources of Law in Roman Egypt," *ANRW*, vol. II, 13, pp. 807–844

Keaveney, A. "Civis Romanus Sum," *Critica Storica* 21 (1984), 345–372

Keck, L. E. *Social World of Early Christianity; A Bibliography*, unpublished bibliography, Yale University Divinity School, 1981

Keck, L. E. and Martyn, J. L. *Studies on Luke-Acts* (Nashville; Abingdon Press, 1966)

Kee, H. C. *Christian Origins in Sociological Perspective* (London: S.C.M. Press, 1980)

Kehnscherper, G. "Der Apostel Paulus als römisher Bürger," ed. F. L. Cross, *Studia Evangelica* ii (Berlin: Akademie Verlag, 1964), 411–440

Kelly, J. M. *Roman Litigation* (Oxford: Clarendon Press, 1966)

Studies in the Civil Judicature of the Roman Republic (Oxford: Clarendon Press, 1976)

Kelso, J. L. "Paul's Roman Citizenship as Reflected in his Missionary Experiences and His Letters," *Bibliotheca Sacra* 79 (1922), 173–183

Kennedy, G. A. *Classical Rhetoric and its Christian and Secular Tradition from Ancient to Modern Times* (London: Croom Helm, 1980)

The Art of Rhetoric in the Roman World, 300 B.C.–A.D. 300 (Princeton: Princeton University Press, 1972)

Knox, J. *Chapters in a Life of Paul* (New York: Abingdon Press, 1950)

Knox, W. L. *Some Hellenistic Elements in Primitive Christianity* (London: Oxford University Press, 1944)

Koester, H. *History, Culture, and Religion of the Hellenistic Age* (Philadelphia: Fortress Press, 1980)

Kraabel, A. T. "Paganism and Judaism: The Sardis Evidence," in *Paganisme, Judaïsme, Christianism: Influences et Affrontements dans le Monde Antique*, Mélanges offerts à Marcel Simon (Paris: Editions E. De Boccard, 1978), 13–33

"The Roman Diaspora: Six Questionable Assumptions," *JJS* 33, Essays in Honour of Y. Yadin, 1–2 (1982), 445–464

"Social Systems of Six Diaspora Synagogues," in J. Gutmann (ed.), *Ancient Synagogues, The State of Research*, 79–91

Kunkel, W. *An Introduction to Roman Legal and Constitutional History*, trans. J. M. Kelly (Oxford: Clarendon Press, 1966)

Untersuchungen zur Entwicklung des römischen Kriminalverfahrens in vorsullanischer Zeit. (Munich: Verlag der Bayerischen Akademie der Wissenschaften, 1962)

Kyrtatas, D. J. *The Social Structure of the Early Christian Communities* (London: Verso, 1987)

Ladouceur, D. "Hellenistic Preconceptions of Shipwreck and Pollution as a Context for Acts 27–28", *HTR* 66 (1973), 435–449

Lampe, P. "Paulus-Zeltmacher," *BZ* 31 (1987), 256–260

Lee, C. L. "Social Unrest and Primitive Christianity," *Catacombs and the Colosseum*, 121–138

Leeman, A. "Die ideale bürger in der Romeinse republiek," *Lampas* 18 (1985), 43–65

Lenski, G. E., "Status Crystallization: A Non-Vertical Dimension of Social Status," *ASR* 19 (1954), 405–413

Lightstone, J. N. *The Commerce of the Sacred: Meditations of the Divine Among Jews in the Greco-Roman Diaspora* (Brown Judaic Studies 59 (Chico, Calif.: Scholars Press, 1984)

Lindemann, A. *Paulus im ältesten Christentum* (Tubingen: JCB Mohr (P. Siebeck), 1979)

Lintott, A. W. "Provocatio From the Struggle of the Orders to the Principate," *ANRW*, vol. I, 2, 226–267

Lipsett, S. M. "Social Class," in *IESS*, vol. 15, pp. 296–316

Löning, K. *Die Saulustradition in der Apostelgeschichte* (Münster: Verlag Aschendorff, 1973)

"Paulinismus in der Apostelgeschichte," in K. Kertelge (ed.), *Paulus in den neutestamentlichen Spoatschriften* (Freiburg: Herder, 1981), 202–233

Lohfink, G. *Paulus vor Damaskus: Arbeitsweisen der neueren Bibelwissenschaft dargestellt an den Texten Apg. 9, 1–19; 22, 3–21; 26, 9–18* (Stüttgart: Verlag Katholisches Bibelwerk, 1966)

Lohse, E. *The New Testament Environment*, trans. J. E. Steely (London: S.C.M. Press, 1976)

Long, W. R. "The *Paulusbild* in the Trial of Paul in Acts," *SBL Sem Pap* (1983), 87–106

"The Trial of Paul in the Book of Acts: Historical, Literary, and Theological Considerations," unpublished Ph.D. dissertation, Brown University, Providence, R.I.

Lüdemann, G., *Das frühe Christentum nach den Traditionen der Apostelgeschichte: Ein Kommentar* (Göttingen: Vandenhoeck & Ruprecht, 1987)

Paul: Apostle to the Gentiles, trans. F. S. Jones (London: S.C.M. Press, 1984)

Lyall, F. "Roman Law in the Writings of St. Paul – Alien and Citizen," *Evangelical Quarterly* 48 (1976), 3–14

Slaves, Citizens, Sons: Legal Metaphors in the Epistles (Grand Rapids: Zondervan Publishing, 1984)

Lyons, G. *Pauline Autobiography. Towards A New Understanding*, *SBLDS* 73 (Atlanta: Scholars Press, 1985)

MacDonald, D. R. *The Legend and the Apostle: The Battle for Paul in Story and Canon* (Philadelphia: Westminster Press, 1983)

MacKenzie, R. K. "Character Description and Socio-Political Apologetic in the Acts of the Apostles," unpublished Ph.D. dissertation, Edinburgh University, 1984)

Macmullen, R. *Christianizing The Roman Empire (A.D. 100–400)* (London: Yale University Press, 1984)

Enemies of the Roman Order: Treason, Unrest and Alienation in the Empire (Cambridge, Mass.: Harvard University Press, 1967)
Roman Social Relations: 50 B.C. to A.D. 284 (London: Yale University Press, 1974)
Soldier and Civilian in the Late Roman Empire (Cambridge, Mass.: Harvard University Press, 1963)

Maddox, R. *The Purpose of Luke-Acts* (Göttingen: Vandenhoeck and Ruprecht, 1982)

Malherbe, A. J. *Social Aspects of Early Christianity* (Baton Rouge: Louisiana State University Press, 1977, 2nd Printing 1983)

Marshall, A. J. "The Survival and Development of International Jurisdiction in the Greek World Under Roman Rule," *ANRW*, vol. II, 13, 626–661

Marshall, I. H. *Acts*, Tyndale New Testament Commentries (Leicester: Inter-Varsity Press, 1980)
Luke: Historian and Theologian (Exeter: The Paternoster Press, 1970)

Martin, J. "Die Provocatio in der klassichen und spaten Republik," *Hermes* 78 (1970), 72–96

Mather, P. B. "Paul in Acts as Servant and Witness," *Biblical Research* 30 (1985), 23–44

Mattill, A. J. *Luke as an Historian in Criticism since 1840* (Ann Arbor: University Microfilms, 1973)
"Naherwartung, Fernerwartung, and the Purpose of Luke-Acts: Weymouth Reconsidered," *CBQ* 34 (1972), 276–293
"The Purpose of Acts: Schneckenburger Reconsidered," in W.W. Gasque and R.P. Martin (eds.), *Apostolic History and the Gospels*, Biblical and historical essays presented to F.F. Bruce (Exeter: The Paternoster Press, 1970)
"The Value of Acts as a Source for the Study of Paul," in C.H. Talbert, *Perspectives*, 76–98

Meeks, W. *The First Urban Christians: The Social World of the Apostle Paul* (London: Yale University Press, 1983)
The Moral World of the First Christians (London: S.P.C.K., 1986)
"The Social Context of Pauline Theology", *Interpretation* 36 (1982), 266–277
"The Social World of Early Christianity," *The Council on the Study of Religion Bulletin* 6 (1975), 1–5
"St. Paul of the Cities," in P.S. Howkins (ed.), *Civitas: Religious Interpretations of the City* (Atlanta: Scholars Press, 1986), 15–24

Michel, H.-J. *Die Abschiedsrede des Paulus an die Kirche. Apg 20, 17–38; Motivgeschichte und theologische Bedeutung* (Munich: Kösel, 1973)

Miles, G. B. and G. Trompf "Luke and Antiphon: The Theology of Acts 27–28 in the Light of Pagan Beliefs About Divine Retribution, Pollution and Shipwreck," *HTR* 69 (1976), 259–267

Millar, F. "Condemnation to Hard Labour in the Roman Empire, From the Julio-Claudians to Constantine," *PBSR* 62 (1984), 124–147
"The Development of Jurisdiction by Imperial Procurators: Further Evidence," *Historia* 14 (1965), 362–367

The Emperor in the Roman World (31 B.C. – A.D. 337 (London: Duckworth, 1977)

"The Emperor, The Senate and the Provinces," JRS 56 (1966), 156–166

Minear, P.S. "Dear Theo: The Kerygmatic Intention and Claim of the Book of Acts," Interpretation 27 (1973), 131–150

Mommsen, T. "Die Rechtsverhältnisse des Apostels Paulus," ZNW 2 (1901), 81–96

Römische Staatsrecht, in J. Marquardt, Handbuch der Römischen Altertumer (reprinted Graz: Akademische Druk-u. Verlagsanstalt, 1982)

Römische Staatsrecht (reprinted Munich: C. H. Beck'sche Verlagsbuchhandlaung (O. Beck), 1982)

Mommsen, T. and P. Krueger, trans. A. Watson, The Digest of Justinian, 4 vols. (Philadelphia: University of Pennsylvania Press, 1985)

Montefiore, C. G. Judaism and St. Paul (London: Max Goschen, 1914)

Neusner, J. (ed.) Christianity, Judaism and Other Greco-Roman Cults: Studies for Morton Smith at 60 (Leiden: E. J. Brill, 1975)

From Politics to Piety: The Emergence of Pharisaic Judaism (Englewood Cliffs, N.J.: Prentice Hall, 1973)

"Two Pictures of the Pharisees: Philosophical Circle or Eating Club," Anglican Theological Review 64 (1982), 525–538

Neyrey, J. "The Forensic Defense Speech and Paul's Trial Speeches in Acts 22–26: Form and Functions," New Perspectives, 210–224

North, H. Sophrosyne: Self-Knowledge and Self-Restraint in Greek Literature (Ithaca: Cornell University Press, 1966)

O'Toole, R. F. "Luke's notion of 'Be Imitators of Me as I am of Christ' in Acts 25–6," BThB 8 (1978), 155–161

"Luke's Position on Politics and Society in Luke–Acts," PLA, 1–17

"Why Did Luke Write Acts (Luke–Acts)?," BThB 7 (1977), 66–77

Perry, A. M. "Acts and the Roman Trial of Paul," HTR 17 (1924), 195–6

Pesch, R. Die Apostelgeschichte, 2 vols. (Zurich: Benziger Verlag, 1986)

Plümacher, E. "Acta-Forschung 1974–1982," TRu 48 (1983), 1–56

Lukas als hellenistischer Schriftsteller, Studien zur Apostelgeschichte (Göttingen: Vandenhoeck and Ruprecht, 1972)

Pokorny, P. "Die Romafahrt des Paulus und der Antike Roman," ZNW 64, 3–4 (1973), 233–244

Pomeroy, S. Goddesses, Whores, Wives and Slaves: Women in Classical Antiquity (New York: Schoken Press, 1975)

Praeder, S. M. "Miracle Worker and Missionary: Paul in the Acts of the Apostles," in SBL Sem Pap (1983), 107–129

Rabello, A. M. "The Legal Condition of the Jews in the Roman Empire," ANRW II, 13, 662–762

Rackham, R. B. The Acts of the Apostles (London: Methuen and Co., 1925)

Radl, W. Paulus und Jesus im lukanischen Doppelwerk: Untersuchungen zu Parallelmotiven in Lukasevangelium und in der Apostelgeschichte (Frankfurt: Peter Lang, 1975)

Rajak, T. "Jewish Rights in the Greek Cities Under Roman Rule: A New Approach," in W. S. Green, Approaches to Ancient Judaism, 19–36

"Was There a Roman Charter for the Jews?," JRS 74 (1984), 107–123

Ramsay, W. *The Cities of St. Paul* (London: Hodder and Stoughton, 1907)
"Corroboration: The Census List of Quirinius and Augustus and the Family and Rank of St. Paul," *The Expositor*, vol. IV (1901), 321–335
"The Jews in the Graeco-Roman Asiatic Cities," *The Expositor* (1902), 19–23; 92–109
St. Paul the Traveller and the Roman Citizen (London: Hodder and Stoughton, 1908)
"Tarsus," *The Expositor*, series 7, vol. I (1906), 258–277
Reekman, T. "Juvenal's View on Social Change," *Ancient Society* 2 (1971), 117–161
Reese, B. "The Apostle Paul's Exercise of his Rights as a Roman Citizen as Recorded in the Book of Acts," *Evangelical Quarterly*, 47 (1975), 138–145
Rogers, R. S. *Criminal Trials and Criminal Legislation Under Tiberius* (Middleton, Conn.: American Philological Association, 1935)
Roloff, J. "Die Paulus-Darstellung des Lukas: Ihre geschichtlichen Voraussetzungen und ihr theologisches Ziel," *EvTH* 6 (1979), 510–531
Rostovtzeff, M. *The Social and Economic History of the Hellenistic World*, 2 vols. (reprinted Oxford: Clarendon Press, 1959)
The Social and Economic History of the Roman Empire, 2 vols. (Oxford; Clarendon Press, reprint 1966)
Safrai, S., M. Stern, D. Flusser, and W. C. van Unnik, *The Jewish People in the First Century* (Philadelphia: Fortress Press, 1976)
Sanders, E. P. *Paul and Palestinian Judaism: A Comparison of Patterns of Religion* (Philadelphia: Fortress Press, 1977)
Sanders, E. P., A. I. Baumgarten, and A. Mendelson (eds.) *Jewish and Christian Self-Definition*, 2 vols. (London: S.C.M. Press, 1981)
Sanders, J. T. *The Jews in Luke-Acts* (London: S.C.M. Press, 1987)
Schneckenburger, M. *Ueber den Zweck der Apostelgeschichte* (Bern: Druck und Verlag von Chr. Fischer, 1841)
Schneider, G. "Der Zweck des lukanischen Doppelwerks," *BZ* 21–22 (1977–1978), 45–66
Schüssler-Fiorenza, E. *Aspects of Religious Propaganda in Judaism and Early Christianity* (London: University of Notre Dame Press, 1976)
In Memory of Her: A Feminist Construction of Christian Origins (London: S.C.M. Press, 1983)
Seager, A. R. and A. T. Kraabel. "The Synagogue and the Jewish Community," in G. M. A. Hanfmann, *Sardis, from Prehistoric to Roman Times*, 168–190
Sherwin-White, A. N. "The Early Persecution and Roman Law Again," *JTS*, New Series 3 (1952), 199–213
The Roman Citizenship, 2nd edn (Oxford: Clarendon Press, 1973)
"The Roman Citizenship: A Survey of its Development into a World Franchise," *ANRW*, vol. I, 2, 23–58
Roman Society and Roman Law in the New Testament (Oxford: Clarendon Press, 1963)
Smallwood, E. M. (trans.) *Legatio ad Gaium* (Leiden: E. J. Brill, 1970)
The Jews Under Roman Rule (Leiden: E. J. Brill, 1976)

Smith, J. *The Voyage and Shipwreck of Paul* (London: Longmans and Green, 1880)

Smith, J. Z. "Fences and Neighbors: Some Contours of Early Judaism," in *Approaches to Ancient Judaism*, vol. II, 1–26

Spicq, C. "Note de Lexicographie: APETH," *Revue Biblique* 89 (1982), 161–176

Stegmann, W. "War der Apostel Paulus ein römischer Bürger?," *ZNW* 78 (1987), 200–229

"Zwei sozialgeschictliche Anfragen an unser Paulusbild," *Der Evangelische Erzieher* 37 (1985), 480–490

Stern, M. *Greek and Latin Authors on Jews and Judaism*. 2 vols. (Jerusalem: Israel Academy of Science and Humanities, 1980)

Stolle, V. *Der Zeuge als Angeklagte. Untersuchungen zum Paulusbild des Lukas*, BWANT 6 (Stüttgart: Kohlhammer, 1973)

Stowers, S. K. "Social Status, Public Speaking and Private Teaching: The Circumstances of Paul's Preaching Activities," *NovT* 26 (1984), 59–82

Talbert, C. H. *Literary Patterns, Theological Themes and the Genre of Luke-Acts* (Missoula, Mont.: Scholars Press, 1974)

Tarn, W. *Hellenistic Civilization* (London: Edward Arnold, 1927)

Tcherikover, V. A. *Hellenistic Civilization and the Jews*, trans. S. Applebaum (Philadelphia: Jewish Publication Society, 1961)

Theissen, G. *The Social Setting of Pauline Christianity*, trans. J. H. Schutz (Edinburgh: T. & T. Clark, 1982)

Tiede, D. L. *Prophecy and History in Luke-Acts* (Philadelphia: The Fortress Press, 1980)

"Religious Propaganda and the Gospel Literature of the Early Christian Mission," *ANRW*, vol. II, 25.2, 1,705–1,729

Trebilco, P., *Jewish Communities in Asia Minor*, SNTS Monograph Series 57 (Cambridge: Cambridge University Press, 1991)

Trites, A. A., "The Importance of Legal Scenes and Language in the Book of Acts," *NovT* 16 (1974), 278–284

Vanhoye, A. (ed.), *L'Apôtre Paul: Personnalité, Style et Conception du Ministère* (Louvain: University Press, 1986)

Van Unnik, W. C. "Luke-Acts. A Storm Center in Contemporary Scholarship," *SLA*, 15–32

Tarsus or Jerusalem? The City of Paul's Youth (London: Epworth Press, 1962)

Veltmann, F. "The Defense Speeches of Paul in Acts," *SBL Sem Pap* 77, 325–340

Vielhauer, P. "On the Paulinisms of Acts," in L. Keck and J. L. Martyn, *SLA*, 33–50

Vine, V. E. "The Purpose and Date of Acts," *ET* 96 (1984–5), 45–48

Walaskay, P. W. *And So We Came To Rome: The Political Perspective of St. Luke*, S.N.T.S. Monograph Series 49 (Cambridge: Cambridge University Press, 1983)

Wardy, B. "Jewish Religion in Pagan Literature During the Late Republic and Early Empire," *ANRW*, vol. II, 19.1, 592–644

Watson, A. *Law Making in the Later Roman Republic* (Oxford: Clarendon Press, 1974)

"Roman Private Law and the Leges Regiae," *JRS* 62 (1972), 10–105
Welles, C. B. "Hellenistic Tarsus," *Mélange du l'Université St. Joseph* 38 (1962), 41–75
Wild, R. A. "The Encounter Between Pharisaic and Christian Judaism: Some Early Gospel Evidence," *NovT* 27 (1985), 105–124
Wilken, R. L. "The Christians as the Romans (and Greeks) Saw Them," in E. P. Sanders (ed.), *Jewish and Christian Self-Definition*, vol. I, 100–125 *The Christians as the Romans Saw Them* (London: Yale University Press, 1984)
Wilson, S. G. *The Gentiles and the Gentile Mission in Luke-Acts*, S.N.T.S. Monograph Series (Cambridge: Cambridge University Press, 1973)
Wright, N. T. "The Paul of History and the Apostle of Faith," *Tyndale Bulletin*, 29 (1978), 61–88
Ziesler, J. A. "Luke and the Pharisees," *NTS* 25 (1979), 146–157

INDEX OF BIBLICAL AND OTHER REFERENCES